Contact

A GUIDE TO

DEVELOPING EFFECTIVE CALL CENTRE SKILLS

Contact

A GUIDE TO

DEVELOPING EFFECTIVE CALL CENTRE SKILLS

JACK A. GREEN

Australia • Canada • Denmark • Japan • Mexico • New Zealand • Philippines
Puerto Rico • Singapore • South Africa • Spain • United Kingdom • United States

1120 Birchmount Road
Scarborough, Ontario M1K 5G4
www.nelson.com
www.thomson.com

Canadian Cataloguing in Publication Data

Green, Jack A., 1948–
    Contact: a guide to developing effective call centre skills

Includes index.
ISBN 0-17-616797-8

1. Customer Relations. 2. Call centers – Management. I. Title.

HF5415.5.G73 2000 658.8'12 C99-932918-9

Acquisitions Editor	Nicole Gnutzman
Marketing Manager	Chantal Lanning
Project Editor	Mike Thompson
Production Editor	Tracy Bordian
Copy Editor	Claudia Kutchukian
Proofreader	Lynne Missen
Art Director	Angela Cluer
Interior Design	Fizz Design Inc.
Cover Design	Angela Cluer
Cover Image	Wei Yan/Masterfile
Production Coordinator	Hedy Later
Composition	Daryn Dewalt, Erich Falkenberg
Printer	Webcom

Printed and bound in Canada
1   2   3   4   03 02 01 00

BRIEF CONTENTS

CONTENTS

CONTENTS

CONTENTS

In 1988, I created Entretel, a company focused on helping call centre staff improve their performance. All Entretel programs are customized, requiring that we listen to the centre's calls, "shadow" call centre staff as they work, and conduct focus groups of staff to understand their jobs and training needs. In essence, the goal is to understand what makes the call centre work, and what staff behaviours contribute to making the call centre effective. Many projects have required that I do internal benchmarking to determine what makes the top performers more successful than their peers, and to assess which characteristics contribute to call centre success off the telephone as well as on. Consequently, over the course of the last 12 years, I have had the privilege of working with scores of call centres and thousands of call centre staff.

My experience has taught me that success in a call centre position is a result of more than simply using particular techniques for managing customers on the telephone, although good telephone techniques are certainly important. Success in the call centre is the result of the right attitude toward the customer, toward the role of the call centre representative, and toward the other call centre representatives who are part of the team.

Contact is intended to help aspiring and current call centre representatives to optimize their success on the job. Consequently, it is more than just a collection of techniques, and more than a collection of theories about what a call centre should be. This book is a "how-to" manual that will guide the reader to success in the call centre role. By working through the material and the exercises included in this book, and by being honest in assessing yourself, you can ensure your improvement and success in the call centre role and become a true telephone professional.

Each chapter builds on the base developed by the previous chapter. Chapter 1 is a general introduction to the world of the call centre that aims to help the reader understand and appreciate the significance of the call centre phenomenon and the technologies that make it possible. Chapter 2 talks about the call centre "climate"—the atmosphere in which call centre representatives must perform their job responsibilities, and how each rep's contribution can enhance the climate. Chapter 3 introduces the critical importance of a positive attitude and discusses the elements that contribute to a positive attitude and making a good first impression on the telephone.

The call centre representative's voice is critical as the instrument of communication with the customer. Chapter 4 therefore examines how to use one's voice effectively. Chapter 5 explores techniques for establishing and maintaining rapport with the customer during a call. Before we can resolve the customer's issue, we must understand what it is, so listening and questioning skills are essential for the call centre rep. Chapter 6 reviews techniques for listening and questioning effectively. Managing the call length is another important element of the rep's role. High call volumes are always an issue in successful call centres, so skill in keeping calls focused and resolving customer issues in a time-efficient way is important. Chapter 7 discusses how to establish and, if necessary, regain control of the call, how to manage transfers and call "holds," and how to effectively say "no" to the customer when necessary.

Professional call centre reps are able to adjust their style to the customer's style. This increases rapport and minimizes the potential for the customer to become upset or angry. Chapter 8 provides a process for assessing the most appropriate style to use with a customer, explains how to connect with various types of customer, and provides insight into the rep's own most comfortable interaction style.

The role of the call centre rep can be stressful, especially when dealing with the stressed behaviour of some customers. Chapter 9 helps the reader understand the source of customers' difficult behaviour, and provides techniques for dealing with several different behaviours that can be encountered on the telephone. This chapter also provides input on managing stress and becoming less susceptible to the potential stressors in the call centre.

Each representative of the company contributes to the customer's decision of whether to continue to do business with the organization, so each rep influences the company's sales and is therefore, to some degree, a sales representative for the organization. Chapter 10 addresses the role of sales in the call centre and how to be effective in telephone sales.

Because a good deal of terminology is specific to call centres, a glossary is included at the back of the book. Terms that appear in the glossary appear in bold type at their first mention in the text.

Throughout the book are three types of boxed features: "Learning Application Exercises" get readers to examine and apply the various call centre techniques and issues discussed in the text. "Have You Ever?" boxes use examples and anecdotes to illustrate concepts, and "On the Job" boxes look at specific aspects of work in the call centre, providing a look at how issues covered in the text may arise in the "real world."

Teachers and trainers can also supplement this book with an *Instructor's Manual* available from Nelson Thomson Learning.

Acknowledgments

I wish to thank the following people for helping to make this book a reality:

My wife Maria and sons Patrick and Peter, who have endured my being a very distracted husband and father during the months of writing this book; the staff at Entretel for their commitment, support, and input, and in particular Linda MacKenzie and Jan Vialoux, who have been incredibly supportive throughout; the staff of the client organizations with whom I have worked over the years who have been the source of the information shared in this book; and my mother, Lorraine, who was there at the beginning and whose untimely death due to cancer prevented her from being here to see the final result.

Jack Green

Nelson would like to thank the following reviewers, whose time and input helped to make this a better book: Jeannine Lajoie, New Brunswick Community College; Adele Maizels, Pitney Bowes; Cara Musgrave, Cape Breton Business College; Janice Pearson, Toronto School of Business; and Rena Posteraro, Niagara College of Applied Arts and Technology.

CHAPTER 1
Introduction

After successfully completing Chapter 1, you will be able to:

— Discuss how the telephone and the computer have shaped the call centre role, and how this technology continues to evolve the role of the call centre representative.

— Describe the effect of "paradigm shift" in the evolution of the call centre as a business venue.

— Define "call centre" and describe how it is evolving, as well as the trend to large call centres and the variations on that trend.

— Describe the role and functions of the automatic call distributor and contact management software in a call centre.

— Describe the growing role of the Internet in the call centre.

— Discuss the role of call monitoring, the processes for call monitoring, and the ways in which a call centre representative can benefit from call monitoring.

— Recognize and define a number of basic call centre terms.

— Identify the three phases through which new call centres typically grow, and describe why and how a call centre grows this way.

— Identify the ways in which the call centre role has evolved.

— Explain the characteristics of a successful call centre representative.

Evolution of the Telephone as a Business Tool

Invented in early 1876 by Alexander Graham Bell, the telephone broke down the two inter-related barriers to doing business: distance and time. The telephone was a critical factor in society's evolution from the **industrial age** to the **information age**. It helped the work-force change from a production and manufacturing base to an information and communica-tion base. In the process, the types of skills necessary for success in the job market and consequently the focus of the educational system changed in a major way. This may seem like a lot of impact to credit to this one invention. In truth, this evolution was fuelled by the extensive enhancements in **telecommunications** technology, the advent and amazing growth of computer technology, and the blend of these two disciplines (among others). But the first step into what is becoming an amazing future was the invention of the telephone.

Before the telephone, business had to be done face-to-face (and so from a short distance) to be completed quickly. As distance increased, the time it took to complete a business transaction also increased. There was mail, which was—and some claim still is—notoriously slow (hence the term "snail mail"). The time required to complete a business transaction was even longer when the deal required back-and-forth discussion or negotiation, and so more mailing and waiting. Mail was, for most types of business, an inefficient business tool. Yet, because it was the only tool that could overcome distance, some organizations did busi-ness via **mail order catalogue**.

There was also the **telegraph**. Invented in 1837 by Samuel Morse, it was faster than mail, but couldn't be accessed by everyone as messages were sent and received only at Western Union offices or large firms. The telegraph also greatly limited the effectiveness of commu-nication, which requires a message to be transmitted by the communicator and understood by the recipient. Simple meanings can be communicated with words alone, and even com-plex meanings can be communicated by talented writers with words alone. But for most of us, using tone of voice, phrasing, and other cues available through speaking is essential to fully communicate our meaning. So people attempting to do business from a distance could transmit the words, but this took time and didn't always ensure good communication.

Until the telephone, commerce was slow and cumbersome by today's standards. Yet our society, and the commerce around which society is structured, had evolved without the tele-phone and had accommodated to a way of doing business without it. Business was typically conducted through small, local companies. For larger businesses, sales and product support were conducted through a network of branch offices, distributors, and travelling sales repre-sentatives. Because the producers of the products were far from the users, they could interact only through intermediaries, who were removed from the producers by time and distance as well. The telephone—and the technology that evolved to support it—changed all that.

A hundred years ago, communicating with someone who was even 20 km away was a daunting process. The telephone has made it fast, easy, and commonplace to connect with people halfway around the world. It has allowed businesses to decide where to locate based on factors other than proximity to market, such as labour costs, availability of raw materials, shipping costs, and tax regulations or incentives. In an extremely short period of time—particularly when one considers how long humanity has existed—the community-based marketplace has evolved into an international marketplace, largely because of the telephone.

Yet even though the telephone was the beginning, it didn't stimulate an instant change in the way people did business—it couldn't. Telephone communication required an infrastructure, it required that the telephones be connected, and it required deep market penetration so usage was widespread (it doesn't work if the company has a telephone but its customers do not). It also required mental **paradigm shifts**, not only to a technology-based way of communicating (talking into a mechanical device rather than face-to-face), but also a shift in the way people perceived business should be done.

By the end of 1877, Bell Telephone had 3000 telephones installed. By 1903, Bell managed over 1 million telephones, and independent telephone companies managed 2 million telephones. Bell had established a reputation for high prices and poor service well before this time, which helped its competitors to flourish. Bell went on a buying spree in the early 1900s to acquire these generally smaller, localized competitors. It wasn't until 1956 that the first transatlantic telephone cables started carrying calls (previously, transatlantic service was by radio wave), and telephone communication became truly international. Today, computer technology seems to be so much a part of the telephone industry, yet it was only in 1972 that the first computerized **switch** was put into service as part of the telephone infrastructure. Since then, the growth of computer technology has contributed greatly to the increased expansion and efficiency of the telephone industry.

The use of telephones as a business tool has been greatly enhanced by the introduction of 1-800 toll-free calling. Introduced in 1967, this service took awhile to become popular, but by 1992, traffic on 800 lines had swelled to 11 billion calls a year, or 40 percent of telephone-line traffic. By 1996 it was 60 million calls per day in the United States alone. We have since outgrown the 800 exchange, and 888 is the exchange for newer toll-free numbers.

With the application of wireless technologies, infrastructure is less of a barrier to entry into the information age. Developing nations can join in the information age without the time and expense it has taken other nations. Wireless technology is relatively less expensive in areas where there is no existing telecommunications infrastructure. And **wireless phones** are available for use now—the user does not have to wait for the lines and **exchanges** to be built.

As the barriers decline, the telephone has become universal. Along with increased use—which has been enhanced by the recent increase in competition between long-distance carriers and by more effective and efficient technology—has come a significant reduction in the cost of telephone communication and commerce. While the costs of staff, travel, and distribution have gone up, the costs of telecommunications and computer technology have come down. And as the costs of telephone use have come down, use has increased.

SHIFTING TO THE TELEPHONE IN BUSINESS TRANSACTIONS

The final requirement for the telephone to take its place as the major business tool of the 1990s has been the paradigm shift toward public acceptance of the telephone as a tool for doing business. We all try to make sense of our world by developing a set of mental rules about how things work. A paradigm is a belief so fundamental that it is taken to be a truth. We don't even think about it—it is just the way things are. It is not easy to change this sort of belief.

A paradigm shift in how we do business has been essential for the telephone's evolution from a personal communication tool to a business tool, and this shift is one that many have not yet made. For example, the banking industry has moved toward less personal service at the branch level: branches have been closed and customers persuaded to use banking machines or to do their banking by telephone. Some customers resist these changes in spite of their many benefits, not the least of which is greater convenience. Their vision or paradigm of banking is to be across the counter from a live teller, not punching numbers into a machine or talking about personal business to a voice on the other end of a telephone. In spite of these **paradigm-shift resisters** (remember, though, that these people are still customers whose needs our institutions must continue to respect), most of us see the telephone as a principal business tool. In fact, as we get more and more comfortable with changing our old paradigms, we find it easier to shift. For example, note the amazing growth of e-commerce—doing business over the Internet.

The Computer in the Call Centre

While the telephone was the beginning and without it we wouldn't have **call centres**, call centres would be a very different place to work if it weren't for the computer. The computer is such an integral part of business today that it's hard to imagine doing business without it. In the year 2000, an estimated 6 million people worldwide work in the multi-billion-dollar call centre industry. And almost all of those employees will work in a large room that is subdivided into **workstations**, each containing a phone line and a computer.

The computer stores and provides access to customer information, product information, **scripts** (answers to questions, ways to word messages to the customer), shipping information, inventories—basically everything call centre representatives need to do their jobs effectively. So the computer is integral to performing the call centre rep's job duties.

The growth of call centres would have been impossible without the growth in computer technology, which has been a major contributor to the increased effectiveness and capability of our telephone systems, as well as a critical business tool on its own. The first multipurpose electronic computer (ENIAC, or Electronic Numerical Integrator And Computer) was built between 1943 and 1946. It was 3 m tall, occupied 305 m of floor space, weighed 27 t, used more than 70 000 resistors and 18 000 vacuum tubes, had 5 million soldered joints, and needed enough power to light a small town to operate. It was essentially a huge electronic calculator. In 1976, Apple introduced the Apple I (200 units were built in a garage). Apples II, III, and IV followed, and Atari and Commodore introduced their lines of home computers into the marketplace. Then, in 1981, IBM introduced its first **personal computer** (or **PC**). A new and improved model was introduced only a few months later—a trend that has continued to frustrate buyers to this day. In 1984 Apple introduced the user-friendly Macintosh, emulated by IBM's Windows 3.0 in 1990 so that users no longer had to memorize **commands**. With mass production and competition, the cost of a personal computer plummeted and demand skyrocketed. In 1998, 2 million personal computers were sold in Canada alone. This same pattern of cost reduction and technology growth has characterized the use of computer technology in the telecommunications industry.

Call Centres

DEFINITION

We will talk about a call centre as if it is a real place, and for the most part it is. But call centres can be **virtual places** as well. That is, the call centre is the place a caller reaches. The call doesn't go directly to a person, however—in most cases it goes to an **ACD**. An ACD, or **automatic call distributor**, is the device that takes the incoming call and passes it to the next available call centre representative. This rep may be in the same building as the ACD, or in another building, city, province, or country—or even the rep's home. The call may not even reach a person at all, but a computer system that can provide certain regularly requested types of information (such as flight schedules or account balances) through **IVR**, or **interactive voice response**. You've heard an IVR system on the phone when you've been asked to "Press 1 for a new account inquiry, press 2 for your account balance." So the call centre may not be a place at all. This has led Call Centre Consultant Rob Forneri to define a call centre as "the mechanism through which an organization transacts business with an identified group of customers, or potential customers, using the telephone as the primary method of communication."[1] Most typically, the mechanism that is a call centre involves a group of staff who are responsible for those business transactions.

THE TREND TO LARGE CENTRALIZED CALL CENTRES

Call centres have tended to be centralized in one or two locations. With modern technology, a centralized call centre no longer needs to be near the customer. Centralization offers the advantage of **economies of scale**, which basically means that the more of something you make, the less expensive each item is to produce.

Applied to a call centre, economies of scale means that in a large centralized call centre, the average cost per call is reduced. One big area of savings a larger centre enjoys is in staffing, and staffing is the biggest cost in a call centre. For example, if you have 10 locations with 2 reps at each, and each location receives enough calls for 1.5 reps, you still need to have 2 people at each location or a third of your customers won't get through and you'll lose business quickly. And if one of your two reps is off sick or on vacation, the other is overwhelmed with calls and the service level goes down. If you pull those centres together, you have enough calls for 15 people, so you don't need 20 on the payroll.

In addition, if you take all the money you spent on installing telephone and computer equipment at 10 different sites and put that money into one site, you can improve your system and save money while still improving efficiency, further reducing the cost per call. Instead of managing 2 people at each of 10 sites, you only have to manage 15 people at one site. Thus you can have one manager whose only responsibility is the call centre, rather than one whose main responsibilities are elsewhere or who may be located away from the branch staff he or she supervises. This allows you to manage more effectively and to use management tools such as **performance standards**, training, **call monitoring**, and coaching that ensure better and more consistent service. You can also locate your centralized call centre for sound business reasons other than proximity, such as cost and availability of labour, building cost, or local government incentives. Overall, centralization allows for a reduced cost per call, increased effectiveness in providing customer service, and increased efficiency.

Many organizations have call centres that are not called call centres. They may have names like claims department, order desk, help desk, customer assistance centre, or customer care department. Sometimes managers are surprised to discover that their department has evolved into a call centre. Departments that started out as mail-based often change as they use the telephone more and more.

The "bigger is better" trend in call centres is still common. In fact, when companies are establishing call centres, it's a good idea to allow room to grow, because call centres have a tendency to grow. Once they are established and the organization sees how well they work, management tends to find other functions that could be handled through the centre. In contrast to this trend to bigness is the emergence of networked **satellite call centres**, or **home-based** or **virtual agents**. Satellite call centres are smaller centres that are closer to the labour source and are networked—electronically linked—so that they are part of a large **queue**. The customer doesn't notice the different locations. A satellite call centre has greater appeal to the call centre labour market, as it can greatly reduce the travel time to and from a job in a large, centralized call centre. The satellite centre also expands the geographical area from which a company can draw its staff, avoiding using up the labour market in an area with a limited market of potential employees (low unemployment in an area tends to drive up the cost of labour in a market where low labour cost may have been a deciding factor for a company's initial decision to locate there). The technology that was originally one of the factors behind the "bigger is better," economies of scale decision to be big has advanced so quickly, and gone down in cost so dramatically, that these alternate structures can be considered.

Home-based call centre representatives come with an additional cost. Equipment at a workstation that might be shared by a number of reps working different shifts in an office is devoted to just one rep who works only one shift or part of one. Home-based reps do, however, allow a company greater staffing flexibility. For instance, a peak period of many calls may be only a few hours a day, separated by slower periods. The person at home may be willing to **log on** to the system and be ready to take calls for the hours 8:00 to 9:00, 11:30 to 2:30, and 4:30 to 8:00, for example, whereas it would be difficult to find an employee willing to travel to work and back for these shifts. The home-based arrangement also allows organizations to hire people who are **physically challenged** and cannot travel easily to and from the workplace.

As a term, "call centre" will eventually go the way of the outdated term **telemarketing**. Telemarketing, which originally referred to telephone sales, became identified with high-pressure telephone sales used on more vulnerable people, such as the elderly. "Call centre" is losing ground to terms such as **customer contact centre**, **customer care centre**, or **business centre** as the centre becomes the point of contact for the customer no matter what the mode of communication: telephone, letter, **fax**, or **e-mail**. While the term will eventually fade out, it is currently still very much alive and will be used throughout this text.

It is not critical for an effective call centre representative to know the history or the impact of the telephone or of computer technology. However, understanding some of this history can help reps appreciate the newness of the field, understand the rapid and massive change that characterizes this business, and know that they are working on the exciting front edge of two fields of technology: telecommunications and computers.

Basic Call Centre Technology

It is also useful for call centre representatives to have a basic understanding of how their phone system works, because this system drives the call centre.

There are three basic technological elements in handling an inbound call (a call that comes in from a customer): the ACD, the **contact management software**, and the **Internet**. After discussing these topics, this section will address call monitoring, which is also part of the evolving call centre technology.

ACD

When a customer calls in to the centre, the call is answered by an automatic call distributor, or ACD. The ACD is common in larger call centres. A **PBX**, or **private branch exchange**, was originally designed to replace the in-house **switchboard operator**, whose job was to distribute calls from a limited number of outside lines among a greater number of internal telephone users, and to connect internal staff calls to one another without using external lines. Some of the more sophisticated PBXs today can perform some of the more basic ACD functions, like simple call **routing**. The PBX is more commonly associated with smaller centres, since it has lower capabilities and tends to be lower in cost. The ACD passes the call to the representative who has been without a call the longest, or to the next rep to become available, or to the next rep who matches criteria based on information collected about the caller. Different ACDs have different features; many nowadays are PC-based.

Here are some capabilities of the ACD:

- It can greet the caller and advise the caller if there will be a wait, and even how long a wait to expect.

- It can collect caller identification information (such as an account number entered by the customer via the telephone **keypad**), crosscheck the number with the **customer database**, and bring that information to the rep's computer screen when the call is connected. The appearance of this information on the screen is called a **screen pop** and is available through **CTI (computer–telephone integration)**, in which information from the telephone is matched to information from the company's internal computer system.

- CTI can also provide **ANI**, or **automatic number identification**, which can match the customer's telephone number to the company's database and produce the customer's account as a screen pop when the rep receives the call or slightly before, if the system is so programmed. This allows the rep to review the file briefly before the call comes in, without having to ask the caller to provide any identification.

- ANI may also allow the system to review the customer file and route the call to the appropriate rep, such as the rep responsible for that customer, a particular region, or a particular function (such as collections).

- The ACD may use IVR, or interactive voice response, to query customers and direct their calls by asking callers to press certain telephone keypad numbers. IVR can even answer a customer's question without the rep's help, providing such information as the customer's account balance.

- IVR can also be used to interview job applicants, allowing information about different applicants to be standardized, efficient processing of many applicants in a short period of time, and the convenience of 24-hour-a-day access to the application process. IVR is also used to conduct surveys, avoiding the bias of a human interviewer.

- The ACD can also provide the supervisor with **real-time**—as it is happening, not after the fact—information about what is happening in the call queue, such as how many calls are currently waiting, how long they have been waiting, the number of representatives available to take calls, and the types of calls that are waiting. The supervisor can use this information to make decisions and respond to problems now rather than wait until a report comes later, when it is too late.

- The supervisor can listen in on a call and even join the call or signal the rep when there is a problem. The reps' telephone, computer screen, or **display board** (an electronic sign that is linked to the ACD) can be fed information by the ACD to give the reps real-time information about the call queues, helping them make decisions about when to take a break or do after-call work.

- The ACD can be programmed to allow the reps a period of time after each call to complete work related to that call before the next call is passed through.

- Many different kinds of call centre and individual rep performance reports are available to the supervisor from the ACD.

Not every call centre ACD, however, has the capability or is programmed to do all of the above.

CONTACT MANAGEMENT SOFTWARE

Call centres need a shared system of access to customer information, since with queuing we typically don't know which representative will receive the customer's call, so all must have access to this information. This system can be designed internally or adapted from one of the software packages available on the market. When a call is received by a rep, he or she asks for identification information that will either show the customer's account or allow the rep to set up a new customer account.

Contact management software can provide the rep with information necessary to deal effectively with a customer. The types of information—or **fields**—are established to support the rep in handling the customer. This information may include address and telephone/fax/e-mail numbers, records of previous contacts with the call centre and previous orders, and an indication of the customer's status with the company (for example, a preferred customer, or one who is behind in payments). Some contact management systems do the following:

- Work with other computer software systems to give the reps quick access to inventory levels, the status of shipments, and other information that can help the reps better serve customers.

- Organize customer documentation (agreements, prices, typical orders, and so on) for easy access and reference during a call.

- Print reports or letters by merging the appropriate customer information fields with standard letter or report **templates**.

- Produce statistics or lists of certain types of customers for analysis.

- Schedule follow-up calls and present the file for the customer to be called at the appropriate time. Contact management software can even dial the customer's phone number for the rep.

- Forward files to appropriate people in the organization and bring the files to their attention.

- Provide a reference system of scripted call introduction statements, responses to customer objections, answers to common questions, or resource information so reps don't have to remember all of this or use potentially outdated **hard-copy** references.

- Fax or e-mail information directly to the customer right from the workstation PC.

- Provide supervisors with performance activity reports on their staff for feedback, coaching, and assessment purposes.

THE INTERNET

The telephone opened the public's awareness to new ways of doing business, and consequently the acceptance of the Internet as a way to do business has been relatively rapid. The process by which customers shop and place orders through a company's **Web site** by completing an electronic order form themselves and e-mailing it to the company greatly reduces the cost of each transaction. Since call centres are the point of contact for customers, they are typically assuming the responsibility for all customer contact and becoming customer contact centres or customer care centres, including the responsibility for written correspondence, fax contacts, and e-mail interaction. Internet contact with customers may be **batched** (e-mail messages are collected and reviewed periodically, much like most of us manage our personal e-mail) or real-time (the rep receives the e-mail as soon as it is sent and responds immediately, allowing for an electronic dialogue between the rep and the customer).

E-mail, or electronic mail, has become such an accepted method of communication that Canada Post is becoming concerned over revenue loss, and even with reduced rates telephone companies can't compete with the zero long-distance costs of e-mail. Some governments, recognizing that e-mail is so widely used, are investigating ways to levy a tax or fee on e-mail.

Here are some other advantages the Internet provides:

- A **restricted-access Web site** allows reps to keep up-to-date on inventory levels, prices, and so on and can allow them to place real-time orders that go directly to the fulfillment department or warehouse rather than to an order desk for processing.

- Customers can not only place orders through a Web site but also get guidance or information by interacting with a rep by e-mail. For example, a customer can have technical problems resolved by an Internet-enabled **help desk** rep, have a complaint resolved by an Internet-enabled customer service rep, or have his or her needs analyzed and an appropriate product explained by an Internet-enabled sales rep.

- Customers can have information instantaneously e-mailed to them by requesting this information by e-mail.

- Customers who have the appropriate systems and sound equipment can click an icon on the company's **interactive Web site** and speak to a live rep who is looking at the same screen the customer is viewing. This can be simulated by simultaneous telephone and Internet contact between the customer and the rep.

- Call centre rep training can be done over the Internet, allowing greater and more cost-effective customization and flexibility than computer-based training (which becomes outdated quickly in our changing times) while providing all the benefits of self-directed study.

As the Internet becomes part of the way call centres do business, call centres in turn facilitate the Internet becoming an important tool of business. Once again, the call centre is on the leading edge of new technology. The Internet adds to the variety and depth of the call centre role.

Call Monitoring and Assessment

In most jobs in which staff communicate with customers, the supervisor or coach cannot observe staff without being noticed. Having a supervisor observe from nearby usually results in the staff being nervous and not performing normally, or being on their best behaviour so that the supervisor doesn't get a true representation of their performance and any opportunities for improvement. As a result, coaching is less effective because it's not based on true performance.

Call centres present a wonderful opportunity for more effective coaching, because technology allows any or all calls to be monitored by the coach. Typically in a call centre, coaching takes several formats. These include the following:

- **Drive-bys**, in which the coach or supervisor overhears a rep's response to a customer while passing by and stops to either reinforce or redirect the rep's performance. This is beneficial because it is timely, and it provides the rep with clear direction. The rep knows which behaviours are good and should be continued, and which need to change. However, because this coaching happens by chance, it's inefficient. The rep may handle calls less than effectively many times before this comes to the coach's attention.

- **Side-by-side coaching**, in which the coach or supervisor sits beside the rep, usually listening in on a headset to both sides of the call. The supervisor can give immediate feedback to the rep right after a call or, if necessary, during the call. In some cases, the coach may become involved in the call and speak directly to the customer. This type of coaching is most effective with new reps who find the coach's presence reassuring. That same presence can, however, bias the rep's performance, so the feedback may be less useful.

- **Remote monitoring**, in which the supervisor or coach listens to calls from a location away from the rep's workstation. The supervisor can listen in on a rep's calls through a monitoring line. Feedback is provided on calls that are unbiased by the supervisor's physical presence, ensuring that coaching is most efficient and beneficial. Usually the supervisor doesn't tell reps when their calls will be monitored, only that they may be monitored at any time. The supervisor may provide feedback to the rep immediately after a call or later, in the form of a report (which has more value as an assessment tool than as a coaching tool, since the report is about a call the rep may have forgotten about).

All of these monitoring systems lack in one key area: when reps are involved in a call, their attention is focused on effectively responding to the customer, and less on the style or behavioural aspects of the interaction. If the rep had known, for example, that her or his tone of voice was less than effective, the rep would have used a different tone during the call. The most significant benefit of using telephones is that calls can be tape-recorded. This allows reps to listen to and assess their own performance.

Taping can happen right at the rep's workstation by having a **phone jack** spliced into the rep's line and connected to a tape recorder (a voice-activated tape recorder is best, as it is less distracting than having to turn it on and off). Alternately, calls can be recorded remotely so the rep is unaware of the taping. Again, this can be done by a simple jack connected to the supervisor's monitoring line. More sophisticated taping systems can collect all the calls of all the reps, to be listened to later by the supervisor (sometimes the nature of a business requires that it have a record of what the company and the customer have verbally agreed to, so all calls are taped). Or the system may selectively tape calls from different reps at different times and days to get a random sample to assess.

Some sophisticated systems collect and store each call assessment, record supervisory feedback comments, splice them into the call for the rep to review later, and provide reports that track rep performance on various criteria over time. Where there are many assessors of calls in an organization (such as in many large call centres) and consistency among assessors is important (for example, because these assessments are part of the reps' performance records and are used for determining pay levels), these sophisticated systems will track and compare assessors to identify any biases. Some systems can even capture the screens the rep used during a call so the assessor and the rep can determine if the entries were made accurately and most efficiently.

Call centres struggle to be objective in assessing calls. For example, if a call is assessed for the rep's listening skills, rather than have the supervisor rate it a "3" out of "4" based on his or her experience, it is more meaningful if the criteria for a "3" or "4" score is clearly laid out. This allows the assessor to be more consistent in assessments and, even more importantly, the reps to know what behaviours they performed got them the "3" and what they need to do differently to attain a "4." Clear, objective performance criteria allow for more effective coaching and improved performance, the real purpose of assessing calls at all. Clear objectives allow reps to take ownership of their performance—they know exactly what is expected of them, and can listen to their own calls and know whether they did what is required or where they need to improve.

To be effective, criteria for effective performance must be as objective as possible and must also assess the behaviours that yield the desired call results. For example, if keeping customers is a key objective of the call centre, the behaviours that result in customer retention must be represented in the performance criteria or standards. The behaviours that correspond to success in meeting call centre objectives are called **competencies**, and performance standards must incorporate these competencies to be meaningful.[2]

Evolution of the Call Centre

Sometimes a call centre happens before it is planned. Staff in some departments (such as order-taking, sales support, or customer service) use the telephone more and more because it is faster and more efficient than mail. The jobs gradually change from being paper-based into mostly computer- and telephone-based. When this happens, management must begin adjusting systems, job descriptions, and so on, to fit the new reality.

When the call centre is created, either based on a perceived need to centralize the organization's telephone contacts or to offer a new or improved service, it experiences a series of growth steps or developmental phases. These steps are distinct from, yet influenced by, the evolution of the new call centre staff members (discussed in Chapter 2). The steps include the quality phase, the quantity or efficiency phase, and the balance or performance phase.

QUALITY PHASE

In this phase, the new call centre tries to get customers to use the services of the call centre. During this phase, the call centre also aims to establish credibility with the rest of the organization. Quality service drives this phase—every attempt is made to ensure that each customer is satisfied. Customers who are not used to doing business over the telephone often have a "help me" attitude that allows the rep to assume the role of guide and company/call centre advocate.

The calls during this phase are often longer, because quality service is the main consideration, and because when calls begin to come in, there are often fewer of them, so average call length is less of an issue. Reps are encouraged to make a good impression, so they may adopt a call-handling style that is not the most time-efficient, but this is also not an issue at this stage. In the quality phase, call statistics are not usually kept. Instead, management's aim is to develop a base upon which to establish standards of performance.

As the call centre evolves through its developmental phases, so too do the members of the call centre team. The team goes through its **forming phase** (or honeymoon phase), discussed in Chapter 2. This stage of team growth is followed by one that involves conflict and resistance to leadership.

If the call centre team moves into the conflict or **storming phase** before the call centre has moved on to its next stage, staff will feel very repressed and will be very resistant. This is often a problem in call centre development: the team's storming phase coincides with management's attempt to move the call centre toward greater efficiency. The storming phase can be so upsetting to reps that their attitude on the phone is affected. It is often this decrease in quality that causes call centre management to introduce measures of performance and move the call centre into the second, or quantity, phase.

QUANTITY OR EFFICIENCY PHASE

The quantity phase results from call centre management feeling pressured to account for the centre's performance. At this stage, management introduces processes to measure staff performance. Typically, because ACD statistics are so readily available, they are the basis for call centre performance measurement. Here are some of the statistics that are typically analyzed:

- **Average handling time (AHT):** The average length of time it takes the rep to handle each call, including talk time and after-call work time.

- **Average talk time (ATT):** The average length of time the rep spends talking to the customer in each call.

- **Average work time (AWT):** The average length of time the rep spends out of queue doing wrap-up work on a call after the call has been completed.

- **Average hold time:** The average amount of time the customer was on hold per call.

- **Adherence to the staffing schedule:** A measure of whether the staff in queue are ready to take calls during the period of time they are expected to do so.

- **Average speed of answer (ASA):** The average time a caller was on hold before his or her call was answered by a rep.

When these measures aren't introduced or used appropriately, staff may react negatively. Some of these measures cannot be directly affected by the rep and are therefore inappropriate to use in measuring individual performance. For example, individual reps can affect the ASA by lowering their ATT, but without guidance on how to effectively do so, the reps usually lower average talk time by speaking more quickly, cutting customers off, or not asking the probing questions that should be asked. With only these quantitative ACD data to measure call centre performance, reps feel pressured to produce quantity at the expense of quality. When the company's mandate for top-quality customer service continues, it can seem like management pays lip service to quality but actually wants quantity, making the reps resentful.

This phase can go on indefinitely as the team fuels the controversy, creating a very poor call centre climate. Staff and management become frustrated as customer satisfaction decreases, and management may become more controlling and autocratic. The only way out of this problem is for call centre management to create the basis for movement into the balance or performance phase.

BALANCE OR PERFORMANCE PHASE

In this phase, the call centre accomplishes a real sense of balance between the seemingly conflicting objectives of quality and quantity. This phase is most easily achieved when

- Call centre management introduces measurement standards that assess call quality. Such standards are ideally based on those behaviours that contribute to efficient (in a timely and productive manner) as well as effective (in a way that provides appropriate problem resolution and customer satisfaction) call handling, such as listening, questioning, and call-control skills, and the skill with which a difficult caller is handled. These standards should measure **core competencies**—those observable behaviours that result in the rep meeting the job objectives and achieving the quantitative performance standards.

- Call centre management makes reps accountable only for those factors that they can individually control. For example, individuals cannot control the average speed of answer. Management is responsible for this.

- Call centre management does not use the measures of performance as a tool to punish reps, but rather as a basis for coaching to improve performance and for rewarding when reps do well.

Telling the reps that they can achieve qualitative as well as quantitative goals is not as effective as showing them how. Implementing quality standards and showing reps how to perform the behaviours associated with each, along with clear qualitative expectations, establishes a balance and sets the call centre on the road to high performance.

Evolution of the Call Centre Representative

The role of the call centre representative has evolved from one in which low-knowledge (and often low-skill) reps provided or collected simple bits of information, or in which "boiler rooms" with row upon row of unskilled reps **cold-called** large numbers of **prospects** to recite a tightly scripted sales pitch (cold calls are made to people who don't currently do business with a company). While those roles certainly still exist, the majority of call centre positions are now high-skill and high-knowledge roles. A very repetitive job is no longer the norm.

More and more, call centre reps are knowledge workers who have college or university degrees. They have typically trained and educated themselves for other vocations, largely because most education for the working world was developed in pre–call centre days, although that is changing and many people are entering college call centre programs. The available jobs are in the call centre industry, and as this industry becomes more established and call centres develop their own histories, managers are becoming more effective at meeting the needs of a group of workers who are relatively new to the workforce. The people applying for call centre jobs want more than just a job—they want a career, they want fun, and they want to feel they are making a contribution and that that contribution is recognized. Call centres are working to meet these challenges, creating development opportunities in a number of ways.

JOB TIERING

Greater numbers of call centres are moving from a totally flat organizational structure that doesn't allow for much career development to a structure with job levels and job progression. Such a structure increases the high-end growth potential within the call centre, and also allows for entry-level reps at the low end to develop skills rather than having to enter the centre with all the necessary skills and knowledge. **Job tiering** also provides the organization with a broader range of hiring possibilities, because it is usually easier to find new employees who are lower-skilled and develop them in-house than it is to find high-skilled ones. Often, the tiered call centre structure involves horizontal career moves, a number of which are required before the rep can move up in position. This provides the organization with a number of **cross-trained** reps who can be reassigned to cover other areas that are short-handed while providing the reps with variety and a range of learning experiences.

BLENDED/SALES REPS

As call centres establish themselves in organizations, elements of the sales role often migrate to the centre. Reps have the opportunity to develop their sales skills and take on either a telephone sales function (see the wide range of sales functions described in Chapter 10) or a **blended** role in which reps are in an outbound role—often involving making sales calls—until the inbound call volumes require them to start answering calls. Both these roles give the reps the opportunity to expand on their skills, increasing their interest in and rewards from the job and their chances for career growth.

FUN

Call centre management is also adjusting to a younger workforce. Senior managers who have come from the older "baby boom" generation often have different expectations of a job, but they must understand that the younger workforce generally views work differently. The process of change in call centres has increased as older managers who can make this shift gravitate to call centre management and as younger people move into call centre management positions.

As a result, while work is still important and productivity is key, call centres today are typically fun, high-energy environments with a high degree of camaraderie and a steady stream of campaigns, contests, and parties designed to keep the environment and the work stimulating and to create an "extended family" feeling. Organizations that encourage such an environment are rewarded by higher productivity and lower employee turnover.

CALL CENTRE COACH/SUPERVISOR/SPECIALIST

In a call centre with a tiered internal career path, the reps progress through a variety of internal positions until they come to the point of choosing between the coaching and specialist streams. The coaching stream, with its focus on people and performance management, typically leads to supervisory positions, while the specialist stream does not. In the past the only opportunity for career advancement was in coaching and supervising. Usually the more effective reps were offered the opportunity to move into coaching or even directly into supervising, with the only consideration being their effectiveness as a rep. Often people who moved into these roles were poor coaches and supervisors because these involve many different skills from those required to be a good rep. Essentially, companies rewarded good "doers" by promoting them to poor supervisors, leading to career frustration and lower effectiveness of the team.

Several variables affect a person's effectiveness as a supervisor. Some of these skills and traits can be taught, others come with maturity (which doesn't necessarily mean age), and others are part of a person's personality. Rather than set up a good employee for failure, effective call centres are increasingly recognizing that some people are more suited to one role than they are to another. These organizations have established a career stream that allows reps to progress as specialists without having to supervise others, yet still provides the opportunity to learn new skills and enjoy a fulfilling career. The specialist role typically involves advancing job knowledge in a specific area, assuming responsibility for high-value accounts, or taking on project management responsibilities.

Characteristics of a Successful Call Centre Representative

The days when call centre managers were happy just to fill call centre positions with unscreened, off-the-street applicants are gone. Too many of these hires did not work out, and the result was high employee turnover or performance problems. The hiring process has a greater profile in call centres today. The following employee characteristics and skills are prized by hiring managers, and aspiring call centre reps can benefit by developing their abilities in these areas.

ABILITY TO LEARN

To be successful today, a call centre rep must be able to learn and must enjoy learning. The call centre environment is one of ongoing change, so reps must be able to learn quickly to keep up with new information, responsibilities, policies and procedures, and technology. Call centres typically grow into **one-stop shopping** centres or a single point of contact in an organization, so the responsibility for more and more information or types of customer issues is given to the reps.

ABILITY TO MULTITASK

Today's call centre typically does not allow a person to stick with one task until it is done. Call centre reps must be able to **multitask**—keep track of a number of projects, ongoing cases, or calls to be followed up on, and not forget about these or let them get behind while they give their full attention to the current customer.

STRESS RESISTANCE

Today's call centres operate at a hectic pace. For the successful call centre rep this environment is energizing and exciting; for the less successful rep the pace and activity level can be overwhelming and lead to stress. Customers can be demanding and the call volume high, which can be sources of personal reward and continued interest and satisfaction in the job, or causes of frustration, anxiety, and stress.

FLEXIBILITY

No matter how much training new reps receive or how prepared they are, it is likely that on their first day on the job they will encounter something that wasn't covered in the training. A fact of the job is that reps will not always know how to handle every situation. The effective rep overcomes the initial fluster this can cause and uses her or his skills to explore and deal with each situation, taking skills and answers developed for one set of circumstances and applying them to a new set of circumstances.

ABILITY TO GET ALONG WITH PEOPLE

If a person does not genuinely like people but instead distrusts them, considers them lower in status, or fears them, then working in a call centre is not appropriate for them. The call centre rep must interact with a variety of people constantly. A rep may be able to fake an interest in people for a while, but the daily demands of the job will make this impossible— and frustrating—to keep up for a long time.

COMPUTER/KEYBOARDING SKILLS

Keyboarding skills are a must in most call centres. The task of managing a call is simply too consuming for the rep to concentrate on finding the right key. The keyboard should be like an extension of the rep—he or she needs to be able to use it without consciously thinking about it.

Each call centre uses a different contact management system, but reps who are comfortable with computers and with one of the major word-processing packages can usually easily learn how to use a new system.

POSITIVE ATTITUDE

Effective call centres seek reps who are positive about the job. Hiring is essentially a screening process—managers look for signs of potential problems to avoid hiring the wrong applicants. If a person does not display a positive attitude at the outset, odds are things will only go downhill from there.

INTERPERSONAL SKILLS

A person can genuinely like people but be ineffective in communicating with them and in managing calls, so hiring managers try to select applicants who exhibit good interpersonal skills.

The remainder of this book will go into more detail on the characteristics that can help a call centre rep to be successful.

Learning Application Exercise

1. Which aspects of a call centre appeal to you the most? Which do you feel will give you the greatest satisfaction as a call centre rep?

2. Which call centre rep characteristics are strongest for you already? Which do you see as being the most important for you to develop or improve?

3. Develop a plan with clear goals and achievement dates to develop the characteristics you identified in question 2.

Summary

The telephone and the infrastructure behind it have been key to the growth of call centres. Among the other major contributors to this new way of doing business have been the exponential growth in computer technology and the paradigm shift to seeing the telephone as a legitimate tool for conducting business.

A call centre is the "mechanism through which an organization transacts business with an identified group of customers or potential customers, using the telephone as the primary method of communication." For economies of scale reasons, the call centre business tends to be conducted at large, centralized locations.

ACD technology drives the call centre, collecting calls as they come in and, at a minimum, passing each to the next available or most appropriate representative. Computer technology has greatly enhanced the services available through the ACD and has enabled the many features available through CTI, or computer–telephone integration, many of which use ANI (automatic number identification) to allow the computer to find customer information based on the customer's telephone number.

Contact management software allows all call centre reps to access customer information and other information sources that may help reps service customers.

The Internet is having a profound effect on how we do business today. Through batch or real-time e-mail and interactive Web sites, call centre reps are connecting with customers through yet another medium, adding variety and depth to the call centre role.

Call monitoring allows coaches to improve the team's performance by identifying and reinforcing areas of effectiveness and giving timely recognition and coaching in those areas where performance could be enhanced. Effective coaching based on call monitoring helps the rep to improve more quickly and achieve greater job success and satisfaction sooner. As reps learn to assess their calls, they can take ownership of their performance and continue to grow professionally.

Call centres typically evolve through three phases:

1. the quality phase, in which a new call centre establishes itself with the customer

2. the quantity phase, in which the call centre becomes more efficient in providing service

3. the balance phase, in which the call centre balances quality and efficiency and moves to optimal performance

Call centres have evolved into more "rep-friendly" environments by providing career growth within the centre through job tiering, providing the challenge of sales or blended customer service and sales roles, providing a more fun environment, and allowing reps to follow career streams as specialists or supervisors.

The characteristics that make a rep successful in today's call centre include

- ability to learn

- ability to multitask

- stress resistance

- flexibility

- ability to get along with people

- computer/keyboarding skills

- positive attitude

- interpersonal skills

Endnotes

1. Rob Forneri, "Creating a Call Centre from Scratch." Presentation to the International Nortel Networks Users' Group Conference, June 1998, Anaheim, CA.

2. For a fuller description of how effective call standards are established, refer to Jack Green, "Using Qualitative Performance Measurement to Achieve Performance Improvement," in Stanley Brown, ed., *Breakthrough Customer Service: Best Practices of Leaders in Customer Support* (Toronto: John Wiley and Sons, 1997), 319–331.

CHAPTER 2
Creating a Positive Work Climate

Learning Outcomes

After successfully completing Chapter 2, you will be able to:

- Describe the importance of the call centre "climate."

- Discuss the factors that contribute to the call centre climate.

- Describe the benefits when a call centre works as a team.

- Explain the four steps of call centre team evolution.

- Understand how to maximize those behaviours that contribute to team effectiveness, and minimize those behaviours that undermine team effectiveness.

- Understand how to resolve interpersonal conflicts that can arise in a call centre.

Call Centre Climate

UNDERSTANDING CLIMATE

Every call centre evolves its own **climate**. Just as geographic climate is the result of a number of factors, such as rainfall and temperature variations, that affect what it feels like to live somewhere, the call centre climate is the result of a number of factors that affect how it feels to work there. Every organization and each department or work unit in an organization develops its own climate, which you can often sense when you walk in.

The call centre is like the heart of the organization. Its function is to interact with the company's customers, to be the company's voice and face to the customer—essentially, it is the human side of the organization. The rest of the organization handles the creation, marketing, and distribution of the product or service, while the call centre deals with customers' questions, concerns, problems, and frustrations.

There is a sense of energy and urgency in a call centre. It deals with the customer in real time, not abstractly as a demographic statistic or profile. The customer must be dealt with now, and in a manner that reflects positively on the organization. Thus, the call centre is always "on"—there is no **downtime**. It must always be active and ready to respond to the customer.

No matter how much we rely on technology in our call centres, all that technology merely enables people to communicate with other people. In his book *In Search of Excellence*, Tom Peters talks about the many "moments of truth" in organizations, those small ongoing decisions that together create the image of the organization to its customers.[1] No part of the organization has more moments of truth than the call centre, where each representative makes numerous decisions every minute that contribute to each customer's perception of the company and create the organization's complex persona.

The **call centre climate** can range from dynamic to apathetic, from caring to impersonal, from efficient and proactive to constantly reactive, from customer-focused to procedure-focused, from calm to constant panic. The call centre culture cannot be ignored, as it influences the reps' attitude toward their work. The culture can make the call centre an enjoyable or a terrible place to work. Because attitude is so critical to success as a call centre rep and is so influenced by the climate, it is important to understand how this climate is formed, how people can affect it, and how the team can protect itself from factors that make the climate negative.

FACTORS THAT SHAPE CALL CENTRE CLIMATE

Many factors contribute to a call centre's climate. Consider the following.

Level and Type of Technology

Does the technology support or hinder efficient call centre operations? Is the call centre technology slow, so that there is a lot of **dead air** (periods of silence) while reps wait for a particular computer screen to appear? Are there many software systems, and do they work well together? Is there too much technology, so that customers are turned off by the lack of human contact or reps feel—and interact—like parts of the machine? Is the technology so out of date or inappropriate that staff are scornful of it and feel constrained by it? Does the technology enable the work or does it drive the work, so that the call centre staff facilitates the technology rather than the other way around?

Management Style

Is the style autocratic ("Staff should be seen and not heard")? Does it allow only top-down communication from management to staff? Is the management style disrespectful of people ("You should be thankful you have a job")? Or is the style people-oriented, motivating, and empowering? Does the style fit the staff, or does it fit the needs of the senior manager? Is it trusting, or does it exhibit a "See if I can catch you doing something wrong" attitude? Is management supportive or abusive? Does it lead by example or by directive?

Presence of Management Tools

Does the organization have clear staff performance expectations against which managers can assess and coach performance, or is assessment subjective? Are the measurements system-generated and after the fact (such as average call-handling time statistics), or do they assess the qualitative skills (such as the ability to control the call) that are necessary to achieve quantitative results? Do managers know how their employees are doing, or does the lack of measurement tools leave them unable to give meaningful performance feedback? Can the managers tell who is effective and who is not? Employees who contribute little can bring down morale and must either be coached to improve or weeded out. Are systems in place so that the right people get promoted, or are promotion and recognition based on politics or favouritism?

Number of Reps in Relation to Call Volume

Is the organization's planned **service level**—how quickly calls are expected to be answered and what level of call attrition, or customer hang-ups, is acceptable—consistent with its staffing policy or capability, or is the call centre held responsible for a high service level that it has insufficient staffing resources to meet? Is front-line management so frustrated by the lack of resources required to meet their goals that they give up trying, or are they able to manage performance and staffing levels in order to meet corporate expectations?

Procedures and Systems

Are there clear procedures for handling different call centre situations, or are staff just expected to know what to do and then reprimanded when they guess wrong? Do the procedures and systems for getting the work done fit the call centre environment? Are they efficient? Are procedures inflexible, or is there opportunity to change them to fit changing call centre and customer needs? Does the company try to have a procedure in place for absolutely every situation, which the staff must memorize and follow, or does the company communicate values within a framework of basic procedures, giving staff the tools to interpret and think for themselves? Is there a process for collecting and incorporating staff input about improvements to the system or procedures? Is the organization run in a bureaucratic manner, or can decisions be made in a timely way? Customers want their answers now, but this is difficult to accommodate when the company forces its bureaucratic style on the call centre.

Complexity of Calls and Diversity of Customer Issues

Are the calls frequent, short, and routine, requiring less knowledgeable call centre reps, or are the calls longer and more complex, requiring the reps to be specialists? Is the call centre an **outsourcing service**, in which each rep represents a number of clients, or is it a one-product-line, one-customer-base, in-house call centre?

Customers and Reasons for Contact

Are calls initiated by customers or by reps? Do customers contact the call centre when they are dissatisfied with something, or are there more positive reasons? If the reps are involved in selling, is this a key part of the call centre function, or is the call centre role focused on resolving customer service issues? Does the role of the call centre mean that customers who call are likely to be demanding and impatient, or are they more likely to be accommodating and understanding?

Organizational Perception of the Call Centre

Does the company's management see the call centre as having strategic importance, or as a "necessary evil" for responding to customer or competitive demands? Is the call centre viewed as a cost centre (requiring constant efforts to keep those costs down), or as a profit centre (adding value to the organization)? Do other departments share the organization's view of the call centre, or does the organization see the benefits while other staff view the centre as the lowest level of the organization?

Call Centre Design, Layout, and Location

Is the call centre attached to the company's factory, or is it located in an upscale office building? Do the layout and the workstations encourage the reps to interact and use one another as resources, or do they isolate reps? Does the design fit the needs of the particular call centre? Is the call centre easily accessible by public transit, is it near where the employees live, or must the employees have a car, travel long distances, and spend extra time commuting? Is the furniture and equipment ergonomically appropriate for spending hours in front of a computer screen, or is it dated and uncomfortable? Is the call centre well-lit with natural light, or are there few windows or ones that are blocked by workstations? Are supervisors located so they are accessible to workers without being intrusive, or are they in "guard towers"—raised areas in the call centre where they can watch everyone?

Corporate Image in the Community

Is the company and, by association, its call centre viewed as a good place to work, a prestigious place to be employed, a preferred employer, or the reverse? Is the company's type of business viewed unfavourably by the community, or is it seen as a positive type of business with which the community is proud to be associated?

Employment Environment and Hiring Policies

Is the call centre located in a low unemployment area where reps can leave a job at the slightest provocation and be hired elsewhere, or in a community where jobs are more scarce and staff are willing to work through problems to ensure their continued employment? Is the company responsive to this situation, or does it abuse it? Is the company able to recruit highly skilled people whose experience or background ensures greater success in the call centre role? Or is the call centre a low-end employer that hires people who are inexperienced and unskilled, and then tries to coach or train them to success? Does the company bother to train inexperienced people, or does it just keep the ones who show natural skill and let the rest go? Typically, this type of company will say it cannot waste time and money on training staff because they just leave anyway. Does the company rely heavily on contract or part-time staff, or does it maintain a team of full-time employees? If the call centre is unionized, this can have a major effect on its climate.

Nature of Supervisory Role and Coach Availability

Is the supervisory role one of policing to ensure call volumes are met and staff adhere to their scheduled on-phone time, or are staff treated as adults, with supervisors offering support and coaching? Are supervisors expected to coach when they don't have time to do so, or is coaching a designated part of someone's job? Is the supervisory style one of respect for the staff, or are employees seen as lazy "children" who must be told what to do and when?

Job Level Positioning in Organization

Is call centre rep a senior clerical position, so that staff work their way up to this job and then stop there, or is there opportunity to advance? Is this a high-level entry position in the organization or a low-level entry position? How do pay levels in the call centre compare with those of other jobs in the organization?

Career Pathing, Job Opportunities, and Turnover

Is there a career path in the call centre, or must an employee leave the call centre or even the organization to advance (leaving only new hires, ineffective employees, and non-growth-oriented reps to staff the centre)? Is employee **turnover** high? If turnover is low, is this for good reasons or because staff have no other opportunities or are trapped by "velvet handcuffs"—are dissatisfied and would like to leave, but the money is too good? If there is a high ratio of long-term staff, are they there for positive reasons? Is the majority of the call centre new reps who are unsure of their jobs and learning as they go, with all the mistakes and chaos that can create?

Sense of Team and Cooperation among Staff

Do employees cooperate and feel like part of a team, or is the environment one in which competitiveness rules and employees are into secretiveness or one-upmanship? Which type of environment do the management style and reward systems encourage? Are staff "cliquish," or do they welcome new members? Is there a negative and influential core group? Do people have time to help one another, and is this seen as part of the role, or is mutual support neither possible nor encouraged?

Flexibility to Meet Personal Needs

Does the call centre discourage schedule changes that might be useful for accommodating personal needs, such as child-care problems? Are start and end times flexible enough to accommodate different transportation arrangements, or is strict adherence to a preset schedule expected? Is time off for family matters expected and understood, or is it discouraged and frowned upon? Are staff members encouraged to personalize their workstations, or are they required to maintain a pristine look to achieve a uniform appearance?

The above list of factors that affect call centre climate is only a partial one. Most of these factors cannot be controlled or even influenced by the call centre reps. In most cases, reps can only learn to live with and make the best of whatever factors exist. There are, however, some climate-shaping factors that the reps can influence. Since they will spend a good part of their time in the call centre, each rep has a vested interest in working to make the climate as positive as possible. The factors that reps can influence relate to the call centre team. A positive, productive, and cohesive team can balance the potentially negative influence of any or all of the factors that influence the call centre climate.

The Team

BEING A TEAM PLAYER

A team can be defined as "a group of people working together toward the same objective." Some call centres require that their staff work together extensively, others less so. Being together in the same room doesn't necessarily mean that the call centre reps must work together. Their job involves interacting with customers, not necessarily with other reps. Some call centres have their staff work together as teams, assisting and coaching one another, and meeting periodically to share ideas and support one another. Other call centres have **self-directed work teams** that plan the responsibilities of each team member. Some organizations have their staff's workstations organized so that the reps sit as teams to give one another emotional support even though they work relatively independently. Still other organizations do none of the above, and the only way the reps "work together" is that they share the same call queue, so that each needs to carry her or his share of the load or the others' share gets bigger.

At a minimum, call centre reps must work together to manage the calls in their queue. In addition, there are many ways in which the actions of one can affect the job of the others:

if one rep is out of queue unnecessarily, the rest have to manage more calls; if one rep doesn't handle a customer well and that customer calls back, another rep may have to take the call and deal with the repercussions; if one rep is speaking loudly or sounds upset, the others have to deal with the effect of that behaviour on their own attitude and ability to communicate with their customers.

The "same objective" referred to in our definition of a team may be that part of the company mission statement or objectives that can be influenced by the call centre, such as sales targets or customer satisfaction levels. In many organizations these objectives are clearly communicated by top management. More typically—although call centre department mission statements are becoming more common—the objective of the call centre is not directly stated. Instead, the reps must guess the call centre's objectives based on management comments, the call centre's performance expectations, or the coaching process. Consequently, the call centre's objectives may be understood differently by different reps. However, most reps share the goal of having the department function smoothly so the day's work passes with fewer problems. It's fair then to say that generally call centre reps work toward some common objectives.

Call centres qualify as teams by our definition, some much more so than others. The ability to function as a team benefits the call centre and the reps who staff it. These benefits are listed in Table 2.1.

TABLE 2.1

The Benefits of Teamwork

Benefits of Teamwork to the Call Centre	– more efficient, as staff support one another to get the job done – more effective – reps know more due to sharing information – few problems from individuals adopting a "not my job" attitude – less turnover – staff feel good about the people they work with – greater customer satisfaction as customers deal with more satisfied reps
Benefits to the Reps	– greater motivation and team spirit – emotional support and help with the workload during stressful times – learn more and grow in skill due to sharing information and receiving informal coaching from teammates – the job is easier as everyone's skills improve, and is therefore less stressful – positive feeling from being part of something successful and from helping and supporting other staff and customers – enjoy work more (feel more connected, more a part of something)

Learning Application Exercise

1. *Think of at least two teams in which you are or have been a member. Outline how each fit the elements included in our definition of a team.*

2. *Discuss your answer with a peer.*

TEAM EVOLUTION

A simple way to understand team evolution is to use the **Normative Model**,[2] which says that teams grow through, potentially, four steps: forming, storming, norming, and performing.

Forming

The forming stage for teams is like the courting phase in personal relationships. In this stage, team members look for the positives in one another, for the commonalities. They politely put on their best face to fellow team members, and it is common to hear them remark on how much they have in common. This is a happy, pleasant time as team members look for reasons to bond and feel good about one another. It is not, however, a very realistic time, because people do not see teammates as they really are—real people with all the imperfections of real people. In this stage, team members see others—and often strive to present themselves—the way they'd like them to be rather than how they are. In the forming stage, people look at their team and teammates through "rose-coloured glasses."

Team members all strive to cooperate during this phase. Yet this is not the time of greatest team efficiency: roles have not been defined, the processes for dealing with one another and coping with conflict have not been established, and without recognizing one another's strengths and weaknesses, members cannot delegate or assign tasks most efficiently. In this stage, teams are so anxious to get along that they can develop "groupthink," in which people go along with decisions they don't agree with simply to feel like part of the team. The consequence is that dissenting opinions, which may be valid and may appropriately reshape decisions, are never discussed.

At this phase, team members have a dependency relationship with the designated or emerging leader and look to her or him for direction. If the team is together long enough, they will move on to the storming stage.

Storming

The storming stage has been compared with adolescence. While previously team members were trying to see similarities and were willing to sacrifice self for cohesiveness, at this stage they seek to regain their individuality. Instead of looking only for the good and the similarities in others, the team members' differences and less positive traits get excessive attention. The team members jockey for power or influence within the group, and are stereotyped as their worst selves by other team members.

As team members struggle to find their place in the group, leaders are rejected. The team becomes counterdependent on their leaders. The team members resist the need to work as a team, to collaborate; arguments and petty squabbles are common, as are defensiveness, cliques, competition, jealousy, and tension. They will stay in this counterdependency phase until they can move on to interdependency, where they give to and take from one another according to the skills and knowledge of each. Team members are disillusioned about themselves and one another, doubt whether they have accomplished anything, and wonder whether they should even stay together as a team. These are common reactions to the group's inability to resolve issues in the storming phase.

Many teams don't grow out of the storming stage. Often teams will hit a crisis in this stage, pull back to independence (noninvolvement in the team) for a brief period of time, then begin the process again with the forming stage, doomed to a future of repeating the first two phases. Other call centres exist perpetually in the storming environment and do not move on. Both of these situations create a very negative call centre climate in which the only way out is for staff to move from counterdependence to independence (and at least save themselves), or else leave the call centre completely.

To move beyond this phase, call centre staff need to create processes for decision-making in the group or for handling conflict effectively. They must gain a realistic perspective of what they have accomplished and start working on the difficult issues by taking them one at a time. The members need to start seeing one another as real human beings, not the perfect people of the forming stage and not the caricatures of the early storming phase, but basically as good people with strengths and imperfections. As teams begin to resolve these issues and mature, they gradually move into the **norming** stage.

Norming

After the negativity of the storming stage begins to be put into perspective, team members can move from the independent state (where they went to avoid the conflict of the storming phase) into a more realistic establishment of relationships. Instead of seeing only the bad in others, they see good people with human imperfections. They start to realize they can work with the good and accommodate the not-so-good in their teammates. Norms of team behaviour are established at this stage. The team creates processes for dealing with interpersonal issues and conflicts in a manner that is constructive rather than destructive.

In this phase, optimism and commitment flourish, and the team becomes productive. Functional relationships are established, and roles are carved out. The team begins establishing some interdependency, which at this stage is cautious and fragile and easily pulled back into independence at the slightest provocation. This is the first stage in which the group truly works as a team. Before the members can become a truly productive team, their understanding of one another must deepen. Trust must evolve—a realistic trust that can only be based on understanding and acceptance. The mutual appreciation must become less superficial. Many teams feel they've reached the best stage in the norming phase, but it can get even better.

Performing

In the final phase, **performing**, the team is truly mature and fully productive. Members realistically appreciate, accept, and trust one another. They value and use one another's unique talents. The team develops a personality and strength all its own, and membership in the team becomes a source of pride. The members experience a sense of belonging and uniqueness. Like a sports team, everyone plays their position and intuitively knows where all their teammates are at a given time.

BENEFITS OF KNOWING THE NORMATIVE MODEL

Knowing the Normative Model of team development is beneficial for a call centre rep: the rep knows what to expect, and knowing what phase the team is in helps to keep what is happening in perspective. Each phase must be experienced, and how well a team handles the growth necessary in each phase dictates how long the team must stay in that phase. The rep who understands the process can also see the light at the end of the tunnel—even in the depths of the storming phase, the rep knows that if the group works through the issues, norming and performing wait on the other side.

Also, the rep knows what needs to happen to move beyond each phase. This is particularly useful when the team is in the storming stage. While the rep may not be able to lead the group out of this stage (because at this stage the team members rebel against leaders), he or she may be able to model the effective behaviours for teammates and influence the team's evolution.

The rep who knows the model knows also that to some extent the cycle is repeated when the group changes or after a major accomplishment. Knowing this can help the rep keep a positive perspective and motivate him or her to adopt a style that softens the effects of each stage.

Learning Application Exercise

1. *For the teams you identified in the previous Learning Application Exercise, list and explain the stages of team evolution that you experienced.*

2. *To which stage did your team evolve? What prevented it from evolving further?*

Positive and Negative Behaviour

Individual behaviours can either contribute to a positive team environment or undermine it. Behaviours that undermine team effectiveness are not a result of someone being "bad"; in fact, typically it is "good" people who have adopted habits that have negative results for the team, their teammates, and themselves (see Table 2.2). The effects of their behaviour on the team are usually unconscious.

TRUST

Some people mistakenly think trust is like a light switch that's either on or off—one either totally trusts or totally distrusts. In reality, since trust involves people it is necessarily more complex than that. Everyone can be trusted with certain types of things, to a certain extent, and in certain circumstances. Change the type of thing, the extent of trust required, or the circumstance, and the degree to which a person can be trusted changes.

TABLE 2.2

Team Behaviours

Behaviours that Contribute to the Team	– Trust—expect the best of others, yet know their limitations and adjust your trust expectations accordingly. – Offer to help. – Thank others for their help. – Respect peers. – Share information and ideas. – Have a positive, professional, "can-do" attitude.
Behaviours that Undermine the Team	– Form cliques—"We are 'in,' they are 'out.'" – Spread and encourage rumours. – Be dishonest with peers, supervisors, and customers. – Be a "minimalist"—do the minimum to keep the job, don't carry a full share of the load so that others have to do extra.

It is wise to give trust gradually, and as you determine that a coworker is comfortable with the level of trust you are offering and can react appropriately to that level, you may choose to offer more. Don't bare your soul to everyone and then be hurt when some don't understand the importance to you of confidentiality. On the other hand, don't assume that a coworker will understand that you want something treated confidentially—ask first if it is appropriate to share with him or her something you don't want others to know. Some people who aren't good with secrets know it and will tell you so. Make it okay, with your tone and words, for people to let you know if they aren't good at keeping confidences, and even then, begin with less important secrets.

Don't blindly trust that a coworker will follow through on a project, and then get upset when at the last moment you find it was not done. Instead, be clear with instructions and deadlines and check progress along the way, at least until you know the person is able to follow through.

If a coworker doesn't keep a secret or doesn't meet a deadline, simply accept that this has helped you identify the level to which you can trust that person. It's useful to be aware of others' limits. Like them for their good characteristics and for the level of trust they can handle; don't base your relationship on the other person's ability to pass your "test."

Recognize that you may tend to share personal information too freely. This can lead to difficulty with others, particularly with coworkers who handle confidences differently from you. Even if you are good at keeping confidences, it may be inappropriate to do so, and the person sharing a confidence with you needs to know that. This can help to prevent "you and me against her or him" situations, or the development of cliques.

If you tend to assume that everyone has the same commitment to deadlines that you do and the same ability to plan for deadlines, it is important to recognize that this is not true.

People have different abilities in planning and structuring their time to meet commitments, and different working styles. Some tend to procrastinate and have trouble motivating themselves until the pressure is on, so every project is frantic around delivery time. That doesn't make these people bad or untrustworthy; it simply means you have to accept and anticipate this different work style. Know yourself and your own work style. How good are you at keeping others' secrets? Do you work toward deadlines or only generate energy at the last minute? Be conscious of the effects of these behaviours on others.

If you are the type of person for whom trust is an "all or nothing" proposition, recognize that this can lead to much personal disappointment and to alienating the basically good people you reject. The problem is yours, not theirs. Accept your responsibility for at least some of the problem. Positive relationships with coworkers are important in a call centre, and understanding and effectively using trust can help create and maintain productive relationships.

HELP COWORKERS

Call centres are busy environments. It is easy to feel so overwhelmed with your own work that you have no time to help others. The working world has evolved so much that people can rarely, if ever, leave at the end of the day with everything finished so that they can start fresh the next day. More typical is being responsible for multiple projects at the same time, and working to resolve the most urgent or at least to prevent any from becoming bigger problems than they already are. Most jobs today feel like a balancing act that requires us to constantly juggle tasks and projects.

In today's complex work environment, it is also easy to feel that we are under too much of our own pressure to be able to offer help to others. It is easy to believe that we have more to do or are under more pressure than our coworkers. Much of this pressure is self-imposed. We expect ourselves to get everything done, and we can't. A better approach is to address what is critical and deal with the less important matters later.

Offers to help a coworker should be made when

- The coworker is busier than you, and is up against a deadline that she or he may not be able to meet and that is more critical than any deadline you might be facing.

- The coworker is showing signs of stress from the workload.

- The coworker is new to a task and could benefit from your experience, skill, or coaching.

- You are not up against a deadline that cannot be changed or that requires your total involvement at this time.

Don't offer your help in a way that says you really don't want to help. Your manner and words should communicate the sincerity of your offer. For example, "Let me help you with that" is better than "You don't need any help there, do you?" Don't force your help on people who resist your offers. Respect their wish to do things on their own or their discomfort with receiving help, but leave them with a sincere, "If you change your mind, just ask."

Remember, you are more likely to receive help from others if you offer help to others.

THANK OTHERS

Make a point of thanking anyone who helps you. Ensure that the way you express your thanks is not excessive in relation to the help you receive. Excessive thanks may make the other person feel uncomfortable and reluctant to help you again.

RESPECT PEERS

If you look for the good in everyone, people feel better being around you, and you bring out the best in people. If you look for the likeable in everyone, you will be much more effective in interpersonal relationships. People who always look for the flaws in others and then comment on them could begin in a process of positive personal growth by adapting a more positive outlook and actively looking for positives. Respect, a positive attitude, and avoidance of negatives are all critical for effectively dealing with customers, and are essential for positive interpersonal relationships and effective call centre teams.

SHARE INFORMATION AND IDEAS

Sometimes a call centre representative comes across information or a resource that is useful for certain types of customers, or she or he may stumble across a technique that works particularly well.

This information, resource, or technique could be useful to the rest of the call centre team, improving the effectiveness of the entire team by affecting more customers. Yet some reps refuse to share their information with others, for a number of reasons.

- The reps may be so intent on doing well and making a positive impression on management that they want to use this information to stand out or have a competitive advantage over the rest of the team. These people are more concerned with their image than with the success of the call centre—they do not work toward a common goal and essentially cease to be team players.

- Some people whose previous life experiences have been competitive don't see that the call centre's success hinges on cooperation. They may not realize that management may, instead of being impressed, be concerned about their lack of ability to work with others.

- Some people are so busy they don't think to share things or don't want to take the time to do so. If anyone else is working less efficiently because they don't know of something that would help them, then this attitude undermines team efficiency.

- Some people don't know how to share information or ideas appropriately. They don't want to seem pushy or be seen as a know-it-all, so they don't tell others what they know.

HAVE YOU EVER?

Among a group of kids who got together to play hockey, John was a wonderful player. He could skate as well as or better than the rest of the kids, he could stick-handle better than the others, and he had all the moves. Yet, when picking teams for a neighbourhood game, John was never the first one chosen. His team usually won, but the others didn't like playing on his team. With all his skills, John was a "grandstander"—he always played so he looked good, so he could show off. He was a bit too in love with his own ability. Worst of all, he hogged the puck. His team got fewer goals than they might have because John would always try to score himself, often losing the puck when a pass to another player would have resulted in a goal. Players were always calling for him to pass the puck, which he never did, and no one wanted to pass the puck to him because he always kept it. John just wouldn't share.

To contribute positively to the growth and success of your call centre team, develop the habit of sharing anything you encounter that might be helpful to others. To communicate ideas and information appropriately,

- Offer information, but don't insist on others using your input.

- Don't treat your information as bigger than it is—be humble in outlining your idea.

- If you've learned something based on the cues of others, give them credit.

- Suggest ideas for improving your department in a way your boss will find comfortable, typically when the two of you are alone, not by surprising her or him at a meeting or on the way to one.

HAVE A POSITIVE AND PROFESSIONAL ATTITUDE

Be optimistic with teammates, look for the bright side of a situation, and look for ways to deal with an issue rather than have your mood negatively affected by it. Treat fellow workers in this positive friendly manner, and always act professionally.

CLIQUES

When a call centre team is large, it is difficult to feel a sense of camaraderie with everyone. You will interact with some people more than with others, and some will have personality traits or interests that match yours better. You will naturally gravitate to some people more than others. Such a tendency is understandable and certainly not counterproductive to effective group behaviour, as long as other people in the larger team do not feel excluded in the process. Cliques, on the other hand, do exclude people, undermine the sense of team, interfere with team cohesiveness, and inhibit team growth. They are elements of the storming phase. To avoid the negative effects of a clique:

- Recognize the negative symptoms of "cliquishness," the feeling that because you and your closer coworkers have some things in common this makes you the best, while those who aren't part of your group are somehow inferior. This attitude characterizes adolescence, which some people never grow out of. We all tend to feel that people who share our interests or characteristics are "right,"because they validate the way we are. The key is to not view people who are different from you as bad or inferior.

- Avoid limiting your interactions to a few people to the exclusion of others. When your small group becomes the only group you lunch with, talk to at breaks, seek help from, offer to help, and in general interact with, others can feel left out. Be friendly and interact with everyone, even if members of your circle of friends try to exclude others. Let them know that while you like them, you like other people as well.

- Resist the temptation to think negatively about the people who are in a clique or about yourself because you are not. Recognize the reasons for the situation, and be as friendly with the members of the clique as you are with others, accepting that they may be unable to be as friendly to you because of their clique's "code of conduct."

RUMOURS

Many people want to know things that really aren't any of their business. Most people have some interest in rumours, but others have such a consuming interest that they constantly feed rumours with new information to share with others to keep the process going. The problem is that there are very few good rumours—they are usually about something bad that is about to happen or about someone's ugly little secret. Rumours bring down morale in the team and can hurt people. A good rule of thumb when you are attempting to over-come the rumour-mongering habit: review the rumour, and if it doesn't say something good about a situation or person, don't pass it on. Imagine what better places our workplaces would be if everyone applied this rule.

DISHONESTY

When people lie to a coworker or supervisor to protect themselves or put down someone else, then the morale of the team is brought down and the general level of trust is damaged.

When you've spoken a small lie and it is evident that you'll have to lie again to cover up the original lie, it's best to cut your losses and get out while you can: just confess, apologize, explain, and promise not to do it again. The consequences of the lie get bigger with each additional deceit. Better to clear things up before creating a lasting negative effect on someone's impression of you. Whatever the immediate benefit of lying, it's not worth it in the long run, for the individual or for the team.

"MINIMALISM"

Minimalists are people who have convinced themselves that they should do no more than is absolutely necessary to keep their job. These people often see their employer as the enemy, and to do more than the minimum feels to them like "selling out to the other side."

In a call centre in which everyone is responsible for handling a share of the calls, this attitude in one or more people requires others in the team to do more than their share. If coworkers complain to the minimalists, they will usually shrug it off, saying it's not their issue and that the company should hire more staff. Minimalists put more energy into avoiding doing a full day's work than they would expend if they simply did their job.

Why would someone adopt this attitude? This behaviour may be rooted in some deeply held but wrong-headed beliefs about the relationship between the worker and employer, or about the evils of big business, or about an individual's "right" to be taken care of rather than have to make his or her own way, or it may simply be an attempt to rationalize personal laziness. The reasons for minimalism are often very ingrained, and it can be very difficult to dissuade someone from this attitude, in spite of the fact that it is neither fruitful nor satisfying for the minimalist. Whatever the cause, people who suffer from minimalism are their own worst enemy. Typically these people are not respected by most coworkers or management and are not considered for advancement, if they are able to keep their job at all. Their own negativity and complaining that often accompany their attitude keep them from getting ahead in their jobs and in their personal lives.

The worst problem with minimalists is that they manage to seduce others into sharing in their misery. They encourage others to adopt their negative beliefs and bring themselves down to the minimalist's level of disrespect and dissatisfaction. Again, there is no gain in adopting the minimalist attitude except the friendship of the minimalist.

If you are a minimalist, look for reasons to get past that block. Start with "I'd like to have some respect from others" and "I'd like to keep my job," and go on from there. Look at what others are accomplishing in a day, and set yourself targets to get your productivity up. If you must work with a minimalist, make performance requirements clear, and hope your boss sees and acts on the situation.

Learning Application Exercise

1. Assess for yourself which of the 10 behaviors described on the previous pages apply to you as a member of a team, either as a "contributing behaviour" that you don't do or don't do consistently or as an "undermining behaviour" that you have slipped into in a team environment. Be honest with yourself.

2. For each of the 10 behaviours, determine what you can do to either sustain it in each team you join, or limit its potentially damaging effect on the team. Pay particular attention to those behaviours you identified as most relevant to you in question 1.

3. Discuss your responses with a peer.

Handling Interpersonal Conflict

GETTING THROUGH THE STORMING PHASE

Put any group of people into a highly charged, stressful environment, and you are bound to have interpersonal conflicts. This is particularly true when they have to work as a team, relying on one another to get the job done. Conflict is a major part of the storming phase—conflict with people who, in the forming phase, you may have felt good about and close to, and with whom you felt you had a lot in common. In the storming phase, emotions run wild and resolving conflicts is made more difficult by the hurt feelings, anger, resentments, and blaming that can all be part of this very uncomfortable phase of team growth. To move on to the norming phase, structures must be put in place to resolve conflicts. Too often, the structures that evolve are not the most effective and don't lead out of the storming phase. They are "blind alleys" that get away from the main issue but don't take the team anywhere. Consider these techniques for "resolving" conflict:

- not talking to another person until the other gives in and apologizes
- telling everyone else how upset you are, but not the person who is the source of the frustration, hoping that word will get back to that person or others will take it upon themselves to mediate to resolve the issue
- doing nothing to resolve the issue, but harbouring resentment that can come out in other ways, such as general frustration with the job, a feeling that you no longer like working with these people, or a general disinterest in what you seek to accomplish on the job
- coming to a compromise that deals with the surface issue but doesn't make anyone happy and doesn't deal with the underlying issue
- being generally nasty to the other person, disagreeing over any issue, making negative offhand remarks, yet never confronting the real issue
- getting upset and shouting at the other person in a process aimed more at venting than resolving the problem

None of these is an effective way to resolve conflict. They are all counterproductive in that the conflict remains unresolved. Having settled on one or more of these ineffective ways to solve problems, better ways to deal with conflict are not explored and therefore not discovered, and the team's growth out of the storming phase is delayed. Let's consider a better way to resolve conflict.

STEPS IN CONFLICT RESOLUTION

1. Agree on the Benefits of Resolving the Conflict

Generate a list of reasons why the conflict should be resolved. Include reasons that are potentially relevant for the team and for the other person. Approach the other person with your request to resolve the conflict, along with the reasons why it might be to her or his and the team's advantage for the two of you to do so. If the person is not ready to work on resolving the conflict, respectfully explore the reasons why, repeating the advantages. If the person still resists, keep the door open to this opportunity, and revisit it later.

2. Understand Your Own Position

Often conflict is fuelled by emotions. Consider the following:

- What are your feelings about the situation?

- What aspect of the conflict are you particularly upset about? Are you more upset than the situation warrants?

- Are any of the feelings you have associated with this situation really based on other experiences you have had?

- Separate your feelings from the facts of the situation. What are the objective facts of the situation once emotions have been removed?

- Are there areas in this conflict where you have acted inappropriately, where the other person might have justifiably reacted as she or he did?

- How would you like to see this problem resolved so that it will stay resolved? What do you need to get from a solution?

3. Understand the Other Person's Position

Typically in a conflict, both parties believe their position is the correct one. It's important to understand that the other person believes he or she is right. It is also important to realize that the person feels your position is wrong and that you are the one who is stubborn. A critical step in conflict resolution is to understand the other person's position and reasons for being attached to that position. To achieve this understanding,

- Show your interest in understanding the other person's point of view.

- Collect enough information so you can understand the facts and emotions that make up the other person's point of view.

- Show the other person that you understand his or her position. Do this by asking questions, paraphrasing, and summarizing to confirm you understand the other person's point of view and feelings. Don't ask questions to challenge or criticize the other person.

- Don't react to accusations, criticisms, or blaming from the other person.

- Ask the other person how she or he would like to see this situation resolved, and find out what the person needs from a solution.

4. Share/Clarify Your Position

In terms that describe how you feel and how you see the situation—not about what the other person did and how the person made you feel—outline your interpretation of the situation. Identify the points of agreement and the points of conflict, and share your vision of how you would like to see this issue resolved. Encourage the other person to ask you clarifying questions so the person can be sure he or she understands your position. Be candid about points where you may have responded inappropriately.

5. Identify the Areas of Agreement and Difference in Your Positions

First identify areas of agreement in your positions. Then identify areas in which your positions differ. Explore these, and attempt to reach a better understanding of the reasons for the differences.

6. Resolve the Differences

Explore and brainstorm solutions to each issue until you find one that will satisfy you both. The solution need not be "my way" or "your way" or win–lose, nor must it be a compromise that leaves both of you dissatisfied. You may find it best to give in on issues that are less important to you while the other person gives in on issues that are of lesser importance to her or him. You may opt to "try this first then try this second," or you may be able to combine two or three solutions into one. Be creative and seek agreement.

7. Develop and Implement an Action Plan

Agree on an action plan, then agree on an implementation plan that will make the action plan a reality. Possibly include a trial period with a checkpoint to confirm that the plan is working so that changes can be made early rather than too late.

AN EXAMPLE OF CONFLICT RESOLUTION

Jim's sons, Peter, aged 10, and Patrick, aged 11, were interested in Magic Cards (cards with different characters, powers, and values that are used in a game, but more importantly in trading). Rather than drive them to the card store so they could buy more cards, Jim offered to give them some of the cards he had tucked away to split between them, then he went to work. A short while later, Jim received a call from his wife: one son was in his room upset and the other was on the couch crying. They both wanted Jim's "best" card and had been unable to find a resolution to this impasse. Their first attempt at resolution had failed: they had flipped a coin, with the winner to get first pick of the cards, but when Peter won and chose the card they both wanted most, Patrick became upset. He had assumed that the "first pick" would be a random choice of the cards that would be placed face down. He was upset because he never would have agreed to the coin flip if he had known the rules. Peter was upset because he felt he had won fair and square and now his rightful spoils were being taken away. The only solution they could see was to call the whole deal off and return the cards to their father, but neither one was happy with this alternative either. When Jim got home he sat them down and tried to resolve the situation.

1. They agreed that they wanted to resolve the conflict. If they didn't, they would have none of the cards at all.

2. Patrick explained his situation. He wanted the favourite card, otherwise he was ready to negotiate.

3. Peter felt the same as Patrick, except that he won the flip of the coin and figured he already deserved to have the card.

4. All agreed that the initial instructions for the coin flip left room for confusion. Peter agreed that Patrick doesn't lie, so if he said he misunderstood the plan for the coin flip he was likely telling the truth and not trying to get out of the deal because he lost. Patrick could understand that Peter felt he deserved the card because he won the coin flip.

5. It was clear that they wanted the cards and felt they could trade for the rest with no trouble, but this one card was the bone of contention.

6. They explored a few options for resolution that were rejected by one or the other. Then they hit on the idea of both identifying a group of cards that they felt would be a fair exchange for the best card. Peter saw the cards Patrick was willing to exchange and felt they were worth much more. Jim confirmed that Patrick would be happy with a deal that gave Peter these cards while he got the prized one, and that Peter would feel he had gotten the best of the deal if he got the other cards and Patrick only got the one in exchange.

7. They made the exchange, and both confirmed they were more than happy with the deal. They used a similar process to divvy up the rest of Jim's good cards, and the balance of his deck was split up somewhat less formally. Later in the day they were flaunting their booty with their friends and the entire episode was forgotten.

Learning Application Exercise

1. *Identify a conflict in which you are currently involved. If you aren't involved in one, think of one you had in the past, and walk through as many of the steps in this exercise as possible.*

2. *Apply the seven steps of conflict resolution. Write steps 1 and 2 out as you think them through, and review these with a peer along with your plan for the rest of the steps.*

3. *Implement the steps, and take notes on what worked and what didn't. Discuss each step of the process with a peer. If you are using a previous experience for this exercise, use the conflict resolution steps to assess what worked and what didn't, and why. What could you have done differently?*

Summary

Because the call centre is important as the face of the organization to the customers, the working environment is particularly important. The call centre climate is a result of many factors, most of which are outside of the representatives' control. The factors that the reps can control, however, can have a significant impact on the climate. If the reps can help to create a positive and cohesive team, they can overcome or counterbalance any negative influence on the climate caused by the uncontrollable factors.

A team is a group of people working together toward the same objective. While some call centres are more formally structured as teams, all fit this definition of a team and all can benefit from working effectively as a team. Teams evolve through four stages. Knowing these stages can ease the call centre's transition through them. They are

- Forming: The "courting" phase, in which everyone wants to get along with one another.

- Storming: The adolescent phase, in which the group looks at the differences and creates conflict. Many teams never progress past this difficult stage and instead stay in it indefinitely, or repeat it and the forming stage over and over.

- Norming: This is when teams begin to establish roles and procedures and methods of resolving conflict.

- Performing: This is when teams are at their most productive, working as a cohesive and interdependent unit.

The behaviours of individuals can contribute to or undermine the effectiveness of a team. Such behaviours include

- trusting

- helping coworkers

- thanking others for their help

- respecting peers

- sharing information and ideas

- having a positive and professional attitude

- forming cliques

- spreading rumours

- being dishonest

- being a "minimalist," or performing at the minimum level required to keep one's job

Because of the nature of the call centre rep's job and the call centre environment, interpersonal conflict will arise. The steps required to deal with conflict constructively are as follows:

1. Agree on the benefits of resolving the conflict.

2. Understand your own position.

3. Understand the other person's position.

4. Share/clarify your position.

5. Identify the areas of agreement and differences in your position.

6. Resolve the differences.

7. Develop and implement an action plan.

Endnotes

1. Thomas J. Peters, *In Search of Excellence* (New York: Harper & Row, 1982).

2. Bruce W. Tuckman, "Development Sequence in Small Groups," *Psychological Bulletin* (1965), 63, 384–89.

CHAPTER 3
Addressing the Call: It's All Attitude

Learning Outcomes

After successfully completing Chapter 3 you will be able to:

- *Discuss the importance of a positive attitude.*

- *Recognize the symptoms of a negative attitude.*

- *Avoid the potentially damaging effects of a less than positive attitude.*

- *Prepare, physically and mentally, for each call in order to optimize your attitude and make a positive first impression.*

- *Make every call a success.*

The Power of Attitude

The single biggest difference between an effective call centre representative and a mediocre one is attitude. All the skills this book discusses contribute to one's performance on the job, but if you are lacking one or two of the skills yet have the right attitude, you can still be very successful. On the other hand, if you have all the skills but a poor attitude, you will fail—and fail on a number of fronts.

- You fail professionally. With a poor attitude toward your job, you don't do your job as well, and you don't handle customers as effectively. This affects others' attitude toward you (peers as well as customers), and negatively affects their image of you and, in the case of customers, their image of the company you represent.

- You fail socially. We are each responsible for our interactions with others and for the effects of our interactions with others. These responsibilities are part of what is required to function effectively in the social environment in which you live. If you fail to uphold your social responsibilities, you fail the other people with whom you interact. These people may be customers who are negatively affected by your poor attitude. Likewise, if your coworkers have to work in an environment affected by your negative attitude, picking up the pieces when upset customers you've failed call back, you fail your coworkers. It is not fair for coworkers to have to deal with the consequences of one rep's poor attitude, and this shapes their opinion and treatment of the rep.

- You fail personally. When you are not effective professionally, your self-image is weakened and you set yourself up for failure. A large part of our life is devoted to our job. We define ourselves, in part, by what we do for a living. So when we feel less than effective at our job, we feel less effective as people. The diminished respect from others that our poor attitude inspires further contributes to this weakening of our self-image.

A positive attitude acts in the reverse, setting people up for success: professionally, by performing a quality job; socially, by fulfilling the expectations of our company and coworkers; and personally, by enhancing our own and others' sense of our worth and enhancing our self-esteem. A positive attitude, then, is essential for success.

People with a poor attitude are not happy—who could be with all the negative consequences? They typically try to rationalize their way out of responsibility for their failure. A poor attitude causes these people to put little of themselves into their job, then they find it unrewarding, which reinforces their negative attitude.

Some people blame their poor attitude on their lot in life, feeling that they are working in a position well below their potential. They think a better job will give them a better attitude. The problem for these people is their failure to realize that attitude comes first.

Learning Application Exercise

1.   Do you know any people who don't do their share, who don't care how well they do or how this affects those around them? How does their negative attitude influence your opinion of these people? What do you envision their lives will be like in 10 years?

2.   Do you know people who have a positive attitude about themselves and their job (be sure not to confuse "positive" with "inflated"), even if their job isn't a fast-track, high-powered position? How does their positive attitude affect your opinion of these people? What do you envision their lives will be like in 10 years? How successful in terms of job and personal satisfaction do you expect them to be compared with those who have a negative attitude?

3.   What sort of attitude do you bring to work and to life in general, a negative one or a positive one?

4.   What do you realistically picture for yourself in 10 years?

Overcoming a Negative Attitude

The following are several steps for overcoming a negative attitude or creating a positive attitude.

RECOGNIZE YOUR POOR ATTITUDE

The first step is to recognize that you have a negative attitude, and to forgive yourself. Failure to forgive themselves leads some people to defend or rationalize their counterproductive behaviour rather than deal with it. Rather than waste time and opportunities rationalizing a poor attitude, it is better to take responsibility for it and work on replacing it with a positive attitude.

There are different levels of poor attitude. A poor attitude is not necessarily so negative that it leads to major job failure. It may simply prevent people from being as effective as they could be and working to increase their skills. It may become apparent as a negative attitude toward customers or certain types of customers. The negative attitude may be directed at the company, or it may create the feeling of drudgery that some people have when they come to work.

Watch for the warning signs of a poor attitude. Such an attitude can grow without your even being aware of it. For example, you might start off agreeing with a negative coworker's view of your boss, and then this grows into a negative feeling about your job and a reluctance to go to work every day. A poor attitude can grow so slowly and seem so right that you don't realize you have it until you experience significant effects in terms of job failure and dissatisfaction.

Even a good attitude can benefit from improvement, and even a person with a generally positive attitude can have down periods. Most of us can benefit from a periodic "attitude tune-up." The first step is to recognize if and when one is due.

IDENTIFY THE BENEFITS OF A POSITIVE ATTITUDE

What are the benefits to an organization of its employees' positive attitude?

- Because they are treated better, customers are more satisfied. This leads to an increased sense of loyalty, which can lead to longer tenure as a customer and perhaps doing more business with the organization. The positive attitude of call centre representatives can increase the value of each customer to an organization. The most loyal customer is not one who has never had a problem with the company, but one whose issue was resolved in a timely, effective, and caring manner.

- A positive corporate image is created by a team of positive and effective call centre representatives. This can lead to acquiring new customers who are attracted to a winner. The positive word of mouth that results from this positive corporate image can enhance customer loyalty, because people want to be associated with an organization that is highly regarded. New customers and more loyal customers lead to increased sales.

- When staff work professionally and have a positive attitude, the work environment or corporate culture is improved. It is a better place to work, so the company retains good staff, attracts the best, and enjoys enhanced productivity—all of which contribute to greater cost-effectiveness and enhanced sales. A positive attitude is infectious.

These benefits are important to a company's success and, indirectly, to the people who work for that company. There are also benefits to the customer.

- Customer issues are resolved more efficiently, saving them time and annoyance.

- Customers have a positive feeling about doing business with the organization, and consequently their decision to do business with it is reinforced, removing any anxiety associated with buying.

- Customers feel respected and cared about as people, helping to make their day a little nicer.

These positive effects don't just happen—a consistent positive staff attitude is not easy to achieve. It requires that each individual call centre rep keep her or his positive attitude call after call, in spite of numerous daily frustrations.

Why put all this extra effort into being better and more professional? Why bother trying to achieve personal growth when it's so hard to achieve? What's in it for the rep? There are many potential benefits, though not all will appeal to every rep. It is important to identify those benefits that are most meaningful to you, and to stay conscious of and focused on those benefits, particularly when you are faced with pressures that can negatively affect your attitude. Here are 10 benefits to the call centre rep of having a positive attitude:

- When your team does well and is respected by the outside world, you take pride and feel a sense of personal satisfaction for having contributed to that success. We all like to be associated with a winner, to feel proud of the company we work for.

- Many of us feel good when we are able to help someone else. Call centre reps feel personally satisfied by helping resolve customer issues. You feel good if your positive attitude has caused customers to feel positive about their interaction with you.

- If you contribute to the company's success, it is more likely to grow, and your job and income will be more secure.

- Even if the company restructures—a common phenomenon these days—a positive attitude and job success increase your chances of being retained or being hired somewhere else more quickly. Your successful track record, strong skills, and a positive attitude give you career security.

- If career advancement is important to you, you stand a much better chance of being promoted if you have a positive attitude that enhances your performance and inspires your peers.

- The call centre job is more fun if you have a positive attitude. You have fewer difficult customers, because a positive approach tends to result in a more positive customer response. You are also better liked by your coworkers.

- The job gets easier, partly because you get better at it and partly because you have fewer problem callers. Consequently, a positive attitude results in a job that is more rewarding and less stressful.

- For some of us, knowing that we are good at what we do and that we are truly professional is very satisfying. A positive attitude is an essential ingredient of professionalism.

- You get recognition and positive feedback from your customers, coworkers, and supervisors. This positive feedback is important to many of us. It's one thing to know you are doing a good job, but that much more meaningful if someone else notices it.

- We are motivated to work on enhancing our call centre skills. These skills include interacting effectively with other people, which is a very transferable skill. If we are good at interacting with people, we can be more effective at most jobs. Furthermore, this is a good life skill that can be transferred to our relationships in other, even nonwork, parts of our lives.

With so many benefits to your company, your customers, and yourself, there is ample reason to strive for a positive attitude. The key is to recognize those benefits that are important to you, that can motivate you to strive for that positive attitude.

Learning Application Exercise

1. *Do you see yourself as having a negative attitude? Do you think you have ever had one, even for a short period of time?*

2. *What were the symptoms of your poor attitude?*

3. *What are the benefits for you of a call centre representative position?*

RECOGNIZE AND OVERCOME THE HABITS THAT UNDERMINE A POSITIVE ATTITUDE

Undermining Factor 1: Reality Sets In

Often when we start a new job, we go through a "honeymoon" phase: the new company seems wonderful, the new boss seems wonderful, the coworkers seem to have so much in common with us, and the job seems great. After we are on the job for a while, the honeymoon ends as we start to notice the things that are less than perfect.

Some people can enjoy the parts that they like while recognizing that nothing is perfect. They put these imperfections into perspective, accepting them but continuing to like the job, company, or coworkers for the things that are worthy of being liked, things that far outweigh the negatives.

Other people dwell on the imperfections. The negatives take on such importance that they overwhelm the positives. In effect, for these people, the pendulum swings from being too far in the positive end to being too far in the negative end—they fail to find balance in their perceptions. These people spend so much time and energy focusing on the negatives that they end up developing a negative attitude.

When this happens, it is often useful to step back and put things in perspective. Here are four steps for overcoming a negative attitude:

1. List all the things that you like about whatever is the focus of your negative feelings.

2. List the things you do not like.

3. Deal with each of the things you do not like.

    a. Attempt to understand why it is like it is—for example, why a person did something or why the company made a certain decision.

    b. Assess the impact for you. We tend to mentally blow negative effects out of proportion. If you think realistically about the most probable impact or look at the best case/worst case/most likely impact, often you'll find that the reality is not as bad as your negative imaginings.

    c. Identify the positive elements of the situation. For example, what can you learn from it?

    d. Determine whether the focus of your negative feelings is something you can change. If so, plan how you will deal with it. If not, plan how you can accommodate the situation or otherwise live with it. If it is something you cannot accept, realistically and logically weigh the costs of removing yourself from the situation, make a decision to leave your job or stay, then act on the decision.

4. Once you have made your decision, move on. Stop feeling upset about something you have made a decision to live with. Instead, put it in the background and enjoy the positive elements you identified in step 1.

ON THE JOB

Positive Attitude

Sally's company is changing the call centre's hours of operation from 12 hours a day to 24 hours a day.

Sally does not like the decision because she doesn't want to work overnight. She is so upset about the company's decision that she realizes she has developed a negative attitude toward her job and the company. This attitude is affecting her work and her enjoyment of the job. She decides to apply the steps for overcoming this negative attitude.

The list of things that Sally likes about the job and the company is extensive. Topping the list are the company's medical benefits, which cover her and her family; the fact that she really does believe in the company's products; the fact that she enjoys her supervisor and coworkers; and the fact that she feels rewarded by the positive feeling that she gets from helping customers. She hasn't felt this good about any of her previous jobs.

There are a few items on Sally's negative list, but they are mostly small procedural things that are in the process of being changed anyway. The only real frustration is the change in business hours.

Sally discusses the change with her supervisor and discovers that the company is making the change in response to customer demand and competitive pressures. Sally works for an international call centre, and customers need to be able to access it during their work hours, which means the company has to be available to all customers 24 hours a day. Some major customers have been talking about taking their business to competitors to get 24-hour access, so Sally's company has no choice but to expand its hours.

Sally's worst fear was having to work weekly rotating shifts of days, afternoons, and evenings like her dad had had to work in the local factory. She knows how much her dad hated those shifts, and knew she would as well. In reality, the worst-case scenario is each call centre rep having to work the overnight shift once every two months. The best-case scenario is the company hiring staff to handle the overnight shift (Sally can live with rotating days and evenings). Sally realizes that her emotional reaction to the change is based on her worst-case scenario, which is worse than the realistic worst-case scenario. The most likely scenario is that a number of the reps whose spouses work rotating shifts will volunteer for overnight duty so they can be on the same shift as their spouses. Sufficient interest has already been expressed by people to cover the shifts.

Sally realizes that she can manage the one overnight shift every two months with only a minor adjustment to her lifestyle.

Having done her analysis, Sally puts the upset behind her and focuses on her list of positive aspects of the job, which she posts in her workstation for a couple of weeks as a reminder when her positive attitude slips.

Undermining Factor 2: Getting Caught Up in Negative Self-Talk

Some people have a habit of verbally venting when they encounter minor frustrations. They may vent quietly to themselves (with others in earshot), to a trusted peer, or to anyone who will listen. The longer the habit goes on without being checked, the more it will progress to the most problematic stage of indiscriminate venting. When we get caught up in our negative self-talk, we perpetuate what could have simply been a momentary frustration. By letting it go on and escalating the negative self-talk, the frustration gets bigger until it becomes a negative attitude.

We can also get caught up in the negative self-talk of others. When we hear coworkers express their frustrations, it temporarily brings down our mood. When this happens regularly, it starts to affect our overall mood and we may develop our own negative attitude. If we are the trusted coworker who repeatedly hears the negative person's venting, there is a tendency to join in and look for negative stories of our own. Negative self-talk, whether our own or others', can be damaging and should be avoided.

To overcome your negative self-talk:

1. Realize that you do it and that it is not harmless. It can affect your attitude and that of your peers.

2. Apply the four steps for overcoming a negative attitude discussed previously in this chapter.

To overcome the effects of others' negative self-talk:

1. Identify the behaviour: "Jody, you sound so unhappy with your job."

2. Let the person know the effect it has on you: "When I hear those comments I feel down."

3. Help the coworker put the issues in perspective and see that this behaviour is the beginning of a general negative attitude.

4. Agree on a plan to playfully or empathetically remind the person when she or he is starting to slip into the negativity again.

This same plan may work with coworkers whose negative talk has reached the stage of actively looking for others with whom to share their misery.

1. Change the subject when a person starts to get into negative talk.

2. Tell the person something good about whatever he or she is complaining about.

3. If nothing else works, stay away from the negative person. You may be unable to pull the person out of his or her negativity, but at least you can save yourself from going down too. If the person asks why you are avoiding him or her, explain why.

ON THE JOB

Negative Talk

A consultant was asked to analyze an ineffective call centre in which the negative atmosphere was palpable. It felt depressing just walking into the call centre and was definitely an uncomfortable place to work. No physical causes of the negative atmosphere, such as a lack of natural light, poorly designed workstations, and so on, could be found. The negativity was coming from the staff—they even looked depressed!

One staff member, Jerry, was the exception. He was energetic and always smiling. When interviewing Jerry, the consultant remarked on the negative atmosphere and asked Jerry what he saw as the cause. Jerry replied, "Well, it started a couple of years ago when there was a computer error and all the monthly statements were wrong. Every customer who called was upset. We were going crazy taking all the angry calls—no breaks, no time for lunch. It was pretty hectic. Around this time I noticed people started to talk negatively about the customers, and it wasn't just venting after a difficult call. Every time they spoke, they seemed to be trying to outdo one another with stories of horrendous customer interactions. I wanted no part of it, so every time someone told me a negative story, I told them about a positive call I'd had. After all, 19 out of 20 calls were from reasonable people. After a while the other reps stopped telling me about how bad the customers were. They didn't want their negativity shattered by my positive stories, so they just left me alone, which was fine by me.

"A few months later they started talking negatively about the company and the managers. I handled it the same way, and soon they left me alone. And now, recently, they've started talking negatively about one another. I know that nobody's perfect, but everybody has good traits, so I just tell them something good about the same person they are complaining about.

"So here are all these people getting up in the morning hating the customers they have to talk to, negative about the company they work for, and not liking one another. Whereas I enjoy the customers I work with, I like the company and the supervisors, and I can find something to like about everyone who works here. I think I got the best of this deal."

The consultant had to agree, because she had seen similar situations often. If people stopped to consider the effects of negative talk, they wouldn't start it. If they realized how ultimately unhappy the negative talk could make them, surely they would stop it immediately.

Undermining Factor 3: Looking for the Negative

Some people have a natural tendency to look for the negative in anything. They can quickly pick out the flaws in any plan and tell you why it won't work; they can proofread almost as fast as they can turn the pages, identifying spelling and grammatical errors with uncanny accuracy; they always see what's wrong before they notice what's right. An example is the woman who won two lottery prizes totalling $80 000 and whose remark to an interviewing reporter was "Well, it isn't the million."

Seeing what's missing rather than what's there is a common stress reaction (see the **Valuator** personality type discussed in Chapters 8 and 9) that can become a habit. Such an outlook makes it hard to have a positive attitude. To overcome this habit,

1. Recognize you have the habit.

2. Conduct a self-assessment to determine whether the behaviour results from stress (see Chapter 9) and, if so, work to avoid or minimize the causes of the stress.

3. If this is a non-stress-related habit, work on changing it.

   a. Commit yourself to changing the habit.

   b. Solicit peer support, or attach a cue card saying "AVOID NEGATIVITY" to your computer screen to remind you when you slip into the habit.

   c. Force yourself to identify two positives every time you identify a negative.

4. Use the steps described under undermining factor 1 to help you overcome this cause of a negative attitude.

5. If the negative mood persists or recurs periodically, seek medical advice. With all the recent research on mood and all the mood management products and techniques available, it makes no sense to spend large parts of your life feeling bad.

Learning Application Exercise

1. *Which of the attitude undermining factors apply to you? Have you ever fallen into one of the three habits? Do one or more apply to you now?*

2. *Apply the steps for overcoming whatever attitude-undermining factor is relevant to you. Document each step.*

Creating a Positive First Impression

Because the first impression we create with customers is the most lasting and can be difficult to change, it is critical that our first impression on the telephone be positive. To make sure the first words out of your mouth form a positive image of you and your company, take these four preparation steps before you accept or make a call:

- Prepare your workstation.

- Prepare your information.

- Prepare yourself physically.

- Prepare yourself mentally.

PREPARE YOUR WORKSTATION

Your workstation is your "command centre," the place where you make it all happen. Prepare it in a way that is both comfortable and functional. Make sure the tools you need frequently are close at hand and others are still within reach. Keep binders of resource materials accessible and up-to-date, and hard-copy files well organized for easy reference. Well-organized workstation resources help you respond faster to customer questions. If your resources are computerized, arrive at work in time to log in to your system or start up your computer before your calls begin.

Because call centre jobs require reps to be on the telephone for extended periods of time, headsets are almost a necessity, especially where there is extensive need for computer work or note-taking while on the phone.

Ensure the headset cord is long enough to allow you to stand, move around your work area, or periodically get up and stretch. Regular movement can help to reduce body fatigue. If you often write while on the phone, make sure your phone is on the opposite side of the desk from your writing hand so cords do not cross over papers on your desk.

Make sure your chair, computer screen, and keyboard are placed so you can sit comfortably and with good posture. Inappropriate ergonomics, or a poor relationship between your body, furniture, and computer equipment, can make you physically and mentally tired. Sitting with your back straight, your feet on the floor, your computer screen placed to permit you to look at it at a 90 degree angle vertically and slightly down horizontally, and your forearms parallel to the floor will give you greater comfort and help you avoid the various aches and pains that can result from poor body positioning.

Learning Application Exercise

Is your workstation set up appropriately?

1. *Do you have a system for keeping your tools and resources organized?*

2. *Do you use a comfortable headset?*

3. *Do you have a routine for periodic stretching?*

4. *Is your workstation organized for optimal effectiveness?*

5. *Are your chair, keyboard, and computer screen positioned appropriately?*

PREPARE YOUR INFORMATION

To be effective on the telephone, you need to be comfortable with all the relevant job information.

Understand your software, scripts, procedures, and any product information you may need to refer to during a call. Know where to find information. When you are new to the job, you usually receive training to acquaint you with the information you need to do the job, but learning does not stop there. Keeping up-to-date is a continuous process. It is your responsibility to keep informed—don't wait for your company to give you more training. Use downtime during the workday to read up on new products and other information. A true professional is constantly learning, structuring opportunities to acquire more knowledge that will help her or him to be even more effective on the job. Ensure your reference material is up-to-date and available. Rather than store updated hard copy in your in-basket (to be filed later when you have the time), develop the habit of putting it in the appropriate binder or file immediately so you don't waste time looking for it or, even worse, give customers outdated information. Make time to review e-mailed company notifications and to familiarize yourself with updated material rather than discovering it for the first time as you share it with a customer. At a minimum, your resources should include

- a calendar you can refer to when scheduling appointments, callbacks, deliveries, and so on

- reminders of key procedures

- a list of key telephone numbers to which you may have to transfer a call

- scripts for those points in a call where wording may be critical, including responses to questions or objections you might receive, or introductory statements for outbound calls

- descriptions or summary information on the products and services offered by your company

Learning Application Exercise

In your job (which can include full- or part-time employment, volunteer work, or other positions of responsibility), do you know what you need to know and how to get the information you don't know?

1. *Do you have an established procedure for continued learning on the job? If not, what can you do to ensure that your knowledge of products, scripts, and computer systems is constantly updated?*

2. *Is your reference material up-to-date? Do you have a system for ensuring that it is, and that new material is appropriately filed in a timely fashion?*

3. *Do you make it a habit to review all e-mailed information updates and any additions to your computer-based information system?*

PREPARE YOURSELF PHYSICALLY

To be physically ready to handle a call, finish conversations with coworkers before placing or answering the call. Aim to make customers feel special and like they are your priority.

In-progress, nonphone work that is still on your desk can be distracting. When your attention is drawn to an item on your desk, you listen less effectively and the customer can sense you are not giving him or her your full attention. Remove work in progress from your field of vision so it doesn't distract you. File it, and list all unfinished projects in a schedule or on a "to-do" list so they aren't forgotten.

Never eat, drink, or chew gum when on the telephone. Doing so is rude to the person on the other end of the line.

It is difficult to give your full attention to a call when you have to go to the washroom or your mouth is dry. Take care of these needs before making or accepting calls.

Avoid drinking too much coffee or other sources of caffeine. Find other drinks that quench your thirst without causing caffeine's side effects, such as nervousness or irritability.

Learning Application Exercise

In your current telephone interactions, are you physically prepared for each call?

1. *Do you ensure that no conversations with coworkers interfere with your calls? That a call signals the end of conversations with coworkers?*

2. *Do you have a system for ensuring that work in progress is not on your desk, a system that ensures you don't forget about this work or let it fall behind?*

3. *Do you make sure you don't eat or drink during a call?*

4. *Do you take adequate washroom and refreshment breaks?*

5. *Do you manage your caffeine intake so you do not suffer caffeine's adverse effects?*

PREPARE YOURSELF MENTALLY

Addressing the Call

Have you ever watched golf pros "address the ball" before teeing off? They go through a ritual of shuffling, practice-swinging, looking, stretching, more shuffling, lining up the club head, and then finally taking their swing. For every tee shot, the same ritual is repeated. The process helps pros focus on what they are about to do, and blank out all the external distractions. It is also an "imprinting" process that allows the person to no longer have to consciously consider the positioning of the feet, the angle of the body, and so on—the motion becomes automatic. The pro clears her or his mind, focuses on the task, and imagines success.

Successful call centre representatives do the same thing. They develop a ritual to put them into the right mindset.

Many find that taking a deep breath from the diaphragm before making or accepting a call helps them in "addressing the call." The deep breath clears their mind of the previous calls and external distractions, allowing them to focus on the task and imagine success. The deep breath is also calming—it helps to relax the diaphragm. When we relax physically, we relax mentally as well.

A **diaphragm breath** is a stomach breath, not a chest breath. Place one hand on your stomach and the other on your chest. Take a deep breath. With a diaphragm breath, the hand on the stomach will move and the one on the chest will not. Practise this.

WARNING: If you take five or more fast diaphragm breaths in a row, stop—you are hyperventilating, which is not relaxing.

Professional call centre reps develop their own "addressing the call" routine to use before starting their calls and between each call. The routine may include organizing the workstation, getting a fresh glass of water, reviewing objectives or scripting, or taking a diaphragm breath. Develop your own ritual to use at the beginning of each shift and before each call.

Project a Positive Image

Avoid sounding impatient, hostile, or condescending when speaking with customers. As discussed earlier in this chapter, call centre reps represent the company, and they should strive to project a positive image in order to retain customers and help the company be successful. Customers can be very unforgiving, especially if alternative companies are easy to find. If reps are professional and friendly, customers are more likely to have a positive impression of the company. Remember that on each and every call you create an image not just of yourself but of the whole company.

To avoid creating even one bad impression, professional call centre reps incorporate into their addressing the call ritual a mental image of the impression they want to give the customer. If reps are conscious of this image before beginning each call, the customer's impression is more likely to be positive.

Be Emotionally Ready to Handle the Call

Make certain you are carrying no "emotional baggage" from a previous call. **Baggage** is jargon counsellors use to refer to issues that cause an emotional reaction we cannot easily shake off and so carry with us. Have you ever started off the day with an angry customer or with another stressful situation, like an argument with a coworker or spouse? You probably thought to yourself, "It's going to be one of those days!" and then, sure enough, the day consisted of one difficult call or situation after another. This kind of day tends to be a self-fulfilling prophecy—your stress level affects your mood, which affects your tone of voice, no matter how slightly. When you deal with the next customer, your voice has an edge that the customer unconsciously reacts to, and you have a difficult call. Your mood is then even worse for the next call. As you continue through your day collecting more baggage, you are unconsciously responsible for creating "one of those days."

To avoid this baggage effect, try the following:

- Use an addressing the call routine to clear your mind of the previous stressors and focus on the next call.

- After a difficult call—even one you feel you handled effectively—be conscious of the fact that your mood may be affected. Try to put the call behind you before moving on to the next call. Remember that you can influence the next call to be positive or difficult.

- After a particularly difficult call, take a short break from the phone, stand up and stretch, walk to the water cooler, or have a short chat with your supervisor or a coworker.

- Learn to manage stress and make yourself less susceptible to the stressors (for more on this, see Chapter 9).

Develop a "Showtime" Mindset

Each year, a list of the 10 things people fear the most is produced. Typically, fear of death by some painful means is first on the list. But near the top of the list, consistently higher than just plain fear of death, is fear of speaking in public. Most of us are fearful or at least very uncomfortable with speaking in public.

The only way to overcome that fear is to confront it by speaking at wedding receptions, meetings—everywhere you can. Make a fool of yourself and realize that the world doesn't end, and finally you will get to the point where you may not be a great speaker, but at least you are comfortable with speaking in public. In this state, you can even approach a speaking, teaching, or lecturing engagement feeling physically ill, yet feel a rush of adrenaline and be able to put your physical feelings out of your mind once you begin speaking. This "showtime" mindset is one of the rewards of public speaking. When you're in it, you feel that you are entering a different part of your psyche, or perhaps taking on an alter ego.

This phenomenon can occur in other situations, such as face-to-face sales. With practice you eventually become more comfortable with it, until one day you are able to access the showtime mindset. When you are in that mindset, you are more lucid, you can interact while managing the conversation, and your memory is sharp so that you have the answer to whatever the other person has to say—everything just works for you.

You can attain the showtime mindset on the telephone through much the same process. When you are new to the call centre, your call-handling techniques will probably be self-conscious, feel artificial, and not flow well. But after you have some successes, they begin to get integrated into your style. You no longer have to be conscious of each skill, response, or technique—they just flow for you. In this state, the time on the telephone is enjoyable, you connect well with customers, calls are more successful, and time passes almost too quickly. This is a good place to be for a call centre professional. It is when you know you have made it, and it is worth striving for.

Learning Application Exercise

Are you mentally prepared for each call?

1. *Do you have an addressing the call routine? Does it include a diaphragm breath?*

2. *Do you think, before each call, of the positive image you wish to create for the customer?*

3. *Do you ensure you are emotionally ready for each call? Do you have a system for managing the baggage from difficult calls?*

4. *Have you ever experienced the showtime mindset at work, school, or during sports activities? If so, describe how you felt.*

5. *Have you ever experienced this mindset while working in a call centre? Describe the situation. What are you doing to learn to consistently tap in to that alter ego?*

Smile

Every book or course that offers to teach people how to talk on the telephone advises that you smile. Why? Because callers can actually hear your smile at the other end of the line. Here are some of the things callers hear that tell them reps are smiling:

- They sound happy. This is good, because happiness is infectious. Customers are more likely to feel and react as if they are happy too, making them easier to deal with.

- They sound like they like what they are doing. This encourages customers to have more trust or confidence in the company's product or service.

- They sound like they like the customer. A call has a much greater chance of success if the customer starts off liking the rep back, which is what usually happens.

- It sounds like they are talking *to* the customer instead of *at* the customer. This encourages the customer to feel more connected with the rep and to believe what the rep is saying, making the call go more smoothly.

There are, then, several positive effects of smiling at the beginning of a call, not to mention the effect it has on our own mood. It is therefore a good idea to build smiling into your addressing the call routine. The reason "smile" is on every list that addresses good telephone skills is because it is so effective.

Call centre reps often ask, "How can we get all those benefits of smiling without really smiling?" The question usually arises from people who don't smile on the telephone and don't feel comfortable doing so. Smiling on the telephone is a habit that can be learned. Here's how:

- Appreciate the benefits of developing the smiling habit. Simply by smiling you create the impression that you like your job and the customer, are talking *to* versus *at* them, and are happy—and you get all the benefits that result from these good impressions.

- Experts say it takes three weeks to develop a new habit or break an old one (with the possible exception of an addiction like cigarette smoking). So, for three weeks constantly remind yourself to smile on the telephone even when you don't feel particularly happy. For three weeks you'll probably feel a little foolish and won't feel natural, and people may even make fun of your new smiling image. But then, for the rest of your career and even your life, you will reap all the benefits of smiling.

- Attach a cue card to your computer screen to remind you to smile.

- Ask coworkers to observe you and remind you.

- Fix a mirror near your phone to remind yourself to smile. (One company even handed out mirrors to everyone.)

Learning Application Exercise

Do you smile on the telephone? If not, develop the habit now. Try it during your next phone conversation.

Make Every Call a Success

A positive attitude can be weakened when we encounter a customer who, in spite of all our efforts, is difficult. We tend to take it personally when the customer is hostile. This is understandable, since in our personal life when someone expresses anger or is upset with us it *is* personal. But on the job, particularly on the telephone, you represent your company, your company's product, big business, government, uncaring bureaucracies, or whatever other group the customer has fixed on as the source of her or his frustration. So the frustration is not usually directed at you as a person but at what you represent.

Companies are typically pleased when they encounter a dissatisfied customer. They are not pleased about making the customer dissatisfied, but that they have identified one who is unhappy. Most upset customers just leave and don't do business with a company again. Dissatisfied customers who call represent opportunities to win back their business, or at the very least find out what has caused their displeasure in case it's a problem that may be affecting others as well. So when reps encounter an upset customer, they should view him or her as an opportunity to solve a problem and to bring the person back to the company. This is easier if reps do not react to the difficult behaviour that often accompanies the customer's dissatisfaction.

If reps could convert every upset person into a satisfied customer by the time they finished the call, then some hostility at the beginning of the call would be bearable and would not negatively affect their attitude. That, however, can never be the case. For some customers, their problem with the company represents only part of what has them upset. For others, the only thing that will satisfy them is beyond what can be provided. For still others, the need to vent and express their anger is greater than any need for resolution, and no solution will satisfy them. In all these situations, the rep will be unable to satisfy the customer.

Are calls that do not result in a satisfied customer all failures? If the rep has handled the customer well; has maintained a positive, respectful, and helpful attitude; and has done everything within her or his power to resolve the issue and satisfy that customer, then the rep can still feel the call was handled successfully. Some calls offer no opportunity to win the customer—they only offer the potential to make matters even worse. In these cases, success is measured by how well the rep is able to avoid losing even more ground with the customer. It is not uncommon for customers, after leaving one of these no-win calls, to think about how they treated the rep and recognize that they were wrong. Some have even been known to call back and apologize.

Thus, one key to maintaining a positive attitude is to accept that all customers will not be satisfied, but to consider each call you handle effectively as a success. With this measurement criterion, every call has the potential to be successful. Here are additional criteria for considering a difficult call successful:

- Did you learn anything from the call that you can use to be more effective in a similar situation in the future? Whether or not you handle a call effectively, if you can learn from it and improve as a result of it, it was a success.

- If the customer did not achieve what he or she wanted, did you convince the customer that no further initiative on his or her part would change the response, thus ensuring that the customer will not call back to readdress the issue? If so, your success was in saving a coworker the time and trouble of dealing with this issue again.

Learning Application Exercise

Develop the habit of asking yourself after each call, especially the difficult ones, what made that call successful. Keep notes.

Summary

A positive attitude is critical for success as a call centre rep. Even people with a generally positive attitude can have a less positive attitude at times. With a poor attitude, we set ourselves up for professional, social, and personal failure. We try to rationalize it away rather than work to overcome it.

The steps for overcoming a poor attitude include the following:

1. Recognize when you have a poor attitude, even when the degree of "poorness" is relatively slight.

2. Identify the benefits in having a positive attitude and in doing your job well, then measure the benefits of a positive attitude against the benefits of a poor attitude.

3. Recognize the presence of attitude-undermining factors in your life, and work to overcome them. These include going from an unrealistically positive impression to one that is unrealistically negative; getting caught up in negative self-talk, your own or others'; and looking for the negative rather than the positive.

4. Work to create a positive first impression by preparing your workstation, preparing your information, preparing yourself physically, and preparing yourself mentally.

CHAPTER 4
Voice

Learning Outcomes

After successfully completing Chapter 4 you will be able to:

- Recognize and overcome the problems that can affect voice quality: nasality, throat voice, breathy voice, and high pitch.

- Assess and adjust your rate of speech.

- Recognize and overcome each of the various diction problems.

- Improve your ability to use voice inflection and become better sensitized to others' inflection.

- Adjust your voice volume appropriately.

Voice: The Instrument of Communication

Communication on the telephone consists primarily of speaking and listening. Fax and e-mail may use the phone line for communicating, but play a lesser role in most current call centre positions. Speaking consists of the words we select (along with all the thinking that goes behind that selection) and the voice with which the words are spoken. Our voice is the instrument through which we communicate the words. When that instrument is played well, it is very powerful in enhancing the image or message of our communication. When the instrument is out of tune or played poorly, even a good message sounds bad. Any flaws in the instrument or how it is played detract from the message.

For example, a voice that is nasal and whiny reduces the impact of a message or creates a negative impact. Similarly, speaking so fast that the listener has to mentally play back the message to hear it makes communication less effective. If a person's **diction** is poor—words slurred together, or endings cut off—the listener may get the impression that the speaker is uneducated or a bit slow. Other voice problems include speaking at a very high **pitch**, which can sound childish, or speaking so quietly the listener has to strain to hear. If the speaker's voice combines several of these elements, the impact of the message is even further damaged.

Voice effectiveness is influenced by:

1. **voice quality**
2. rate of speech
3. diction
4. **inflection/tone**
5. volume

These nonword or noncontent elements of a message are discussed in detail later in this chapter.

Marshall McLuhan, an expert on communication and popular culture, stated that "the medium is the message."[1] The voice itself may communicate as much or even more to the listener as the words that are spoken. A study by Albert Mehrabian[2] at UCLA showed that the impact and sincerity of what a person hears is assessed as follows:

- 55 percent based on body language (visuals)
- 38 percent based on voice
- 7 percent based on words

On the telephone, with no body language or other visual cues, all we have left are voice and words to communicate our message. On the telephone the words we choose become more critical, and we must pay attention to the message our voice sends. Yet we still focus more on the content of what we say than on the voice. This neglect can result in misusing the voice so it not only negatively influences the listener's perception of the message, but may even unconsciously damage the voice in the process.

Figure 4.1

Elements of Voice Communication

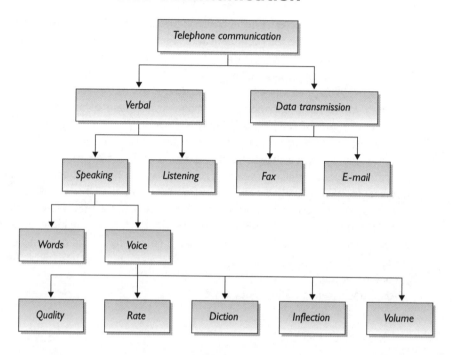

Call centre representatives must use their voice extensively. Reps who misuse their voice have a greater chance of causing associated physical damage, such as sore throat, hoarseness, or even loss of voice. Even if your voice is not in danger of being damaged, it may still be "out of tune" and be undermining the message you are trying to communicate.

PREVENTIVE MAINTENANCE FOR THE VOICE

Just as carpenters must take care of their tools, call centre reps must take care of their voice. The most effective way to care for an important tool is with **preventive mainte-nance**, keeping it "in tune," or in good working order, rather than waiting until there is a problem or breakdown. Here are some tips for preventive maintenance of your voice:

- Drink plenty of liquids.

- Protect your vocal chords from extreme cold, and avoid prolonged periods of shouting, cheering, or loud talking (this may mean reducing background noise rather than trying to be heard over it).

- Assess your voice to identify voice problems. Not all voice problems will damage the voice, but they may damage the communication.

- Work to correct any voice problem before it becomes an even bigger problem.

Voice Quality

NASALITY

Dr. Morton Cooper, a voice therapist and author of numerous books and articles on voice effectiveness, identifies three main areas that contribute to the sound of our voice.[3] The larynx or voice box located in the throat produces the sound, which is amplified by the oral cavity (or mouth) and the nasal cavity. Our ideal or "real" voice is focused in our oral and nasal cavities. You can find this voice by enthusiastically humming the first few bars of "Happy Birthday" (feel your lips vibrating when you do), and then speaking with that voice. When we speak with too much nasal resonance and not enough oral cavity resonance, the voice sounds too nasal, which can also sound whiny or even childish. Dr. Cooper claims that as much as 50 percent of the population speaks with too much **nasality**. This habit can be overcome by doing these exercises:

- Hum a bar of "Happy Birthday," then say the word "one," hum it again, then say the word "two," and so on.

- Open your mouth more when you speak, so less air is forced through the nasal cavity: yawn, then hold the lower jaw down with your hand to keep your mouth open, and read this paragraph or any other. While your pronunciation of words may suffer during the exercise, your tone will be less nasal.

The objective of both of these exercises is to help you hear and reproduce the correct sound. Use a tape recorder to hear the difference in tone before and during the exercise. With regular daily practice, you can develop a fuller, less nasal voice. Nasality for most is a voice habit, and habits take time to change. For all voice issues, including nasality, if the problem is severe and does not decrease with the use of exercises or is painful, consult a professional.

To determine whether nasality is an issue for you, try these techniques:

- Ask a friend you trust to be painfully honest with you about the sound of your voice.

- Listen to an audiotape of you speaking. Don't blame the nasal sound on the quality of the tape recorder—that really is how you sound. Your voice sounds fuller to you as it resonates in your head.

- Hold your nose and say the long vowel sounds a, e, i, o, u (ay, ee, eye, oh, you). If you speak too much through the nasal cavity, this exercise, especially the a, e, and u, will cause your nose to vibrate.

THROAT VOICE

Of the 50 percent of the population who do not suffer from nasality, half have an even more serious problem. These people speak from their throat, a habit that may give them a husky, throaty, or "sexy" voice, but that can also damage the vocal chords. This can produce a sore throat, weak voice (other people have to ask them to repeat themselves), hoarse voice, or even periodic or permanent loss of voice.

Dr. Morton Cooper refers to the habit of speaking from the throat as "voice suicide." He recommends a daily routine of energetic humming interspersed with spoken words to learn to speak from what he calls "the mask"—a balance of the oral and nasal cavities. Humming "um-hmmm" followed by speaking a word from the mask, not the throat, repeated regularly, can help a person overcome **throat voice**.

Hoarseness may also be the result of a dry throat. Call centre reps should drink fluids—preferably noncarbonated and noncaffeinated to avoid problems of gassiness or tension—regularly between calls. To be kind to your vocal chords, avoid drinks that are too cold.

Hoarseness may also be caused by prolonged throat voice or by a cough or cold. Anyone who earns their living with their voice should take extra care of it during the early stages of a cough or cold.

If you have throat voice, it is wise to reduce your smoking and alcohol intake (ideally, eliminate these entirely until you overcome the problem). Be especially careful when speaking with a cold or a sore throat or when you are tired. Avoid clearing your throat, as this only causes more damage.

To determine whether you have throat voice, answer the following questions:

- Do people describe your voice as sexy, harsh, or hoarse? Do they constantly have to ask you to repeat yourself because they cannot hear you?

- Do you regularly have the urge to clear your throat when you speak, but find that this has no effect?

- Is your throat regularly raw and sore?

- Does your throat regularly feel scratchy or dry?

- Do you lose your voice when you must speak a lot?

- Does your voice tire as you go through your day?

BREATHY VOICE

Breathiness in the voice, where the speaker's breathing is so obvious as to be distracting, can be caused by

- The habit of breathing through the nose when speaking. When a large amount of air is forced through this constricted passageway in a short period of time, a sound of rushing air may be produced. This is accentuated if the speaker has any nasal constriction, such as adenoid problems.

- Not breathing regularly when speaking, so that the less frequent breaths have to be bigger to supply the speaker's oxygen needs. The larger breaths force greater amounts of air through the passageways and can be heard over the telephone. This habit also can cause speakers to sound strained or breathless as they try to get the last few words out on the remaining supply of air (words come out as we exhale, so as we talk, we lose air). This breathlessness often is a byproduct of speaking too quickly—trying to get all the words out without taking time to breathe.

- "Chest breathing" is louder than "stomach breathing." Proper breathing is lower in the lungs so that the stomach rises and falls when we breathe. Forcing air into the upper lungs is not only less efficient, it also takes much more effort to raise the rib cage as opposed to simply raising the stomach muscles, as with diaphragm breathing, and it creates more rushing air sound.

- People from some areas of Canada inhale a breath hard with a whispered "yeah" to express agreement. This can be a distracting habit to the listener, particularly if the listener is from a different region.

When speaking, proper breathing is accomplished by inhaling small amounts of air through the mouth often, during frequent short pauses in speaking, in an unrushed way, using the diaphragm muscles of the stomach. Nervousness can contribute to improper breathing, so it is even more important to manage your breathing when you are nervous.

To determine whether you have a **breathy voice**, try the following:

- Pay attention to whether you run out of air as you speak and don't have enough air for the last few words you want to say so that you have to push them out.

- Tape-record one of your telephone conversations. Can you hear your breathing in the recording?

- When you speak, note whether you take large breaths instead of smaller, more frequent ones.

- Ask a friend you trust to tell you honestly whether breathiness is an issue for you.

HIGH PITCH (CHILD VOICE)

High-pitched voices sound childlike. If the high pitch is accompanied by nasality, working to overcome the nasality may affect the pitch. Here are some other methods for lowering the pitch of your voice:

- Humming (use the first few bars of "Happy Birthday" again) until the pitch is lower but your lips still vibrate, so you are using the mask. When you hit the pitch you want, try the hum/speak-a-number exercise described earlier. Gradually expand the speaking part as you develop the memory and habit of this pitch. Make sure you are using the mask, and avoid moving to throat voice to overcome high pitch.

- Use a tape recorder to record your successes.

- Some people develop the habit of speaking with one hand on their chest. This reminds them to think lower pitch. To avoid throat voice, do this with the previous exercises.

- Sit on a chair with a book on the floor in front of you. Bend at the waist to face the floor, hanging your arms and torso between your knees, and read aloud from the book. Retaining the feeling and the pitch, sit up straight and talk.

Gradually, by using exercises such as these, you can change the pitch of your voice. The new pitch will sound and feel awkward for the first few weeks until practice makes it a habit.

To determine whether you have a child voice, ask yourself the following questions:

- Do people regularly mistake you for a child or as being a lot younger than you are when they hear you speak on the telephone?

- When you hear a tape recording of your voice, does the pitch sound higher than other people of your sex?

Rate of Speech

Call centre reps can easily fall into the habit of speaking too quickly. Because reps deal with a large number of calls in a day, parts of what is said can seem repetitive, and the reps may hurry to get past those parts to focus on the specifics of the customer's situation. This is common with the call greeting. Also, reps may feel pressured to handle calls quickly so they can get to the next call and reduce the time the customer spends waiting in queue. Reps will also speak faster to make the call move more quickly.

Many people just naturally speak very quickly. Their mind races ahead, and their words scramble to keep up. Whatever the reason for this habit, the result is not effective for the customer, who may miss parts of what is said and may get a negative impression of the person who speaks too quickly.

Customers may feel the rep does not care about their issue and is trying to get rid of them to get on to something else. This feeling can be supported by the rep's impaired ability to exhibit genuine empathy—it is very hard to communicate empathy when speaking very quickly. Customers may also feel the rep does not care enough to ensure they understand.

The "fast-talking" rep may sound insincere, which can undermine customers' trust. Customers may feel the rep is speaking quickly in an effort to deceive them, moving on to the next topic before it registers on the customers that they have been deceived.

This habit can lead customers to visualize the rep as younger and less credible. Speaking quickly is a common habit of adolescence, and is therefore often associated with youth. Speaking quickly may also make the rep sound nervous. Customers may credit this perceived nervousness to the rep's inexperience, thus lowering customer confidence. Alternately, the customer may believe the rep's nervousness is due to the severity of the customer's situation, or to the fact that the rep is not being entirely truthful, either of which will negatively influence the customer's attitude toward the call and the rep.

If customers are upset when they call, the rep's rapid speech can heighten their anxiety, making the call a more difficult one for the rep to handle.

To determine whether you speak too quickly, follow these steps:

1. Tape-record your voice during a series of telephone conversations. Record a number of conversations over a period of time so you become comfortable with being recorded and it does not affect your performance.

2. Select some calls that take place after you have become comfortable with being recorded.

3. Find sections in which you spoke more than a dozen words.

4. Time each section from the beginning of the first word to the end of the last word.

5. Count the number of words in each section.

6. Determine the average number of words per minute for each section you recorded. If, for example, you spoke 32 words in 10 seconds, divide 32 by 10 to find the average number of words per second. Then multiply by 60 to determine the number of words per minute. For example: 32/10 × 60 = 192 words/minute. Appropriate speaking rate is about 140 to 160 words per minute. If you have any samples that are significantly faster than that, then you may be speaking too fast.

Here are some ways to overcome this fast talking:

1. If you haven't already done so, do the previous exercise. Then practise the taped samples in which you spoke too quickly. Repeat the words so that they fall within the comfortable speed range. Retape them, time them, and calculate your rate of speech.

2. Practise talking at a rate that is within the comfortable range until you can recognize what it sounds like.

3. Continue to record yourself, and periodically select some calls and calculate the rate to ensure that you are within the comfortable range.

4. Practise slowing your speech down when you are off the telephone as well, so that this becomes a life habit.

5. Attach a cue card to your computer screen that says "slow down" so you'll see it when you are on the phone.

If you have discovered that you speak much slower than the target rate, that your speech is hesitant and does not flow evenly, or that you pause frequently, causing you to sound tired or distracted, see Table 4.1.

TABLE 4.1

Speaking Too Slowly

Reasons for Slowness	a. The topic of the conversation is sensitive or complex, and you have to choose your words carefully. b. The information is new or unfamiliar to you, so you have to think more while speaking. c. You are nervous. For some people, nervousness causes them to speak more quickly; for others it causes some slowing of speech. d. You are mentally drifting or distracted from the conversation by something else and are not giving your full attention to your call. e. Speaking slowly may be part of your personality. This is more common for people who are naturally shy and uncomfortable about speaking with people and generally speak at a slow, measured pace.

TABLE 4.1

Speaking Too Slowly (continued)

Solution	
	a. Anticipate sensitive or complex topics or questions, and develop scripted responses for each so that you do not need to search for the right words every time.
	b. Study the information you need to do your job, and know how to quickly access information you do not know. Scripting for "what to say when you don't know what to say" situations is also useful in these circumstances.
	c. Reduce your nervousness by knowing your information and having scripted responses for common situations. Relaxation or addressing the call attitude-shaping exercises before a call (described in Chapter 3) can also help you reduce nervousness. Using a cue card attached to your computer screen reminding you to speak more quickly can also help you to overcome this habit.
	d. When your distraction is communicated to the customer, you sound uninterested. Remove distractions, and commit yourself to focusing on calls. See the nine steps for improving listening skills in Chapter 6.
	e. Typically, people who speak slowly do so more when they are stressed. Chapters 8 and 9 discuss how the "Visualizer" personality type can take care of psychological needs in a positive way and not slip into this behaviour. If you have slipped into this habit because of stress and now speak slowly even when you are not stressed, then try the process described above for assessing and adjusting your speaking rate.

Diction

Diction is the clarity with which we speak. Mumbled, slurred, or shortened words (shortened by leaving off word endings or some of the syllables) can cause messages to be unclear to the listener. This speaking style is often picked up at a young age. The problem occurs when this style is used with people who may not understand it or who may judge the speaker negatively based on it. This often happens when the rules of grammar and pronunciation in a rep's country or region of origin are different from those of the rep's customers. It is the rep's responsibility to adjust her or his diction style to communicate effectively.

ON THE JOB

Taking Responsibility

Who is responsible for ensuring a message is understood—the speaker or the listener? The common answer is "Both are equally responsible," which is wrong. This answer implies that each person is only 50 percent responsible, leading the speaker to make only a 50 percent effort to be understood.

The right answer is "The speaker is 100 percent responsible, as is the listener." This means that when they are speaking, reps are fully responsible for ensuring that their messages are communicated in a way that customers will understand. When the reps are listening, they are 100 percent responsible for making sure they understand the customers' messages.

Even if a rep's inappropriate diction can be understood, it can still make a negative impression on the customer. For example, poor diction may suggest to the customer that the rep is too informal or unprofessional, or that the rep is not very intelligent. In turn, this can cause the customer to lack confidence in the rep's ability to handle the call.

To determine whether diction is an issue for you, tape-record some of your conversations. Listen to a selection of recordings that were made once you were comfortable with being recorded. Assess your diction. Listen with another person who doesn't share your diction style, and ask for that person's feedback.

Ask a friend who will give you honest feedback. Ask someone who has seen you upset or stressed, when diction problems are more likely to surface.

TABLE 4.2
Common Diction Problems and Their Solutions

Diction Problems	a. Lisping "th" for "s": "thith ith hopeleth."
	b. Replacing "th" with "d" or "t": "Jean passed de puck to de centre," "de whole ting is tree and a tird inches too long."
Solution	a. If your "z" sound is accurate, try saying "z" words that rhyme with "s" words (such as "zing/sing" or "zed/said"). "S" is "z" without the voice. Practise saying the "z" word followed by the rhyming "s" word until you get it right. Say "t-t-t-t-t-t" for a time, then say a word that begins with "st," such as "stop" or "stick" (e.g., "t-t-t-t-t-stop"). The tongue is in a similar position for both "s" and "t." The root cause of lisping can be physical or may be more complex than this simple exercise can remedy. As with the other voice quality problems described in this chapter, the aid of a medical doctor or speech therapist may be required.
	b. The "th" sound is not part of some languages (for example, French), and a person for whom English is a second language may have difficulty mastering this sound. The "d" or "t" is the attempt to say "th" without having the tongue far enough forward. The tongue tip should rest on the back of the teeth, rather than on the roof of the mouth just behind the teeth, to produce "th." Practise over and over "the three thin bathers dried with three thick towels."

Learning Application Exercise

1. Try the self-assessment tests for each of the elements of voice quality, rate of speech, and diction. Develop a plan of action for overcoming any problem areas you identify. Discuss your plan with a peer.

2. Implement your action plan, then reassess it weekly. Discuss your progress with a peer, and adjust your action plan as necessary.

Inflection/Tone

Tone of voice is influenced to varying degrees by each element of voice quality, but what primarily defines tone is inflection. Inflection creates tone. The tone attaches an insinuated mood or meaning to the words that may or may not be reflected in the words themselves. The tone can totally change the meaning of the words. You probably already know this from using sarcasm or listening to someone else being sarcastic. Consider how the following sentence changes meaning depending on which words are emphasized:

- "**I** didn't say you stole the money."
- "I **didn't** say you stole the money."
- "I didn't **say** you stole the money."
- "I didn't say **you** stole the money."
- "I didn't say you **stole** the money."
- "I didn't say you stole **the** money."
- "I didn't say you stole the **money**."

Learning Application Exercise

1. Practise saying the "money" sentence with the different intended meanings to a group of peers. See if they can interpret your intended meaning. If they can, then you are likely effective at communicating the inflection and tone you intend. If the others cannot decipher your meaning, then you could improve your use of inflection. If the only way you can communicate your meaning is to really exaggerate the emphasized word, then inflection finesse may be an issue for you.

2. Take a number of simple statements, and try to adjust your inflection and tone to create different meanings or moods. Sentences such as "Congratulations on your promotion" or "I'd love to have your mother come live with us" can be said with a variety of tones to change the meaning. To start, try sincere, angry, hostile, bored, sarcastic, sexy, and indifferent. Then try putting the emphasis on different words and assess how that changes the meaning. Practise these on your own, tape the different inflections, and review them with peers. With practice, you will be able to use inflection more effectively.

Inflection can even turn a friendly comment like "Have a nice day" into something negative. One call centre rep confided, "If I have a customer who is a real pain to deal with, at the end of the call I put on a syrupy sweet voice and say 'Have a nice day!' It makes me feel good and the customer doesn't even know I'm being sarcastic." This rep was advised that customers were likely hearing her tone, and even if they did not confront her on it (it was the end of the call after all), they would leave the conversation with a more negative impression of the rep and of the company.

Our inflection and consequent tone can reveal our true feelings when we would rather not reveal them. Our tone may show our insincerity when we try to sound friendly with a customer whom we feel is not very bright or is wasting our time. Often, the customer will react to such a tone, and reps who are not aware of the tonal messages they are sending are left wondering why the customer is responding so negatively.

In addition to managing your tone and ensuring it gives the messages you intend, you must be sensitive to the tonal messages of the customers. Their tone may communicate impatience, upset, distrust, or confusion, for example, and if you ignore the message, the call can be totally unsuccessful. If, however, you identify the message and respond or adjust to it accordingly, you may be able to steer the call to an effective resolution. In effect, the professional call centre rep who "sees" the message in the customer's tone can be said to have "tonal vision."

Learning Application Exercise

1. *With a peer, listen to a number of your taped calls or record role-playing with a peer who tries to prod you into a negative reaction. See if either of you can detect a tone of voice that communicates a message that contradicts your words.*

2. *Listen to the tone of customers in your recorded calls. Does their tone give you any clues as to their mood? Did you respond appropriately to that tone? If not, what else might you have done to adjust or respond to the tone?*

Inflection that is not consistent with our words can be a problem because it communicates a different message from what we intend. Not enough inflection can create a negative image of the rep or the company.

Too much inflection can cause a rep to seem artificial (e.g., forced enthusiasm: "My boss told me to sound happy, so I am") or superficial (e.g., seeming bubbly and enthusiastic over trivial things, exhibiting a childlike wonder when there is nothing particularly wonderful). Interpretations of excessive inflection can also have a negative effect on the client's perception of the rep and the company. The customer may also find the excessively bubbly rep insensitive when the mood of the client or the content of the call does not warrant a bubbly response.

Excessive inflection is relatively rare; far more common is too little inflection. In fact, over-inflection may be a result of a rep's attempt to overcome a problem with under-inflection. The rep swings too far the other way, and too much inflection is the result.

Some reps' excessive inflection is a result of trying to increase their confidence before making an outbound call. These are usually reps who are less comfortable with outbound calls, who are new to this role, or who have not yet developed self-confidence in the role. This can also happen when reps have had a difficult call or a string of unsuccessful calls—because their confidence is low, they try too hard on the next call and end up sounding insincere.

Often, reps think they have to sound more animated on the telephone—they have a telephone voice or **telephone persona** that is different from how they speak naturally. Other reps' telephone voices are too flat, businesslike, cold, condescending, or indifferent. Yet these same people don't sound like this when they're off the phone. It's best to lose your telephone persona—be yourself and get away from this idea of what you think you should sound like on the job.

Some people's over-inflection is a result of naturally high energy. During a face-to-face interaction, the customer has more time to adjust to this style. But on the telephone, with no visual cues to offset it and no time for the rep's behaviour to soften the impression, a naturally excessive style can be detrimental to the rep's success. This style needs to be softened for phone calls.

Some people feel very excited about what they have to say, causing a natural enthusiasm that creates high levels of inflection. This becomes a problem when the customer is not as enthusiastic or has a lower-key style. You may have had an instructor who gets very enthusiastic about his or her subject, but overwhelms students with too much energy and information.

The solution to all of these problems is to know yourself and adjust to fit the needs of customers.

Volume

Too Loud

There are three types of too-loud reps: those who are always too loud, those who are excessively loud only when on the telephone, and those who get louder as some calls progress. Speaking too loudly can make customers feel that they are being bullied and can make them feel overwhelmed, as though they are being shouted at. Talking too loudly can make it difficult for coworkers to focus on their own calls. It may also make coworkers uncomfortable, especially since loudness is often associated with anger. There have even been situations where a customer on the phone comments to one rep on the loudness of another rep in the background. Loudness can and should be controlled.

Chronic loudness can be a bigger issue than the other two types of loudness. The methods already discussed may help to overcome it, but some physical changes to the environment may be needed as well. Appropriate sound barriers can protect other reps from the volume, as can directing the loud rep's talking toward the sound barrier instead of outward into the room. Adjusting the microphone pickup on the headset or using a telephone that allows the volume to be decreased on the speaker's end will help the customer.

Reps who are loud only when on the telephone may be using a telephone persona, or they may simply be enthusiastic. Managing this type of loudness requires changing a habit. This can be done by the rep becoming aware of when the volume is going up (a cue card on the computer screen saying "Quiet please" or asking coworkers for reminders can help), and consciously adjusting his or her voice level. The rep should practise speaking at an appropriate voice volume when on the phone to get a sense of what it feels and sounds like.

For those who get louder as the call progresses, the volume is a result of stress. They usually get louder on difficult calls as their level of frustration mounts. Typically these people do not realize they are getting louder. It is a subconscious attempt to assert control over the customer, and is a learned habit. If progressive loudness is an issue for you, ask your coworkers to give you a signal when your volume starts to rise. Accept responsibility for responding to those signals—remember not to "shoot the messenger" and not to direct your anger at the coworker who is just doing what you asked.

NOT LOUD ENOUGH

Some voices are too soft, prompting customers to repeatedly ask these reps to repeat themselves. This can be frustrating for the customers and can leave them less inclined to want to do business with the organization.

Some people only speak softly on the telephone. This habit can be changed with practice. For others, the root issue is a need for control. When you speak softly, other people must strain to hear you. If control is the root cause, it is usually unconscious behaviour that can still be overcome with the exercises in this chapter.

The cause can also be throat voice or breathy voice, discussed earlier in this chapter. The remedies for each begin with good breathing and learning to speak from the mask. Finally, confidence may be the issue. The person with the quiet voice is in effect saying, "If I'm wrong and they don't hear it, it will be less of a problem"—again subconsciously. A rep's natural shyness may lead to speaking softly, but she or he can change this habit at work by learning to project or speak "out front." Here are some ways to do so:

- Practise speaking through a megaphone or a paper tube.

- Practise shouting a few words (not when you are on the phone with a customer!), and then speak more loudly than normally for a few phrases afterward.

- Speak into a fake microphone—the objective is to learn to speak out rather than in.

- Speak with more enthusiasm, since often a more calm style accompanies a soft voice.

Learning Application Exercise

1. *Assess whether you use excessive inflection or speak too loudly or too softly. Listen to tapes of your calls, and ask peers for feedback.*

2. *If any of these is a problem for you, develop an action plan to remedy the problem that includes follow-up checks. Review your action plan with a peer.*

Summary

The voice is an important communication instrument, so it must be maintained to ensure it continues to be effective. Preventive maintenance for the voice requires ongoing care, periodic checkups to identify problems, and correction of any problems.

Voice effectiveness is influenced by voice quality, rate of speech, diction, inflection/tone, and volume. Through awareness and practice, most voice problems can be overcome. It is important that they be overcome, since how call centre reps sound to customers affects customers' assessment of the organization.

Endnotes

1. Barrington Nevitt with Maurice McLuhan, *Who Was Marshall McLuhan?* (Toronto: Comprehensivist Publications, 1994), Introduction.

2. A. Mehrabian, *Silent Messages* (Belmont, CA: Wadsworth, 1971).

3. Dr. Morton Cooper, *Winning with Your Voice* (Hollywood, FL: Fell Publishers, 1990).

Customer Rapport

Learning Outcomes

After successfully completing Chapter 5, you will be able to:

- Discuss the importance of rapport building for success in the call centre representative role.

- Deliver your greeting effectively each and every time.

- Use the customer's name as a powerful rapport-building tool.

- Communicate respect to the customer.

- Recognize and overcome the main sources of miscommunication.

- Avoid extended conversation gaps.

- Enhance your ability to carry on a conversation while entering information via the keyboard.

- Recognize and overcome distracting speech idiosyncrasies.

The Importance of Good Rapport

How much could a person spend with you in the course of a lifetime? That's the question we ask every time we meet with a customer. You don't want to deal with somebody just once; you want his business forever. We don't want to sell a customer just one car, but ten or twenty in coming years. Are we going to make an extra effort for someone who might buy twenty cars from us? You bet.... Over the course of [a] lifetime, [the customer will] end up spending a lot of money with us—$332 000 to be exact.

—Carl Sewell and Paul B. Brown[1]

Rapport is the customer's sense of feeling "connected" to the call centre representative and consequently to the rep's organization. Each element of a rep's interaction with the customer forms a link in the chain of rapport that connects the customer to the company. If one link is missing or weak, rapport is not achieved and the customer relationship is weakened. The relationship with each customer is valuable, more valuable than just one interaction. At a minimum, the value of each customer is the amount he or she will spend on a company's products or services for the life of his or her relationship with the company.

A customer who is lost is not easily replaced. The cost of acquiring a new customer can be significant compared with the cost of retaining a current customer. The cost of acquiring each new customer can be calculated as marketing and advertising costs per year, plus sales expenses per year, plus sales and marketing staff costs per year, divided by the number of new customers per year. The cost of keeping a current customer can be as little as a responsive, caring approach during a three-minute telephone call.

Once a company acquires a customer, it cannot take the relationship for granted. Customers

Figure 5.1

Why Do Customers Leave?

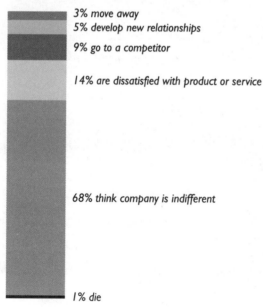

3% move away
5% develop new relationships

9% go to a competitor

14% are dissatisfied with product or service

68% think company is indifferent

1% die

Quoted in Joel Rosen, "Customer Complaints: Are You Getting Enough?" in Stanley A. Brown, ed., Breakthrough Customer Service (Toronto: John Wiley and Sons, 1997), 97.

can easily take their business elsewhere. In most cases, customers don't leave because of anything the company has done, but because of what it hasn't done. A company must, then, make a concerted effort to show customers that it cares. This is clearly in the company's best interest. There are also significant personal benefits for call centre reps in maximizing customer rapport.

TABLE 5.1

Benefits of Good Customer Rapport

Company Benefits	– more satisfied customers
	– positive word-of-mouth
	– positive company image
	– less customer turnover
	– fewer customer complaints, which cost money to process
	– positive staff morale
	– increased productivity
	– increased efficiency
	All of which lead to:
	– new customers
	– continued or increased business with current customers
	– decreased costs
	Which result in:
	– increased revenue and corporate success
Call Centre Representative Benefits	– personal pride in working for a successful company
	– positive feeling from contributing to company's success
	– job satisfaction
	– easier and less stressful job
	– job and career security— effective, skilled reps are a valuable commodity
	– more opportunities for career advancement
	– positive feeling from helping customers
	– recognition from coworkers, customers, and management
	– opportunity for compensation increase
	– positive environment from working with a quality company
	– **halo effect**—as reps feel better about themselves on the job, they feel better about themselves in general
	– sense of self-fulfillment

Learning Application Exercise

The items in Table 5.1 are not equally motivating for everyone. Identify which benefits of good customer rapport are the most important motivators for you.

Many organizations have programs specifically designed to help retain customers. Some of these customer retention programs are retroactive, meaning they are designed to retrieve customers who have decided to leave, rather than simply accepting customer losses as part of doing business. **Retroactive customer retention** programs can be quite successful.

On the Job

Reaching Out to Customers

A large Canadian bank established a program to contact customers who had cancelled their credit cards. The target was to entice back 20 percent of those customers. The plan was to

- Call each ex-customer.
- Express that the bank valued her or his business.
- Inquire into the reason for the card cancellation.
- Resolve any problems or offer a personal apology.
- Offer an incentive to renew the card.
- Sign up the business.

The bank management was surprised at the success of this program—it won back almost 50 percent of the customers who were called.

Customers really do respond when companies show them they care. As Zig Ziglar, an author and motivational speaker, says: "The customer doesn't care how much we know until he [or she] knows how much we care."[2]

Some organizations take a more **proactive customer rentention** approach. Their strategy is to periodically contact current customers. This allows the company to:

- Identify any disgruntled customers who may be considering leaving, resolve their issues, and turn them into satisfied customers. Customers who have had a concern resolved quickly and effectively are more loyal than customers who have never had a concern in the first place.

- Broaden the customer's awareness of the company's products or services. This is done by discussing the products or services that the customer does not use, assessing customer needs, and proposing products and services the customer may not be aware of or introducing new ones. The resulting increased sales can make it worthwhile for the company to implement a proactive customer retention program, and the customer retention department can be a profit centre.

- Show every customer that the company cares about the customer and her or his business. This addresses the large percentage of customers who leave because of a company's perceived indifference, those who don't tell the company why they're leaving but just quietly take their business elsewhere.

Customer retention strategies can be costly to create, manage, and maintain. Consequently, not every organization has a formal retention strategy. Yet every organization with a call centre automatically has a team of customer retention agents. Each call centre representative can and should assume responsibility for retaining customers. Each rep can create a positive customer experience and a positive impression with each and every call. At a minimum, reps can show customers that they care and that their company cares.

This chapter will address six areas that are critical to establishing and maintaining customer rapport:

- greeting the customer

- using the customer's name

- communicating respect for the customer

- matching the customer's vocabulary

- keeping the call flowing

- overcoming speech idiosyncrasies

The Greeting

In Chapter 4, we discussed the importance of the rep's tone of voice in establishing a positive first impression. Also critical to a positive first impression are the words in the greeting—the first words the customer hears from a rep. The greeting affects the extent to which the customer feels connected to the rep and the rep's company.

When a customer initiates a call, the most common greeting consists of four parts, each of which contributes to shaping the customer's perception.

GREETING ELEMENT 1: "HELLO," "GOOD MORNING," OR "GOOD AFTERNOON"

This part of the greeting signals the customer that the rep has answered the telephone. It also says "Please listen. Important information will follow." This is of particular value when customers have been waiting in queue and may be working on or thinking of something other than the purpose of the call.

HAVE YOU EVER?

Have you ever taken a moment from a busy day to call your bank to question an item on your credit card bill? As the phone is ringing, you may think about or be distracted by some-

thing else. Then, when the phone is answered, you go blank for a moment and think to yourself, "Uh oh. Who was I calling?"

This first part of the greeting also makes the call more friendly by personalizing it. This is the way we answer the phone at home, so "Hello," "Good morning," or "Good afternoon" communicates the message that we already like the caller and we welcome the call.

In a national or international call centre, saying "Good morning" or "Good afternoon" may be inappropriate because customers may be calling from a different time zone. Then the call is lengthened as the rep and the customer discuss this time difference and maybe the weather. Also, some customers who think they're calling a local office of the company react negatively when they discover they are speaking to someone in a large call centre in a remote city.

GREETING ELEMENT 2: IDENTIFY COMPANY OR DEPARTMENT

This part of the greeting confirms that the customer has connected to the right place.

ON THE JOB

Signs of a Problem

The president of a mid-sized company received a transferred telephone call. The call had been transferred twice before going to the president. After a couple of questions, the president determined that the call was a wrong number. Describing the situation to a training consultant, the president remarked, "That's when I knew we had a problem. That's when I knew we'd better get help."

When a call is from an external customer—someone outside the organization who is the end user of the company's products or services—it is appropriate to name the company and the department. When the call is from an internal customer—another company employee—the department name alone is usually enough. When the call could be from an internal or external customer, state the company name and department.

Where the company name is long, a shortened version may be appropriate as long as it will be recognizable to the customer. When the department name does not communicate the role of the call centre (for example, sales and marketing), substitute a function name customers will recognize (for example, customer service). Likewise, the name of the subgroup or unit may be more meaningful to the customer (for example, help desk).

GREETING ELEMENT 3: REP'S NAME

When reps state their name, they are in effect telling customers that they are taking responsibility for the call. For some customers, this accountability is important and promotes a sense of trust in the rep, thus immediately contributing to the sense of rapport. Providing your name also meets the needs of customers who like to feel a personal connection before doing business.

Should you offer your first name, first and last name, or title and last name? Usually this is dictated by company policy. Consider what each of these communicates to the customer. The first name sounds the most personal, informal, and friendly of the three options. Also, if the rep's last name is unusual or difficult for some people to pronounce, giving only the first name can help the customer. This option also minimizes any risk of harassment by customers, since the phone book doesn't list numbers by first name. However, giving only the first name may not sound professional or formal enough for the company's customer base, so it may not appropriately present the preferred company image or the rep's role in relation to the customer. Also, if a customer needs to call back, it will be harder to reconnect with the rep if a number of reps share the same first name. Using only the first name can also weaken the sense of ownership and accountability for the call on the part of the rep.

Stating the surname along with the first name maintains an impression of friendliness while sounding a bit more formal and professional. Using both names may overcome any misperception that the rep's role is a junior one, and thus increase the customer's confidence that the rep can provide assistance. Using both names can also help a rep who has a young-sounding voice sound more mature, communicating authority and confidence, and giving the rep greater control of the call. It may, however, be too formal-sounding for the organization's customer base.

Providing only a title and last name is not recommended. It can sound cold or controlling or, when the rep has a young-sounding voice, immature and pretentious, thus having a negative effect on rapport.

If the call centre rep has a name that is complex or unusual, calls may be lengthened unnecessarily by a discussion of the name and its origin. If the customer has difficulty understanding or pronouncing the name, the conversation may be further slowed down, or the customer may feel uncomfortable with or distant from the rep. While discussing a name can increase rapport, typically there are more effective and less time-consuming ways to do so. Here are some tips if you think customers will have problems with your name:

- Speak slowly and clearly when giving your name.

- Give customers a similar-sounding word to help them pronounce your name.

- Provide the spelling of your name.

- Plan a response for each of the common customer reactions. For example, if the customer says, "O'Riley—that's Irish, isn't it?" you might respond, "Through and through, though for me a couple of generations back. How may I help you today?"

- Use a simplified version of your name or a nickname you feel comfortable with, or only your first name.

GREETING ELEMENT 4: "HOW MAY I HELP YOU?"

By asking "How may I help you?" the call centre rep clearly communicates a desire and ability to help. Before an upset or anxious customer has expressed a concern, this element of the greeting also communicates that the rep is on the customer's side, which may help calm down a hostile customer. "How may I help you?" also says, "So what are you calling about?" but in a nicer way. It encourages the customer to focus on the reason for the call and gets him or her down to business.

Simply saying "May I help you?" can result in a "Yes" or "No" response, which just adds time to the call with no benefit. But "How may I help you?" encourages elaboration. "How can I help you?" is not recommended because it gives a different message—"may" is more positive, and more polite, as it requests the customer's permission.

DELIVERING THE GREETING

Using the Full Greeting

Some call centre reps omit one or more parts of the greeting to make it shorter. Usually the greeting isn't too long; it simply feels that way because reps repeat it so many times every day, and they want to get to the point of the call faster. It is important to remember that each element of the greeting has a unique rapport-building purpose and that different elements meet the needs of different customers. There is no way to know which type of customer is on the line until after the greeting, so it makes sense to offer all the greeting elements and increase the chances of connecting with the customer.

When the greeting really is long, maybe because of a long company name, the rep can choose to stop the greeting after giving her or his name, before asking "How may I help you?" Then, when the customer responds, the rep can ask, "How may I help you?"

Some reps become concerned when a customer interrupts them before the greeting is completed. The rep may find the customer rude and get offended. Or the rep may see this as proof that the greeting is too long. Again, remember that the greeting includes elements for connecting with many different types of customers. Some may be rushed when they call or want to get down to business without spending time on the "niceties." The interruption gives the rep useful information about the customer, so the rep can adjust his or her style to express greater urgency, sound more professional, and be more to the point.

The key is to overcome feeling offended when a caller interrupts you. Instead, use this additional caller information to make the call more effective. Don't allow the different needs of a few customers to cause you to change the greeting, or you risk losing all the benefits of the full greeting, as well as an excellent opportunity to build immediate rapport with a larger percentage of callers.

Some organizations require their call centre reps to ask for identification from the customer as part of the greeting, such as an account or authorization number. Typically, this request takes place after the rep gives his or her name.

Keeping It Fresh Each Time

The call centre representative typically delivers the greeting many times a day, so it can start to sound stale, mechanical, and automatic. When this happens, all the benefits of the greeting are lost. Even though it may be today's hundredth greeting for the rep, it is the first greeting for the customer, so it must sound fresh to create a positive impression. Here are some ways to keep the greeting fresh every time:

- Practise the words and tone of the greeting so that it becomes automatic yet sounds fresh each time. Make it part of your addressing the call routine (see Chapter 4), so that the greeting even energizes you.

- Know your own daily rhythm and your low times of the day. For many, the low time is from 3:00 p.m. on, right after lunch, or at the beginning of the day. During your low times, pay particular attention to how your greeting sounds.

- Tape-record yourself practising the greeting, then tape yourself greeting real customers at various times of the day.

- Be aware that the quality of your greeting may deteriorate when you are very busy. Try to make up for this deterioration.

- When your mind is not totally focused on the call, your greeting may sound automatic or you may sound distracted. Always give the call your full attention.

Pacing and Enunciation

Call centre representatives can slip into the habit of saying the greeting too quickly or slurring the words together so they become incomprehensible. This happens for the same reasons that cause the greeting to lose its freshness, with the same results. Often, it is just the rep's name that is spoken more quickly than the rest of the greeting. When the customer is less able to understand what's been said, she or he may get a negative impression of the rep or the company. The customer may feel the rep doesn't care or that the organization doesn't care. Any frustration or upset the customer is feeling is likely to increase when the initial contact is negative.

See Chapter 4 for a detailed discussion of ways to use your voice to create a positive impression. Also try these tips:

- Practise your **pacing** and **enunciation** until the greeting becomes second nature.

- Tape-record your greetings at different times of the day to determine whether your pace and clarity are consistent throughout the day.

- Assess and address the cause of any problem.

CHANGING THE GREETING FOR SPECIFIC SITUATIONS

Providing the Greeting in Two Languages

Some reps work a bilingual line, where they may receive calls from customers in either of two (or more) languages. In Canada, these are typically French and English. If most of the customers speak French, then it is appropriate to give the full greeting in French followed by "How may I help you?" in English, and vice versa. In some organizations, the entire greeting may need to be repeated in both languages; in others, only some elements may need to be repeated. For example, the French "allo" is similar enough to the English "hello," and may be followed by the company name and the rep's name. That leaves only the "Comment puis-je vous aidez?" or "How may I help you?" Where there is a relatively equal volume of French and English calls, it is recommended that French be provided first, followed by the English translation. There is an understandable tendency for French-speaking customers to be more sensitive about language.

Greeting Internal Customers

Some call centres act as help desks or expert resources for other employees in their company. When all calls are from these internal customers, the greeting should include all the elements except for the company name. Positive customer service must be extended to internal as well as external customers for organizations to have a truly service-oriented culture.

Changing the Words to Reflect the Season

During holiday seasons, avoid greetings with a religious connotation, such as "Merry Christmas" (unless, of course, your organization has religious ties, such as a Christian charitable organization). "Season's Greetings" is less likely to offend a non-Christian caller.

Greeting on Outbound Calls

For calls initiated by the call centre rep, the guidelines for freshness, pace, and enunciation apply as for inbound calls. Once you have confirmed you are speaking to the right person, the content of an outbound greeting is as follows:

- "Hello," "Good morning," or "Good afternoon" remains the same.

- Greet the customer by name.

- Introduce yourself and your organization: "This is John Doe calling from Acme Inc."

- Provide a reason for the call that will benefit or interest the customer and be meaningful to the customer: "I'm calling to inform you of our company's new lower-priced combined auto and home insurance."

- Ask a meaningful question that involves the customer in the call, confirms that the reason to call is appropriate for this customer, or determines that this is a convenient time for the customer to speak with you: "Is this a convenient time to talk about how you can save money on your insurance?"

Learning Application Exercise

1. *Practise your greeting until you have perfected it.*

2. *Repeat the greeting 10 times into a tape recorder.*

3. *With a partner, assess the greeting according to the following criteria:*

   a. *Are all four elements included in each greeting? Were any modifications appropriate?*

   b. *Does each greeting sound fresh (positive, friendly, and confident)?*

   c. *Are the greetings consistent?*

   d. *Is each greeting well-paced and clearly spoken, especially your name?*

If any areas were less than effective, practise them and repeat the exercise.

Variations:

1. *Tape your greeting at different preset times of the day to establish your up and down times during the day.*

2. *Call 1-800 numbers (or customer service, reception, or support lines) for five companies, and assess the greetings.*

3. *Tape real conversations with customers at work, and assess your greeting.*

Using the Customer's Name

Our external environment is made up of so many sights and sounds that if we had to be fully conscious of them all, we would suffer attention overload. Our brain constantly scans our external environment and selects the elements we will commit our attention to. Our **attending mechanism** gives the highest priority to things that relate to our personal safety and basic needs, such as the sound of a siren or the smell of food when we are hungry. Once our attending mechanism has scanned the environment for these stimuli, the next strongest magnet for our attention is our name.

HAVE YOU EVER?

Have you ever noticed that often the only way to get people's attention is to use their name? Many times, you can start a conversation with someone else, only to realize halfway through that you're basically talking to yourself because you didn't get the other's attention by starting with her or his name.

Have you ever been at a party where a large number of people and multiple conversations turn the overlapping words into a dull hum, but when someone says your name, your attending mechanism picks it up and passes it through to your consciousness for your attention?

Have you ever been walking along a street or hallway, perhaps involved in a conversation with a friend, when you hear your name separate from the hum of all the other sounds around you, including the conversation you're having? You turn, thinking someone is trying to get your attention, only to see two people you don't know, who don't notice you, walking along having their own conversation, one that includes your name or a similar-sounding word.

Our name is very important to us. We identify with it, and it becomes part of our definition of ourselves. The call centre representative can increase his or her rapport with a customer by effectively using the customer's name.

- Using the customer's name when you first hear it communicates respect.

- Using the customer's name at the end of the call helps you end on a positive note, with the customer feeling good about you.

- Using the customer's name when she or he is dominating the conversation, venting anger, or rambling can help you get the customer's attention and redirect the conversation.

- Using the customer's name when you're about to make an important point, one that you want to make sure the customer hears and understands, will ensure the customer's attentiveness.

- Using the customer's name can be very effective if you want him or her to feel more personally connected to you, when, for example, you are making an empathy statement (e.g., "I can understand your frustration, Ms. Smith").

Yet even though the name is such a powerful tool, it is one of the most underused tools in the call centre rep's repertoire. Why?

REPS DON'T REMEMBER NAMES

Many of us forget a name as soon as we hear it. In fact, many of us have forgotten the first half of the name while the person is telling us the second half. One solution is to use the name as soon as you hear it. Not only does this show respect for the customer, it also helps to commit the name—and how it is pronounced—to memory. Another technique is to write the name down as soon as you hear it.

REPS DON'T KNOW HOW TO PRONOUNCE NAMES

Another reason reps don't use the customer's name is that they don't know or forget how to pronounce it. They don't want to mispronounce it, so they just leave it out entirely. To solve this problem, say the name as soon as you hear it to help imprint the pronunciation on your mind. Write down the name the way it sounds. Use phonetics, or write another word that sounds similar. If you're still not sure you can pronounce it correctly, say it back to the customer and then ask, "Did I pronounce that correctly?" This is much better than repeatedly mispronouncing the name, and it shows the customer that his or her name is important enough to you to take the time to learn to pronounce it correctly. You can also ask the person to repeat his or her name: "I'm sorry, could you repeat your name for me please?" Show that you are taking responsibility for not understanding rather than assuming it is the customer's issue. Speak slowly and clearly so the customer is encouraged to do the same.

With outbound calls, the call centre rep may have a printed record of the customer's name yet not have had the opportunity to hear the customer pronounce it. She or he may resist making the call, fearing an uncomfortable situation resulting from mispronouncing the name. (Often, too, the rep may fear that the customer will have an accent the rep won't understand.) A common consequence is for the rep to call only those customers on her or his list whose names the rep is comfortable pronouncing. Even if the rep makes the call, this minor concern can negatively affect how the rep handles the call. It is important for call centre reps' career growth that they overcome this limitation.

- Consciously and continuously develop your skill at pronouncing names. Multiculturalism is not likely to decrease in Canada, so your skill at pronunciation will contribute to your success in a call centre career. It is useful to start a log of names and their correct pronunciation (e.g., Ng: pronounced "ing").

- The staff in most call centres today are a mix of cultural and language backgrounds. If you can, confirm the pronunciation of a name with a coworker before you call the customer.

- If you are calling the customer at work, call the company's main line rather than calling the customer's direct number first to get the correct pronunciation of the name from the receptionist.

- Call at a time when the customer is unlikely to answer the phone to get the correct pronunciation from the customer's voice-mail message.

- When you must use a name and are unsure of the pronunciation, take time to think through the name and sound it out. Make your best effort at pronunciation when you speak to the customer, and ask, "Did I pronounce that correctly?" If the customer corrects your pronunciation, write it down phonetically, then apologize and repeat it correctly. If your pronunciation is still incorrect, do not keep trying to pronounce the name and add to the awkwardness of the situation. Rather, refer to the techniques in the section "A Name Is Totally Beyond a Rep" on page 89.

Learning Application Exercise

If you have not already done so, begin a pronunciation log of names you have difficulty with. Ask your coworkers for more names to add to your log and your pronunciation expertise.

ON THE JOB

Correct Pronunciation

One customer was very appreciative when a call centre representative took the time to sound out all the syllables of his name and pronounce them correctly. While complicated, the pronunciation was not particularly difficult, but most people simply did not make the effort to try to pronounce the name correctly.

CUSTOMERS DON'T OFFER THEIR NAME

Sometimes customers do not offer their name, and many reps feel uncomfortable asking for it. To overcome this problem, try asking one of these questions in a pleasant voice:

"May I ask your name please?"

"And your name is…?"

"Certainly I can get to that information, Mr./Ms. …?"

"And who am I speaking to?"

It is important to respect the customer who is reluctant to give his or her name. There are many reasons for this reluctance on outbound calls, including the following:

- Periodic media reports of telephone scams have made many people nervous about providing any information over the phone. The customer may think a rep has an ulterior motive for requesting her or his name.

- Older people particularly may feel vulnerable and uncertain of what information is safe to provide, so they provide none.

- Since it is the rep who has called the customer, it may increase the customer's feeling that the rep is being intrusive if he or she doesn't even know the customer's name.

- Some people have a negative impression of telephone solicitation and will not go out of their way to be cooperative, especially if a rep doesn't even know their name.

Many of the above reasons also apply to inbound calls. In addition

- Customers may be upset, and their priority may be to express the reason for the call rather than to provide their name.

- Customers may fear repercussions if they provide a name.

- Customers may be concerned about confidentiality.

If the nature of the calls you handle might encourage customers' reluctance to provide their name (for example, you handle complaints or do outbound telephone selling), the following tips may be useful:

- Present a logical reason for requesting the name, especially one that benefits the customer: "In order for me to log this call for you, may I have your name please?" or "May I have your name please so I can access your file?"

- Personalize your request: "I just find it more comfortable if I can address you by your name."

- Use the techniques for confirming pronunciation: "I want to make sure I'm pronouncing your name correctly." Note that this works only for complex names. If you ask to confirm the pronunciation of "Green," for example, you won't leave a good impression. Be prepared to overcome any defensiveness: "I know nowadays we are getting nervous about giving our name over the telephone. Let me assure you I have no ulterior motive in asking for your name. It's just that I feel better talking to a person rather than a voice."

Most people aren't reluctant to provide their name. Don't allow isolated cases to interfere with the habit of requesting and using customer names. The benefits of doing so far outweigh the potential problems. However, if your purpose in requesting the customer's name is simply to build rapport and you don't need it for another specific part of the job, then respect the customer's wish not to provide it. Just say, "I'm sorry, it wasn't my intention to make you uncomfortable," then move the conversation on.

A NAME IS TOTALLY BEYOND A REP

When pronunciation of a name is totally beyond you, the following may help:

- Address male customers as "Sir." Do not use "Ma'am" for a woman—many women find this offensive. For a woman whose name is totally beyond you, the best recourse is to avoid addressing the person directly, except by using "you." There is no parallel to "Sir."

- Some customers who have encountered problems with others' ability to pronounce their name may suggest you use a nickname or shorter version of the name.

REPS DON'T WANT TO SOUND INSINCERE OR PHONY

We have all met people who overuse our name, a person who sounds like a recent graduate from a memory or sales training program. The overuse sounds insincere and fawning, like the person is trying to manipulate us. Because they don't want to give other people the same impression, many reps avoid using customer names.

Similarly, it's possible to use a first name in too familiar a manner—for example, when someone you do not know begins a call by using your first name and talking to you like you are his or her best friend. Yet, using names is so powerful for rapport-building that reps must overcome these negative feelings. If you use a name twice in a conversation, when you first hear it and again at the end of the call, you will not be seen to be overusing it.

REPS FEEL UNCOMFORTABLE WITH USING NAMES

Some reps are not in the habit of using someone's name when they speak to that person, so they just don't think to do so with customers.

It may feel uncomfortable getting used to the habit. Developing any new habit takes about three weeks. So for three weeks you may need to remind yourself to use customer names. A cue card attached to your computer screen to remind you may be useful during this period. It will be easier to develop this habit if you practise it outside of work as well.

REPS ARE UNCERTAIN ABOUT WHICH NAME TO USE

Using a customer's first name may be appropriate when

- Calls are business-to-business (particularly when there are repeated calls to or from the same person).

- The nature of the business is less formal.

- The rep is mature and has an older-sounding voice.

- The rep is personally comfortable with using the first name.

- A customer offers only his or her first name.

- A customer asks the rep to use his or her first name. In this situation, the rep will seem rude if she or he doesn't use the first name.

Using a customer's title and surname is appropriate when

- Calls are business-to-consumer (unless a customer asks the rep to use his or her first name).

- A customer does not provide a first name.

- A customer provides the title along with the first and last name (e.g., Mrs. Louise Gagnon, Dr. Carlos Diego).

- The rep is personally more comfortable with using a title and surname.

- A customer asks the rep to use her or his title and surname. If the customer has corrected a rep who has used the customer's first name, the rep should offer a simple apology and comply with the customer's wish.

A rep is uncertain about which is the first name and which is the surname (in some cultures, names are given with the surname first). The rep should confirm that she or he is using the correct name with the title.

1. *Of the seven reasons why a rep might not use the customer's name, identify which apply to you. Which reasons currently or might potentially interfere with your use of the customer's name?*

2. *Develop a plan of action for overcoming these barriers. Ensure that your plan includes*
    a. *specific action steps*
    b. *a time line for implementation*
    c. *a way to test that you have overcome the barriers*

Communicating Respect for the Customer

Each and every customer needs to feel respected. The professional call centre representative communicates respect in every call.

Disrespect can be communicated through words or nuances in tone of voice that a rep may not even be aware of, that the rep may think the customer will not identify, or that the rep feels the customer "deserves."

Unconscious disrespect can occur after a period of unusually high stress in the call centre. The rep begins to speak in a way that communicates impatience with the customer; disregard for the customer; the view that the customer is not very bright, capable, or important; the implication that the customer's issue is unimportant; or the impression that the rep believes the customer is misrepresenting his or her position or even lying.

Often these habits persist long after the initial stressors have disappeared and may resurface when the rep is experiencing only minor frustration. The rep's stress may simply be too close to the surface, or she or he has too short a "fuse."

Unconscious habits that communicate disrespect may also include sighing into the phone, yawning, tapping a pencil on the desk, or making sarcastic comments to oneself.

Intentional low-level disrespect is the result of reps feeling annoyed with a difficult customer but not being able to express that annoyance. It may even be a response to dealing with a previous difficult customer and have nothing to do with the current customer. In effect, the reps vent their anger by allowing an edge to enter their tone of voice. Reps rationalize this behaviour by saying that the customer doesn't hear the disrespect or sarcasm—which, of course, is not true.

The customer usually can sense the disrespect, and even though it may not be evident enough for the customer to point it out to a rep, the customer will either respond negatively (and consequently make the call more difficult) or, at a minimum, leave the call feeling dissatisfied with the rep and the organization.

"The customer deserved it" attitude typically arises when call centre reps feel that they are being mistreated by customers. The rep who justifies this disrespect with this excuse has begun to personalize the customer interactions and lose her or his sense of professionalism. It is never constructive or appropriate to show disrespect to a customer.

Customers who are experiencing stress may be oversensitive to negative criticism (see the Valuator personality type described in Chapters 8 and 9), so even a neutral comment by the rep may be interpreted as disrespectful. It is therefore not enough to simply avoid communicating disrespect—failing to communicate respect can undermine the relationship with the customer just as easily.

BASICS OF COMMUNICATING RESPECT

Respect Yourself

Communicating respect for the customer is easiest when we genuinely feel that respect. Typically, before we can feel that others are worthy of our respect, we must feel that we are worthy of it too. A sense of self-worth, then, is important. When reps feel good about themselves, they react less to the stresses of the job and are less likely to be disrespectful to others.

Use the Customer's Surname and Title

As mentioned earlier in this chapter, addressing the customer by name is more respectful and communicates the rep's interest in the customer as a person.

Be Polite

A few simple expressions of politeness are often avoided in telephone interactions, even by people who would normally use them in face-to-face interactions. Make sure "please," "thank you," and "you're welcome" are part of your telephone style.

Show Customers Their Issue Is Important

Even if you have heard the customer's issue a dozen times today, remember that this is the customer's first time. Show the customer that his or her issue is important to you by:

* using **listening responses** such as "yes," "okay," and "I see"
* using **active listening techniques** such as **paraphrasing**, **summarizing**, repeating, and **focused questioning** for clarification
* expressing **empathy** as the customer expresses her or his feelings about a situation
* telling the customer the issue is important to you: "Thank you for bringing this to our attention"
* expressing a sense of urgency and ownership regarding the customer's issue: "I'll take care of this right away"

Ask Permission to Proceed

If a rep pushes on with a presentation or questions without confirming the customer's permission, the customer may feel a lack of control and that the rep is being domineering or disrespectful. The simple solution is for the rep to "position" where she or he is going with the call and confirm the customer's permission to go there by saying, "May I ask you a couple of questions?" "If you'd like, I can explain that," or "May I take a moment to discuss this?"

Confirm Customer Understanding

Rather than pushing on with a customer whose understanding or interest has been lost, it is more respectful to periodically confirm the customer's understanding.

Cues that the customer may not understand include sudden silence, questions that don't fit what you are talking about, or reluctance, hesitation, or negative responses from a customer who had been positive.

To confirm the customer's understanding, ask, "Do you have any questions?" "Did I explain that right?" or "Did I answer your question?"

Allow the Customer to Save Face

It is important that call centre representatives be enthusiastic about what they do and develop knowledge and expertise in their company's products, services, and procedures. It is, however, unfair to expect customers to be just as passionate or knowledgeable. We are disrespectful to customers if we do not allow them to know less than we know about our business and if we treat their questions as naive. After all, if they didn't ask these questions there wouldn't be so many call centre reps! An "education call" is a wonderful opportunity to build rapport with the customer, but the rep's tone of voice must be respectful, not condescending.

Learning Application Exercise

Assess how you communicate respect to others in work, school, or personal environments. Can you improve in any of the areas mentioned in this section? If you are unsure, try asking your friends or coworkers.

Matching the Customer's Vocabulary

Matching the customer's vocabulary refers to choosing words the customer will recognize and understand. It is important for call centre representatives to use words that reflect and enhance the customer's understanding and acceptance of what a rep is saying. The effective rep speaks **humaneze** rather than **techno-talk**, **mycompany-isms**, **familiareze**, or **intellectualeze**.

TECHNO-TALK AND MYCOMPANY-ISMS

Techno-talk consists of terms related to computer systems, software, or technical aspects of the company's products—any words or phrases that may be understood by coworkers and by some of a company's customers, but that many customers will not understand.

Mycompany-isms are terms, acronyms, identification numbers (e.g., for forms or parts), or slang words that are peculiar to the organization and that someone outside could not be expected to know (e.g., "You need to complete a T43").

HAVE YOU EVER?

Have you ever been in a situation similar to this one?

A man made arrangements to meet his girlfriend for lunch at the hospital where she worked. When asked how he would find her when he got to the hospital, she responded with, "No problem, just come in the front door, then I see you."

She eventually found him after he had been impatiently waiting for half an hour in the lobby for her to see him. Having no understanding of hospital terminology, the man did not understand that ICU stands for Intensive Care Unit, where his girlfriend worked and where she had been waiting for him.

To manage techno-talk and mycompany-isms, try the following:

- Find user-friendly ways to express technical issues or company-specific information.

- Avoid using company acronyms and jargon with customers.

- Even if the customer sounds knowledgeable, periodically confirm that she or he still understands you. Listen to the customer's language—is the customer's use of techno-talk consistent, or is the caller just using the odd word she or he has collected and probably doesn't understand well? While the customer's words may be sophisticated, does the use of these words reflect an understanding of what they're about? Are the words misused?

- Verify the customer's understanding of a term that could be unfamiliar: "Do you understand what is meant by…?" "Am I making sense?" (this works well because the rep assumes responsibility for the communication and makes the customer's lack of understanding okay), or "Would you like me to explain that a little further?"

- Listen to the customer's tone of voice as you explain something. Does the customer sound uncertain? Impatient? Does the customer withdraw from the conversation—lead it to closure, change the subject, agree too easily, or lose concentration? Does the customer ask what you mean? The latter is a good sign that the customer doesn't understand, yet many call centre reps in an information-giving role answer a customer question with more technical or insider talk and simply add to the customer's confusion.

- Determine the customer's level of understanding at the beginning of the call: "How familiar are you with…?" or "Have you done this before?"

FAMILIAREZE

Familiareze is the tendency to speak in a less formal manner than customers may be comfortable with. This may lead customers to feel that call centre representatives are being pushy, unprofessional, or insincere. If a rep is too candid, this may undermine the customer's confidence in the company or its products (for example, if a rep says, "We've had a lot of problems with that model").

Call centre reps who speak familiareze may mistakenly see their overfamiliarity as strong people skills. If a customer reacts negatively to this style, the reps ignore or rationalize this away by thinking the customer is tense or rigid.

Reps who speak familiareze tend to have a longer average call time because they are more wordy and take more time explaining and connecting personally. Their conversations typically include slang expressions ("I gotta tell you…."), sentences that are not grammatically correct ("I seen that"), and pronunciation that is not precise ("goin'," "doin'," "yeah").

Customers who are not comfortable with the level of familiarity tend to jump quickly into the conversation as soon as the rep pauses, and speak very quickly so the rep doesn't start up again. The customer's voice may have that "I'm ending the call now" tone in which she or he sounds more distant, the tone drops, the call becomes more businesslike, and the customer starts summarizing. The level of customer interaction also drops, and she or he sounds uninterested or does not respond. The customer's tone also becomes more formal during the conversation, and the customer begins to give short or minimal answers to the rep's questions or comments. These are all cues to the rep that the customer is reacting negatively to the rep's style.

Often reps who use familiareze will show symptoms of the "I've-got-an-example-of-that-same-situation" syndrome, in which the rep responds to every customer comment or story with one of his or her own. This is particularly annoying to a customer when the rep's story always outdoes the customer's. One-upmanship can interfere with expressing true empathy with the customer, which is other-based rather than self-based. Instead of showing that the rep understands the customer's situation, the result of one-upmanship is that the customer feels her or his situation or feelings are diminished by the rep's story.

Familiareze can be an example of too much of a good thing—of taking a natural rapport-building ability a step too far. To overcome this habit, reps need to pay attention to their use of slang and their grammar and pronunciation. A cue card attached to the computer screen can serve as a reminder. Reps should also track the number of times they use the customer's name during a call, and make a conscious effort not to use it excessively. When reps get the urge to share a personal story, they should substitute an empathy statement or question instead.

INTELLECTUALEZE

Intellectualeze is the tendency to use a more difficult vocabulary than the customer's. Its potential effects include the customer feeling inadequate; the rep seeming pretentious, condescending, or just silly; the customer failing to understand what the rep is trying to communicate; and the customer taking up the challenge by pulling out her or his own vocabulary arsenal and turning the conversation into a word war.

Reps who speak intellectualeze usually have good intentions. They may simply have a large vocabulary and have developed the habit of using it with friends and associates. These reps may be striving for perfect communication—using harder words that communicate the nuances of meaning—but instead just end up confusing the issue. Also, sometimes a rep's vocabulary isn't particularly difficult but the customer's vocabulary is weak, and the rep needs to adjust her or his language.

A good way for reps to check for intellectualeze is to listen with a candid coworker to a number of their own tape-recorded calls. The reps can then practise simpler ways of saying things, or use a cue card attached to their computer screen reminding them to follow up difficult words with paraphrasing in simpler language. The objective is to develop the habit of using only the paraphrasing and to avoid the difficult words altogether.

When customers pause for a long time after you speak to think over what you've just said, respond in ways that show they don't understand, sound confused, or state that they don't understand, you may be using intellectualeze. Try to adjust your vocabulary to meet the customer's, taking care not to sound condescending—remember that you're not speaking to a child and shouldn't sound as though you are. You want to sound intelligent and competent at your job, not pretentious.

Learning Application Exercise

1. Call five 1-800 numbers or customer information or support lines, and assess each customer service representative for his or her use of these four uncommunicative "languages."

2. Assess your own calls or conversations for the use of these languages. Have a partner help you assess your style.

3. If you show signs of using any of these languages, develop an action plan to overcome the problem. Ensure that your plan includes

   a. specific action steps

   b. a time line for implementation

   c. a way to test that the problem has been overcome

Keeping the Call Flowing

"Dead air" occurs when the call centre representative's response to the customer is delayed so that there is a noticeable silence lasting three seconds or more on the telephone. Dead air is a pause initiated by the rep, not the pause during which a customer considers an answer to the rep's question. Typically, dead air occurs when the rep is entering customer information into the computer or is waiting for a screen to pop up when the system is slow.

Not all call centre reps effectively manage dead air. The ability to interact with a customer while entering information into the computer or waiting for a screen to pop up is becoming a sought-after skill in call centres. The benefits of having this skill include more time-efficient call management, and therefore lower average talk time; lower average length of call; higher number of calls handled per rep; fewer reps doing the same work, and therefore savings for the call centre and the organization; and increased customer sense of call continuity—the call flows better, the customer feels more connected, so the customer is more likely to be satisfied.

Here are some tips for improving your management of dead air:

- Develop the skill of keying without looking at the keyboard as the other person is talking. This skill has become critical for a call centre career. Tape-record a speech, presentation, or sermon (not one that is spoken too quickly), and practise keying the words into your computer while the tape is playing. From that same tape, create an organized summary of what the person is saying while it is being said. Then, input a summary while listening to a different tape. Alternatively, practise keying while role-playing a "call" with a friend. Practise these skills until they become second nature.

- Learn to fill dead air by talking to the customer while you are completing your computer entry. The easiest way to do this is to encourage the customer to speak by asking questions. Ask the customer to elaborate on the information that he or she has provided. Summarize or paraphrase the customer's situation as you enter information, or ask the customer to confirm your summary. Confirm details as they are provided (repeat the address, account number, name, order, etc., as they are provided). Confirming information is always a good idea whether dead air is an issue or not, since it prevents errors and reassures the customer that you have heard the information correctly. Discuss side issues that are relevant to your business but not necessarily to the purpose of the call, such as the results of previous conversations, general issues about the customer's account, other products or services your organization provides, or new products or company programs. Discuss something personal raised by the customer earlier in the conversation. When a pause is predictable and short, tell the customer what you are doing—the steps you are taking or what you are entering on the computer—to keep the customer involved.

Overcoming Speech Idiosyncrasies

Speech idiosyncrasies are words or phrases we use often or repetitively, usually unconsciously, that can distract customers and cause them to focus on the idiosyncrasies rather than on what we are saying. Some examples include "right," "OK," "see," "you know," "eh," "basically," "obviously" (which can sound condescending), and various regional idiosyncrasies. Some speech idiosyncrasies are stress-induced and can be managed by learning to manage your stress (see Chapter 9).

HAVE YOU EVER?

Have you ever had an instructor who repeated a word or expression excessively? For example, she or he may have made a point then said "right," then made a second point and said "right," and so on through 100 or more points and 100 or more "rights." At the end of such a lecture, the topic of conversation among students is not the instructor's material, but rather "How many 'rights' did you count?"

Learning Application Exercise

1. *Listen to tape recordings of your telephone calls or classroom presentations to identify, with help from a partner, any speech idiosyncrasies you may have.*

2. *Develop an action plan to overcome your speech idiosyncrasies. Ensure that your plan includes*

   a. *specific action steps*

   b. *a time line for implementation*

   c. *a way to test that the problem has been solved*

Summary

The six critical areas for establishing and maintaining customer rapport include

- the greeting
- using the customer's name
- communicating respect for the customer
- matching the customer's vocabulary
- keeping the call flowing
- overcoming speech idiosyncrasies

The standard greeting consists of "Hello," "Good morning," or "Good afternoon"; identifying your company or department; giving your name; and then asking "How may I help you?" An effectively delivered greeting sounds fresh each time, is well-paced, and is clearly enunciated.

Use the customer's name when you first hear it, when you are ending the call, when you need to regain control of the conversation, when you are about to make an important point, and when you want to personally connect to express empathy.

To communicate respect for the customer:

- First respect yourself.

- Use the customer's surname and title.

- Be polite—use "please," "thank you," and "you're welcome."

- Demonstrate to the customer that his or her issue is important to you.

- Ask permission to proceed.

- Confirm that the customer understands.

- Allow the customer to save face when she or he doesn't understand.

To increase customer understanding and rapport, avoid techno-talk, mycompany-isms, familiareze, and intellectualeze. Keep the customer involved and connected by avoiding dead air—develop the ability to type and talk to the customer at the same time, and to fill pauses by encouraging the customer to ask questions, discussing side issues, or explaining to the customer what you are doing.

Endnotes

1. Carl Sewell and Paul B. Brown, *Customers for Life: How to Turn That One-Time Buyer into a Lifetime Customer* (New York: Doubleday, 1990), xviii, 161.

2. Zig Ziglar, *Zig Ziglar's Secrets of Closing the Sale* (New York: Simon & Schuster Audioworks, 1992) (audiotape).

CHAPTER 6
Listening and Questioning

Learning Outcomes

After successfully completing Chapter 6, you will be able to:

- Use a variety of listening responses to show the speaker that you have heard.

- Use active listening skills—restating, paraphrasing, and clarifying—to show your understanding of a customer's issues.

- "Diagram" calls to enhance listening.

- Overcome the tendency to interrupt or "drift."

- Make sincere empathy statements when appropriate.

- Avoid barriers to effective listening.

- Listen through an accent.

- Overcome biases that can interfere with effective listening.

- Communicate effectively when speaking with someone whose first language is not English (or French).

- Use open-ended and closed questions appropriately to manage the call and resolve customer issues.

- Improve your questioning effectiveness by incorporating effective questioning techniques.

Effective Listening

Nobody ever listened himself out of a job.

—Calvin Coolidge

When two people are in a conversation, the speaker can tell if the other person is listening by watching his or her facial expressions and body language. Typically, the listener will add verbal responses as well. These responses show interest and encourage the speaker to say more.

In a telephone conversation, fewer clues are available to the speaker to confirm that the listener has understood the message, so verbal comments are necessary to convey the message that the listener is indeed listening and understanding. Call centre representatives with effective listening skills compensate for the missing visual cues by using verbal responses.

Have you ever been in a telephone conversation in which the other person did most of the talking and then the person asked, "Are you still there?" Because of your silence, the other person could not determine whether you were listening, or whether the line had been disconnected, whether you were still on the telephone. When this happens, the speaker may feel that you aren't listening because you don't particularly care what she or he has to say. This is poor social etiquette on a personal call, and unacceptable service for a call centre rep.

REAL AND PERCEIVED LISTENING

Professional call centre representatives not only listen effectively (real listening), but also show the customer that they are listening effectively (perceived listening). To achieve real listening you must pay attention to what is said and understand the words. You must listen for the meaning of what the speaker is saying—listen for any additional message communicated by the speaker's tone or words. You must also act on what the speaker has said. At a minimum, show you have understood, then apply the appropriate techniques to question, problem-solve, sell, or act on the information in whichever manner is required by your specific call centre role and the nature of the situation.

When you listen effectively and show the customer you are listening:

- The customer will know you are listening and feel as though you are paying attention, and trust you and your company.

- You will have fewer upset customers. Ineffective listeners leave the impression that they don't care about the customer or the customer's issue.

- The customer will feel encouraged to further communicate, providing you with information you need to address the purpose of the call.

- You will have shorter calls, because you will have taken the most direct route to getting the information you need to resolve the customer's issue.

- The customer will not need to call back about issues that were unresolved in a previous call.

Many skills combine to achieve the goal of "effective listening." They range from the simple actions of paying attention and providing verbal listening responses to more complex "active" listening skills.

Some of us are naturally less effective at listening than others. The good news is that listening is a skill that we can all get better at.

NINE STEPS FOR IMPROVING LISTENING SKILLS

1. Recognize That Listening Is Hard Work

Effective listening involves concentration and focus. The average person speaks at a rate of 100 to 160 words per minute. The average person can listen at a rate of 300 to 600 words per minute. So what does the average listener do with all that extra time? When we are face-to-face with a person, part of our extra brain capacity is taking in the visual messages we are receiving. When we are on the telephone, we can do other things at the same time. Some of us, however, waste this available capacity and let our mind drift.

Each of us drifts to some extent. Because we can think faster than customers can speak, we may guess their message by listening only to parts of what they say. We can mentally complete the thoughts before the words are finished. We may form enough of an impression of what the customer is saying without hearing any extra information the customer provides. Then, with the time left over after we have formed our own interpretation of the message, while the customer is still talking, we drift.

Some drifters are planners who drift from a conversation and mentally plan a shopping or "to do" list, or who think about other things or people. Other drifters are fantasizers whose minds drift to a pleasurable experience they have had or would like to have.

Have you ever drifted from a conversation and got so lost in your planning or fantasizing that you stayed there too long? When you returned your attention to the speaker, you found that you now had no idea what the person was talking about. While you were away, the speaker took a turn and you missed it. If you had to ask the speaker to repeat what she or he had been saying, you probably appeared rude. While all of us drift, most people "check in" on the speaker regularly so they don't get lost, and know when to resume full attention. A few people habitually drift and stay away too long. For these people, drifting is a problem. There is a solution. First, recognize that drifting is an issue for you. The cues are as follows:

- Do you get lost in conversations and don't know where you lost them?

- Do you have to regularly ask, "Could you please repeat that?"

- Do you (or others) find that you misunderstand what the speaker is saying?

- Many listeners with a drifting problem blame the speaker. Do you find that a lot of people don't explain themselves well, don't know what they want to say, or seem to change their mind during the interaction?

- Do you find you must regularly guess what the speaker has just said and then act on the assumption rather than with confidence that you have understood?

- Listen to tapes of your calls. Can you (or a friend) identify instances where you missed the point or misunderstood the speaker and did not realize it?

Second, establish a method for reminding yourself to refocus your attention on the conversation. For example, attach a cue card that says "DON'T DRIFT" to the edge of your computer screen.

Rather than drift, true call centre professionals use the extra thinking time to process the information they hear, visualize the customer or his or her situation, think about solutions to the problem, or anticipate opportunities for additional service or sales.

2. Use a Variety of Listening Responses

Responsive listening is more than just making an occasional sound to show the speaker you are still there. Responsive listening is a skill and can be an effective tool to show the speaker that you value what is being said and to encourage the speaker to tell you more.

Listening responses are brief interjections into a customer's speech during a pause or after a complete thought. These let the customer know you have received the verbal message. The responses are subtle enough to not interrupt the customer's line of thought. Repeatedly using any one listening response, even one that is professional, can sound mechanical and may distract the customer or sound insincere. Try to vary your responses based on what the caller is saying. The following are some of the verbal responses used by telephone professionals:

• I agree	• Good	• I see what you mean
• I see	• Thank you	• That's a good point
• Oh	• Yes	• That's correct
• Alright	• Right	• I understand

Listening responses that are superlatives, such as "great," "fantastic," or "wonderful" that are used even when the speaker's comments are not particularly great, fantastic, or wonderful can give the impression that you are insincere or manipulative. Mumbled responses such as "mm-hmm" or "yeah" do not sound professional.

Listening responses are useful for when the caller has asked a question or made a comment to which you should respond. Effective listeners offer a listening response to indicate "message received" before taking a pause to plan their response.

3. Avoid Interrupting

Chronic interrupters typically interrupt with good intention. They believe they understand the caller's point and want to signal that they do not require more elaboration, thereby saving the caller the added effort as well as keeping the call shorter. Sometimes we interrupt because we feel we have something to say that is too important to wait.

The effect of constant interrupting, despite good intentions, is to make the rep sound impolite. The customer isn't given the opportunity to finish, and may find the rep controlling, pushy, and insensitive. Chronic interrupting is considered rude. Most chronic interrupters are aware of what they do, though they often do not realize how rude it sounds. Interrupting is a bad habit that one can learn to control.

Note that appropriate interruptions can be an important part of call control to keep a call from wandering, but here we are referring to interrupting that is chronic or inappropriate.

ON THE JOB

A Hard Habit to Break

Some habits are extremely hard to change. A big part of the problem is simply seeing that the habit exists.

A listening skills workshop was delivered to 20 call centre reps in a customer service department. The two days of the program were separated by two weeks to allow the reps to apply the new skills between training sessions. Before the first day of the workshop, the reps were required to tape-record their calls and assess their listening skills. When the class got together two weeks later for the second day of the workshop, participants each reported on the insights they had collected by listening to and assessing the tapes of their calls. Two of the stronger, more personable, and more skilled reps each confessed, "I am rude." These were nice people who, for the first time, had heard how their interrupting sounded. Both were appalled, and both vowed to stop interrupting.

Later, at the close of the workshop, as the reps took turns sharing their action plans for improving their listening skills with the class, one of the "rude" interrupters again confirmed her concern with that habit and started to explain her plan to overcome it. The other interrupter cut the first woman off with the comment "I do the same thing." Only after the words were out did she look shocked and gasp, "Oh my goodness. I did it again, didn't I?"

To confirm for yourself whether you chronically interrupt, listen to yourself. Listen to some recordings of your phone calls, and ask friends and coworkers for their honest feedback. If interrupting is an issue for you, your commitment to changing the habit is essential. Try the following:

- First, be aware of your interrupting. Work to become aware of it before it occurs rather than after.

- Attach a cue card saying "DON'T INTERRUPT" to the edge of your computer screen as a reminder.

- Make a personal rule to let the customer finish speaking before you speak.

- It may help to write down the thought you planned to interrupt with. That way you know you won't forget it if you don't say it immediately.

4. Listen with Pen and Paper

Some people feel that they must write everything down that a caller says. If they don't write things down, they completely forget what was said. Even if the notes are never looked at again, the act of writing seems to help these people to hear and retain the information better.

Some people take no notes. Then, six months later, they can look at a customer's name and remember every detail about the call they had from that customer.

Another group of people think they don't need to take notes, but really do. These people would be much more effective at their job if they took notes. If you aren't taking notes during calls, you probably should be.

ON THE JOB

Note-Taking

Call centre reps in an office were trained in the importance of taking notes, and the company had built this into its call-handling procedure. Later, their call-handling effectiveness was audited: a number of random calls were selected and taped without the staff's knowledge of which ones would be taped, and then were analyzed. The audit revealed that a large percentage of reps were not answering all the customers' issues, were asking for information that had already been provided, and often responded in ways that showed they didn't accurately recall an item of customer information. All of these are symptoms of a lack of note-taking.

*The trainer went back to the staff, planning to refresh them on the importance of note-taking, only to find out that everyone was taking notes. It was the way they were taking notes that was ineffective. They were taking notes chronologically, writing down information in the order they heard it. They received complex calls, and their lists of information were inefficient for quickly accessing specific items of information. To remedy this, the reps were taught a system for organizing the information: **"diagramming" a call**.*

Not every call requires diagramming—it is unnecessary, for example, for requests for account balances or other very short calls. For longer, more complex calls, however, diagramming is invaluable. Reps who use it cannot understand how someone can effectively manage a call without it. Diagramming may be done on paper or entered directly into computer notes. To diagram a call:

1. Keep blank paper and a pencil close at hand. Be ready to write when a call starts.

2. As soon as you hear it, write down the customer's name (and how to pronounce it, if necessary) in one particular spot on the page (an upper corner is recommended). By developing the habit of writing the customer's name in this spot every time, or somehow giving it emphasis, you avoid confusing it with any other names you collect during the conversation. Then you avoid the embarrassment of calling the customer by the wrong name.

3. Learn to use pictures, abbreviations, and symbols to describe what the caller wants. "Transfer funds" might become an arrow. A request for a "transaction history"

might be an "H." If others will have access to your notes, ensure your abbreviations conform to your company standards so your notes will be understood. If only you will be accessing these notes, you can develop your own code.

4. Collect similar information on specific areas of your page. For example (see Figure 6.1), you might put customer issues on the top left, customer personal information on the top right, questions you want to ask or information you want to collect on the bottom right (and checked off as each is asked or collected), and recommendations, with a reason for each, on the bottom left. The types of information you collect will depend on your job. For example, the reps in one mutual fund investment company use a checklist of potential sales opportunities to be investigated with an area for portfolio analysis.

5. If the customer wants to discuss three issues, make a list with 1, 2, and 3 and a brief outline of each. This way you can refer back to each later in the conversation, and check them off as they're resolved. "I'll deal with your second point first" is an impressive response to so organized a customer.

6. If the customer uses specific language to describe something, jot it down and use the same words later in the call. Such **reflective phrases** are very effective for showing you have listened, and they encourage the customer to accept your (their) point.

Diagrams can be very valuable when a customer has multiple issues, the issue is complex, or the customer is upset and goes into a long story. Diagrams can prevent your asking for information to be repeated, and they can help you summarize a call and provide effective perceived listening.

Figure 6.1

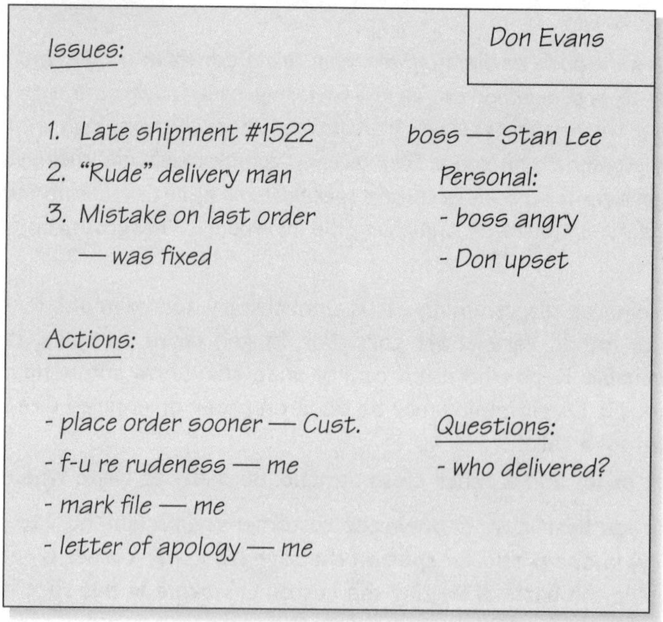

Issues:

Don Evans

1. Late shipment #1522
2. "Rude" delivery man
3. Mistake on last order
— was fixed

boss — Stan Lee

Personal:
- boss angry
- Don upset

Actions:

- place order sooner — Cust.
- f-u re rudeness — me
- mark file — me
- letter of apology — me

Questions:
- who delivered?

5. Use Active Listening Techniques

"Active" listening means that you play an active, as opposed to a passive, part in the listening process. It provides improved real and perceived listening, because it confirms for you that you have understood correctly while showing the customer that you understand.

Restating is repeating back the customer's point or the last few words of the point. Restating is effective for showing the customer you have heard what she or he said. It is also useful if you are unsure that you heard the customer correctly. You say what you think you heard, and the customer then confirms, corrects, or elaborates, thereby enhancing your understanding. Restating also encourages the customer to continue or elaborate.

Paraphrasing is restating using your own words. Beyond showing that you heard what the customer said, this shows you understood. Paraphrasing is a powerful way to show that you understand the thoughts behind the customer's words, or to identify where the intended meaning is different from your interpretation. Paraphrasing also encourages customers to share more information with you. Often callers are not sure what they want to say, and hearing someone else speak the words can help them clarify in their own mind the message they are trying to communicate. Start with phrases like

"In other words...."

"So, what you're saying is...."

"Let me see if I understand...."

Summarizing involves identifying the key elements of the caller's position or argument and either paraphrasing or restating those key elements back to the caller. Summarizing ensures you understand the essentials of the caller's position. It either shows the caller that you have been listening and understand, or helps the caller identify what key elements require clarification. Summarizing is also an effective way to handle a situation in which you do not understand the caller's position or argument. By feeding back a summary of what you think is the caller's intent, the caller can focus his or her clarification. If, instead of summarizing, you opt to simply ask the caller to repeat him- or herself or tell the caller you do not understand, he or she may just repeat the same words back that you didn't understand the first time. Summarizing is much more effective if you have taken notes while the other person was speaking—and best if you have diagrammed the call.

Questioning as an active listening skill involves exploring elements of what people have said so you can "flesh out" their position, or understand what meaning they intend, with certain words or ways of describing something. Focused questioning communicates to people that you are listening and shows them you are working to understand their position. For example, "And do you want to know how to apply for an increase in your credit card limit?"

6. Confirm That Your Response Is Appropriate

Checking the appropriateness of your response confirms that you listened to and understood the customer's communication. Without such confirmation, customers may leave the call without having their needs met, causing them to feel poorly serviced and requiring that they call back to get the answer they need. Such callbacks add unnecessarily to a call centre's workload. Use questions like "Does that answer your question?" "Does that give you what you need?" "Does that work for you?" or "Does this fit your needs?" Confirming the appropriateness of your response is not only polite, it could save you a lot of time.

7. Summarize Responsibilities at the End of the Call

At the close of the call, always restate what actions you will take, what actions the customer needs to take (if any), what results will occur, and when they will happen. This helps the customer feel confident that you have been listening, have understood, and are taking responsibility for carrying out your part of the plan. It also reminds the customer of her or his agreed-upon actions.

8. Demonstrate Empathy as Appropriate

Generally, using the right tone, positive wording, and responsive active listening skills demonstrates to the customer that you are courteous and that you care. Some situations, however, require sincere empathy.

Some customers' descriptions of their situation involve not only the facts, but the feelings that result from the situation. The customer may, for example, be disappointed, frustrated, upset, or angry. If the call centre representative is so focused on the facts of the situation that these feelings are ignored, the customer may feel that the rep is insensitive. Acknowledging these feelings will help the customer put them aside so that the facts can be discussed. Your main objective in showing empathy is to build trust between you and the customer so that you can communicate better.

ON THE JOB

Avoiding Insensitivity

After a customer called to cancel her recently deceased husband's credit card, a rep at the bank's credit card call centre responded to the obviously distraught customer with a stony "Card number please?" This response was likely less a consequence of the rep's insensitivity and more a result of his being focused on the task at hand and pressured by call volumes. But the customer likely felt alienated from the bank and that the bank was insensitive.

HAVE YOU EVER?

Have you ever become aware that someone was speaking to you, but you were not really listening, though the speaker thought you were? Good listening habits are crucial to being a successful call centre representative.

In his book The 7 Habits of Highly Effective People, Stephen R. Covey says that we really listen at different levels.[1] Sometimes we aren't really listening at all, but saying "Yeah, uh-huh" anyway. When we are otherwise occupied, we are selective and listen only for the issues that are important to us. Then, there is what most of us consider really listening—

paying attention and focusing energy on what someone is saying. Covey says empathic listening "gets inside another person's frame of reference. You look out through it, you see the world the way they see the world, you understand their paradigm, you understand how they feel."[2] Try to be conscious of this the next time you find yourself in a meeting or listening to someone tell you a detailed story on the phone.

An empathy statement

- refers to the situation that caused the emotions

- paraphrases the customer's emotion

- expresses your understanding or appreciation for the emotion

Showing empathy does not mean that you agree with the customer. It does tell the customer that you appreciate how she or he feels and that these feelings are legitimate. Here are two sample empathy statements:

"I can understand how frustrating it must be to misplace your credit card."

"I see why you're concerned about your shipment."

Try to avoid the following:

"I know exactly how you feel." You don't, and a distraught customer may tell you that.

"You're right. You shouldn't have been treated like that." This agrees with the customer's interpretation of the situation, which might not be valid.

9. Avoid the Barriers to Effective Listening

Listening effectiveness can easily be undermined. One barrier to listening is allowing yourself to be distracted. We all have a natural "scanning" mechanism that monitors elements of our external environment to identify what is most important for us to focus on. When we are on a telephone call and actively listening, we need to pay attention to the customer by paying less attention to nearby, attention-grabbing distractions.

Deciding what the other person means before he or she has finished speaking is another listening barrier. While call centre professionals must anticipate the direction of the call to effectively handle the caller's needs, they do not jump to conclusions. When we form a conclusion before the customer finishes, there is a tendency to "own" that conclusion and defend it against reality. We tend to stop listening except for evidence that reinforces our assumption. It is critical to keep an open mind.

Thinking about what you are going to say instead of listening to what the other person is saying is a common listening barrier. Unfortunately, the customer could disclose a valuable piece of information that you will miss while planning your response to what you thought the customer was saying.

People do not listen well when they are upset or emotional. When the customer is upset or angry, a call centre professional knows that to provide the best service he or she must listen effectively, and to do that the rep must remain calm. Chapter 9 provides further information on how to handle upset or angry customers.

Learning Application Exercise

1. Which of the effective listening techniques is your weakest? What can you do to strengthen each?

2. Do any of the barriers to effective listening apply to you? If so, which ones, and what actions will you take to overcome them?

3. Tape your calls or pay attention to your conversations with friends, and listen for evidence of listening skills. Ask others to assess your listening on these calls (see Table 6.1).

TABLE 6.1

Listening Skills Assessment

Score yourself on each achievement as follows:

0 = not used or ineffective
1 = used, but could be improved
2 = used effectively, no improvement necessary

Achievement	Self	Coworker 1	Coworker 2
– uses ample verbal listening responses			
– uses varied verbal listening responses			
– restates, paraphrases, summarizes, or questions when required			
– acknowledges customer's comments and questions			
– confirms interpretation fits customer's intent			
– allows ample time for customer to respond, does not interrupt			
– summarizes action plans at end of call			
– makes sincere empathy statements when appropriate			

Communicating through Accents

We are dealing with God's mix....Each of us is part of the same family. Each of us is an ingredient in a great, cross-cultured mix.

—Max De Pree[3]

The cultural mix in Canada is diverse. For many Canadians, English or French is not their first language. The ability to listen through different accents to understand the speaker's message is a skill that can be developed with effort and practice.

Think of a friend or associate who speaks with an accent. Think back to when you first met that person. The accent that is now familiar to you likely gave you difficulty when the two of you first met. You may think your friend has lost some of her or his accent, but most likely you have developed an "ear" for that accent.

If, on the other hand, you know you have an accent that some people find difficult to understand—and even if you don't—you can help them understand if you

- Speak more slowly, especially when you are speaking to someone new or to whom you speak rarely.

- Take care to enunciate clearly.

As listeners, we can encourage the speaker to slow down and enunciate by speaking slowly and clearly ourselves. The speaker will typically "mirror" or copy our speaking style.

It does not take long to develop an ear for an accent. It can be as quick as listening to the same words said two or three times. The following are some tips to help you improve this skill.

KEEP AN OPEN MIND

The willingness to really listen through an accent stems from a positive attitude and an openness toward people who may have a cultural background that is different from your own. Be aware of your own biases for or against people from specific cultures or backgrounds, and take responsibility for overcoming them.

There are three categories of bias. The first is to have a bias against people of certain cultures or backgrounds and be unaware of it. When you are unaware, you cannot do anything to "fix" the problem since you don't know it's there. In this case, the bias will continue to have a negative impact on your interactions and decisions, but you will not be able to do anything about it—you'll be less effective and not know why.

Perhaps even worse is to be aware that you have a bias, but rationalize it as being true. Again, if you do not believe this problem needs to be fixed, you are unlikely to fix it, and your performance—not to mention your customers—will suffer as a result.

In the third category, you realize you have a bias and that it is inappropriate, and you take steps to overcome or minimize it.

It's possible that you really aren't biased against anyone. But it is also possible to be simply unaware of your bias, or unwilling to face that it exists. That's why it is important to know yourself.

ON THE JOB

Becoming Aware

A rep in one mid-sized call centre consistently scored higher than her peers when "mystery callers" posing as customers to test the reps' performance spoke unaccented English. When, however, a heavily accented mystery caller asked about the same issues, this rep's tone became less friendly and more impatient, and she became more directive and asked fewer questions. When presented with this finding, the rep was shocked—she herself was a member of an ethnic minority. She had to hear the tapes of the calls before she could believe this was true. This rep was in the unawareness category. She quickly moved to the acceptance category, and was anxious to work on overcoming her bias.

Suppose you are unsure whether you are biased against some people. To determine whether you have a bias,

- Assess your response to "humour" that involves a racial or ethnic putdown. Does it make you feel uncomfortable?

- Are your parents or other close family members biased against certain groups of people? If so, you may have absorbed some of their biases.

- Consider situations where you interacted, or had the potential to interact, with a person from a different ethnic, religious, income, or other group or even from a different region of Canada. Have you ever made a generalization about someone, negative or positive, based on these factors?

- Have you had a negative experience with a person from a particular group and assumed that one of the reasons for that negative experience was the person's membership in that group? Or have you generalized your negative impression of that person to other members of that person's group with whom you have had no experience?

- Ask a friend or coworker for honest feedback on whether you show any bias.

- Listen to tapes of your calls or pay attention to your daily conversations to assess whether you handle specific groups of people differently. Have a trusted coworker listen as well.

To overcome a bias, it's helpful to educate yourself about the group you're biased against. You might also consider the groups you belong to—not only your ethnic background, but also your age group, your neighbourhood, the region of Canada you're from, your occupation, your sex, and so on—and how it makes you feel to be stereotyped by others based on these factors. Whether you decide to work on your biases or not, to be a professional and to succeed as a call centre rep you must put these aside at work and treat all customers with respect.

Be Patient and Polite

Effectively listening through an accent requires creating an atmosphere that shows the customer you are involved and attentive. It also involves showing respect for the customer.

Politeness is an integral part of most cultures and is reflected in their languages. In Québécois French, for example, one should address a stranger as "vous" rather than the less formal "tu." To a Quebec Francophone, the "vous" shows greater courtesy. Acadian French, however, uses "tu" more liberally.

In English, politeness is demonstrated by asking rather than telling and through the use of words such as "please" and "thank you." Often in call centres these words are used less frequently than they should be, perhaps due to rushing and trying to be "efficient." Yet when speed hampers politeness and call quality, efficiency is also impaired.

It is best to err on the side of greater rather than less respect. In a call centre where call volumes are high and time is at a premium, it can be frustrating to accept that a conversation with a caller who has an accent will take longer, but you must accept this and be patient.

Assume Responsibility

People with accents generally know they have an accent, but the responsibility for understanding is still yours. Apologize to customers when you don't understand them, and, speaking slowly and clearly, ask them to repeat what they said: "I'm sorry. Will you repeat that for me, please?" This gives you another chance to develop an "ear" for that accent.

Listen to the Entire Message

Some people give up when they hear the first words spoken with an accent. Reps who keep listening even after they have failed to understand the first words often find that they can put together the meaning of the message based on words and phrases they understand later in the customer's message. The key is to keep working at it.

Listen for Contextual Clues

Use words or phrases that you do understand as a base from which to put together what the customer is trying to communicate. This is called using **contextual clues** to ascertain meaning. Be patient and listen for a while. The customer will almost always be calling about something to do with the purpose of your call centre, so the words you must listen for and identify are a small subset of all the words in the language.

Use Active Listening Skills

Usually when someone is not fluent in a language, their comprehension is stronger than their speech. People who have studied a language (but not necessarily practised it) may have an excellent aural and written vocabulary and grammar.

Instead of asking customers to repeat what they said, you will accomplish more by repeating back or paraphrasing what you think they said and allowing them to confirm or correct you.

If the customer doesn't understand what you have said and asks you to repeat something, don't say it exactly the same way. Try repeating the message using slightly different words, and concentrate on using common words and speaking slowly and clearly.

When customers are concentrating on speaking a language in which they are not fluent, it is easy to mix up words. Clarify any key points during the conversation, and summarize to make sure the message is correctly received by both of you.

LEARN HOW LANGUAGES DIFFER

Sentence structures of languages often differ. In some languages, asking a question is simply a matter of using the same words with a difference in tone. In the romance languages (e.g., French, Spanish), descriptive words typically follow the word they describe ("Rio grande" for "big river"). Often, a customer whose native language is not English or French will use English or French words but their own language's structure: "I to the store go." Try not to be confused by the order of the words.

Various phonemes (sounds) exist in some languages but not others. For example, French lacks the "th" sound, and English lacks the rolling throat "r." A customer who is learning English or French will usually approximate the sounds that are missing or substitute sounds that are close in his or her native language.

AVOID USING NEGATIVES

Positive wording is easier to understand. So "Enter your password" is clearer than "Don't enter your name until you've entered your password," and much clearer than "Don't miss entering your password or you won't be able to enter your name." In fact, the human brain operates in the "positive." If you don't believe this, try this test:

> *Close your eyes and don't think of the colour red!*

What happened? Most people will have a difficult time not thinking of the colour red.

Different languages treat negatives differently. Negatives may be difficult to understand when you're learning a new language. So, "That's probably not a good idea" could be misunderstood. It is better to say, "That is a bad idea."

AVOID USING POPULAR EXPRESSIONS OR SLANG

People who are still learning a language usually have to concentrate and pay special attention to every word. Expressions, slang, and idioms may not be understood by someone who has limited experience in the country or culture that has popularized the expression. "That blew me away" may, for example, be taken literally or just be confusing. Keep your language simple and direct.

USE SIMPLE WORDS AND SHORT SENTENCES

This is not the time to impress anyone with your extensive vocabulary! When people learn a new language, they typically learn "conversational" language and may not understand complex sentences.

It is not, however, necessary to act as though you are talking to a three-year-old. Avoid talking down to your caller. For many people, this can happen automatically. As soon as they adjust their vocabulary, their tone of voice changes too, and the customer may interpret it as condescending.

SLOW DOWN AND ENUNCIATE

Speaking more slowly and clearly does two things: it makes your own message easier to understand, and it may slow down the other person as well, which can help you understand better. However, avoid slowing down so much that you sound condescending.

AVOID SPEAKING LOUDER

Usually when we have to repeat something, it means the other person did not hear us. Consequently, many people automatically repeat a sentence louder. Avoid doing so, as the customer may think you are yelling at her or him. Remember, people who don't understand your language aren't deaf—they just don't know the language as well as you (just as you probably don't know their language either).

HAVE YOU EVER?

Have you ever had someone say something to you from another room just as you started a loud appliance, like a washing machine? The sound of the appliance drowns out the other person. After you walk over and say, "I'm sorry. What did you say?" the person repeats what was said but louder, even though you're standing right there. This is done out of habit.

AVOID MIMICKING ACCENTS

We are natural mimics. That's one reason young children learn so quickly. Some of us take our strong mimicry skills into adulthood. After a week in England or Georgia, these people are unconsciously imitating the local accent. In some cases, this mimicry can be taken to the extreme, such as when a call centre rep unconsciously mimics a customer's broken English. Resist any tendency to mimic in such a situation—you are likely to offend the customer.

Learning Application Exercise

Tape your calls and listen for evidence of listening through an accent. Get input from your coworkers as well, and summarize your findings in Table 6.2.

TABLE 6.2

Listening through an Accent Skills Assessment

Score yourself on each achievement as follows:

0 = not used or ineffective

1 = used, but could be improved

2 = used effectively, no improvement necessary

Achievement	Self	Coworker 1	Coworker 2
– shows politeness, says "please" and "thank you"			
– requests that customer repeat words only once and prefaces with "I'm sorry"			
– uses excellent active listening			
– uses few negatives			
– uses no slang			
– keeps sentences simple			
– speaks slowly and clearly without being condescending			

Questioning Skills

The higher the quality of communication the more information you will garner from it, the better you will remember it and the more comfortable you will be communicating.

—*Jacquelyn Wonder and Priscilla Donovan*[4]

When call centre reps are asked, "What type of calls do you prefer?" the responses consistently include "The kind where the customers do not really know what they want." When asked why, the answers are "Because I have to work hard at digging for information," "Because it's like figuring out a puzzle," and "I get a real sense of accomplishment from providing them with information and helping them realize what they need."

Life would be simple if all customers knew and could clearly express exactly what they want to accomplish with their call. If this were the case, however, either most call centre roles would be totally computerized or the job would become very boring. The fun and challenge of a customer service or support role is helping people. To do this, you need to collect the right information, so effective questioning is critical for success.

Questioning is a fundamental skill in interpersonal communication. It is a powerful way to search for meaning, information, and understanding from another person. Asking the wrong questions will often limit you and make you ineffective in your search for understanding. Similarly, rapport with your customer suffers if you don't ask the right kinds of questions or you don't ask them in the right way. The way you word a question and the questioning technique you use can make a big difference to its effectiveness.

Questioning can help you

- Uncover facts.

- Guide a conversation in a certain direction.

- Confirm that you've understood the speaker.

- Learn what the speaker is thinking and feeling.

Asking too many questions can make the interaction feel like an interrogation. To prevent this from happening, combine your effective questioning skills with active listening. Alternately, instead of asking a question, substitute an empathic statement or restate what the customer has just said. These techniques encourage the customer to elaborate and can work as effectively as questioning in the appropriate situation.

Questioning is a listening skill. Asking the right questions at the right time will initiate the information-gathering process and structure the flow of the call so that you have positive control over the discussion. That is, rather than the customer calling and telling you his or her issue (the customer's control), the customer calls and answers your questions (your control).

The information-gathering process typically includes

- asking questions near the beginning of a call to gain information

- listening to the answers

- thinking about the answers and comparing this information with the information you need

- asking more questions to get specific information, to focus on a specific problem, or to get more detail

- listening to the responses and analyzing them by breaking them into smaller parts, or tracing the implications of a situation

- deciding on the appropriate action and explaining it to the customer

- asking questions to ensure your solution suits the customer

- asking a final question to find out if the customer has any additional issues

OPEN-ENDED AND CLOSED QUESTIONS

Open-ended questions and **closed questions** get different types of responses. Open-ended questions encourage the customer to provide information—they open the door to the customer's involvement. They also give the impression that you are interested in hearing what the customer has to say. Table 6.3 lists some examples.

TABLE 6.3
Open-Ended Questions

Purpose	Open-Ended Question
– to get the caller talking	– "How may I help you?"
– to expand on information	– "And then what happened?"
– to direct information collection	– "I'm not clear on why your client is upset. Will you please explain that to me?"

Closed questions, on the other hand, elicit more specific information—often a mere "yes" or "no." The response required of the customer ends her or his input or closes the door on her or his involvement, bringing the conversation back to you for more direction. For this reason, closed questions are particularly useful when trying to establish a structure for the call. Table 6.4 lists some examples.

TABLE 6.4
Closed Questions

Purpose	Closed Question
– to learn specific information	– "May I have your account number, please?"
– to get permission to continue	– "Do you mind if I ask you a few questions?"
– to confirm the information provided	– "Let me be sure I understand the situation.... Is that correct?"
– to verify acceptance of a suggestion or plan of action	– "Does that take care of it?" or "Is that what you were looking for?"
– to control the call	– "May I make a suggestion?"

IMPROVING YOUR QUESTIONING SKILLS

Use Questions Early to Control the Call

It is best to set the tone and pace by starting with questions. That way, the customer is responding to you and you are in control of the information-collecting process. Most customers will follow your lead. Typically, the first question you will ask is part of your greeting: "How may I help you?" is an open-ended question that encourages callers to provide the reason for their call.

Fit the Questions to What the Customer Says

After you ask the first question, "How may I help you?" the nature of the customer's response will dictate your approach. The customer could be in a hurry and want information quickly. In this case, you are likely to receive precise and brief comments, and you may offer focused questions for verification or elaboration. Or the customer may be in no hurry and may feel that your purpose is to chat with him or her. Remember the results that open-ended and closed questions will bring. If customers ramble at the beginning of the call, asking some appropriate closed questions will get them back on track. Be sure to ask open-ended questions only when you are willing to give control to the customer.

IF YOU ARE NOT GETTING THE ANSWERS

YOU ARE SEEKING,

REASSESS THE QUESTIONS

YOU ARE ASKING!

Be "Fresh" for Each Customer

There will likely be days when every call feels the same. This is when you must really take care to listen to the customer's answers to your questions. The customer may surprise you with a different answer than you had anticipated. Questioning for detail can bring out the unique nature of each call or each customer.

Allow Enough Time for Responses

Not all customers know what information you need to solve their issue, and not everyone plans before making a telephone call. Resist the temptation to fill a pause after your question with multiple-choice suggestions. Doing so will make you seem impatient, and it may encourage the customer to hurriedly choose an answer that may be inaccurate.

Avoid Giving Orders

Sometimes in trying to speed up the process, reps slip into telling rather than asking. Many people are more than happy to comply with a request, yet stubbornly resist when that request is presented as a command. Consider these examples:

- "May I have your account number?" versus "Give me your account number."
- "Would you please send me the application by fax?" versus "Fax that to me."

"Position" Your Questions

Sometimes people react negatively to being questioned. They may feel that you are invading their privacy, or they may react as though you are accusing them of something. Questions will seem less invasive or accusing if they are appropriately **positioned**.

Positioning means to lead into the questions by explaining or stating the purpose for them first, thereby putting them in perspective. You might explain the reason for the question or the reason why you need the information. This prepares customers by letting them know what is going to happen. Positioning is particularly useful when you need to ask a sensitive question or a series of closed questions, or if a customer seems resistant or hesitant. Some examples are listed in Table 6.5.

TABLE 6.5
Positioning Questions

Rather Than	Positioning the Question This Way
"What is your address?"	– "Let's see if we can determine why you haven't received your statement. First of all, will you tell me your address so I can verify it with our records?"
"When did you put the transfer request through?"	– "Do you mind if I ask you a few questions so we can figure out how the transfer was made to the wrong account?"
"What is your birth date?"	– "Mr. Leonard, our company takes every precaution to protect your investment. We collect information to use as a security check to confirm that it is you who is calling in the future. Will you please tell me your birth date?"

Use an Empathic Statement

If you have posed a series of questions and sense that the customer feels uncomfortable with the questioning, try an empathic statement. Connect with the customer's feeling that her or his privacy has been invaded: "I'm sorry, Mrs. Yan. I know some of these questions can feel a little personal. The information is important for me to understand the root problem here."

In some situations, empathic statements can work as well as open-ended questions to get a customer to provide additional information. This is because you are laying the foundation of understanding, compassion, and trust: "It must be frustrating to have received such poor service."

Avoid Asking "Why?"

Most questions that begin with "why" can be heard as accusing, invasive, or rude. "Why did you do that?" asked of someone who is upset could be misinterpreted as "Why were you so stupid?" To solve customers' problems we typically do not really need to know why they did something. Move on, and focus on what can be done now to resolve the issue and ensure it will not happen again.

Learning Application Exercise

Record some of your telephone calls, or role-play calls with a friend. Using Table 6.6, assess them yourself, and ask your coworkers or friends to provide feedback regarding each of the effective questioning skills.

TABLE 6.6

Question Log

Score yourself on each achievement as follows:

0 = not used or ineffective

1 = used, but could be improved

2 = used effectively, no improvement necessary

Achievement	Self	Coworker 1	Coworker 2
– uses open-ended questions to gather information			
– positions a series of questions or a sensitive question			
– uses closed questions to direct the conversation			
– asks no "why" questions			

Summary

Effective listening requires that you hear the words, listen to the meaning, and act on the information. To increase your listening skills, recognize that listening is hard work. Use a variety of listening responses to show the caller you are still there, but avoid mechanically repeating "mm-hmm" and similar expressions. Avoid interrupting a person unless you are using this technique appropriately to control the call. Take notes as you listen, or, even better, diagram calls that don't involve simple or repetitive requests. Practise active listening, which means taking responsibility for trying to understand the speaker's message by restating the message, paraphrasing, and summarizing. Check the appropriateness of your responses with the customer. At the end of a call, summarize what you will do, what the customer will do, what results will occur, and when they will happen. Use empathic statements when appropriate, such as when a customer's feelings about a situation are as important as the facts of the situation.

All callers have a right to be listened to and respected. When you are having difficulty understanding a caller's accent, keep an open mind, be aware of any biases you may have against certain groups of people, and work on overcoming those biases. Be patient and polite, and take responsibility for understanding the caller's message. Speak slowly, clearly, using simple words, but be careful not to sound condescending. Encourage the caller to do the same, perhaps by modelling this kind of speech. Remember that speaking louder will not help.

Questioning is another critical component of listening. Use open-ended and closed questions appropriately to obtain the information you need and keep the call focused. Fit your questions to the caller, and be careful not to sound mechanical if you've asked the same questions many times already during the day. Be aware that your questions can seem personal or intrusive at times—lead into these questions with an explanation of why you're asking them to ease the customer's concerns. Allow the customer time to respond to your questions, and watch that your questions don't turn into commands when you are feeling rushed.

Endnotes

1. Stephen R. Covey, *The 7 Habits of Highly Effective People* (New York: Simon & Schuster, 1989).

2. Ibid., 240.

3. Max De Pree, *Leadership Jazz* (New York: Currency Doubleday, 1992), 57.

4. Jacquelyn Wonder and Priscilla Donovan, *Whole Brain Thinking: Working from Both Sides of the Brain to Achieve Peak Job Performance* (New York: W. Morrow, 1984).

Managing the Call

Learning Outcomes

After successfully completing Chapter 7, you will be able to:

- *Discuss the importance of positively controlling the call.*
- *Establish control early in the call.*
- *Overcome the habits that threaten loss of control.*
- *Use the "wedge" to regain control of the call.*
- *Effectively use the "hold" feature.*
- *Use voice mail effectively—yours and the customer's.*
- *Minimize "telephone tag."*
- *Transfer calls effectively.*
- *Effectively say "no" to customers, or tell them something other than what they want to hear.*

Positive Control

Effective control of a call by a professional call centre representative is not obvious to customers. All the customers experience is being heard and having their issue resolved in a timely and professional way. A well-managed call will run smoothly from one phase to the next in logical steps. The customer will not feel that he or she lacks control of the call, because the rep's control is positive. **Positive control** is assertive rather than aggressive, and cooperative rather than domineering. Positive control

- moves the call in a direction that is in the customer's best interest as well as the rep's
- moves the call in that direction without control being an issue for the customer
- involves the customer and is not rep-dominated
- gains customer permission to proceed as necessary

The rep knows what information is needed to resolve the customer's issue, so it makes sense that the rep should be the one to manage the call. The rep's role requires collecting and understanding the customer's information. This in turn requires that the customer be involved and talking, but that the talking be focused on information that is relevant for resolving the issue. So, if the customer is already providing the required information, the rep need expend little effort to control the call. If the customer is providing inadequate or unnecessary information, the rep's control is aimed at redirecting the customer, not on stopping the information flow, so the customer is still talking. Control by the rep becomes more active when the rep is required to establish her or his role at the beginning of the call, reestablish this role after a customer has taken the call off-topic, or understand the customer's issue and how to resolve it.

While it is logical and understandable that reps be responsible for managing calls, customers may seek control because

- They are upset or emotional.
- They believe that they must assume control or the rep will take advantage of them.
- They have an agenda other than issue resolution, such as wanting to chat or vent about an issue that involves the rep's organization or industry.
- They believe, because of the rep's role or behaviour, that the rep will not manage the call effectively, so they must take the lead.
- They have all their information stored in their memory in a certain order, and that's the order it must come out in, regardless of the rep's attempts to structure the flow.
- Their personality is such that they are used to being in control and will assume that control in any situation, whether that is the most productive strategy or not.

If the customer is in control but is providing the information that the rep needs, it might be expected that the rep should be less concerned about who controls. However, there are important benefits to be gained by the rep that warrant establishing at least an image of control. First, the transition from a customer-driven information-collecting process to a rep-provided resolution is smoother. This can be a difficult transition, particularly when the rep's resolution may not match the customer's demands or expectations. If the rep has not controlled the conversation to this point, the customer may find the rep or the rep's solution less credible. Second, when the rep has control, he or she can put an end to the information-collecting process once sufficient data is collected. The customer is more likely to accept this if the rep has already established control of the call. When the customer provides the needed information without any prompting, the rep's control style is more passive and provides more of a perception of control than true control (for example, interjecting with "I see, please tell me more about that" when the customer is already determined to tell everything anyway). This creates the impression that the customer is responding to the rep's request for information, which puts the rep in the lead role when the time comes to assume real control.

ESTABLISHING CONTROL AT THE BEGINNING OF THE CALL

Control of the call begins with the first words you speak. There are several ways to establish control at the outset.

Sound Confident

Your tone of voice should communicate confidence that you can handle any customer and any situation, and that you have the responsibility, authority, and capability to do so. The best way to sound confident is to be confident.

- Know your product or service.
- Know your scripting for introductory statements, initial questions, and handling objections.
- Know your resources and where to find out what you don't know.
- Know how to quickly access your reference materials and systems.
- Know how to deal with the various types of interpersonal issues you may encounter on the job.
- Know the limits of your authority and what you can do and can't do to satisfy the customer.
- Practise your greeting so it consistently communicates confidence.

But suppose you are new to the job or have had a bad morning and you just don't feel confident. To sound confident when you don't feel confident, act like you are confident until it becomes real. Practise a confident tone of voice in your greeting—rehearse it until it captures the right balance of all the necessary elements: confidence, a positive attitude, enthusiasm, and friendliness. If your first few words sound confident, the customer will think you are confident and will be less inclined to try to take control of the call. If you fake confidence, real confidence comes more quickly than if you don't fake it. That's because you have fewer customers challenging you and knocking your confidence down. Note that you should not fake information—only a confident tone of voice.

Initiate the Information-Collecting Process

Ask questions, beginning with "How may I help you?" This puts the customer into the pattern of responding to you right from the beginning of the call. Use questions to direct callers who ramble: "Did you get the name of the attendant you were speaking to?" "What happened just before you offered your card?"

Reassure the Customer That You Will Help

"How may I help you?" in your greeting gives the message that you intend to help. In some cases, this needs to be reinforced even more directly: "Mr. Janacek, you're speaking to the right person. As a customer service representative, my role is to help customers in your situation," or "Mr. Janacek, as a customer service representative, I have the responsibility and authority to resolve customer concerns."

Empathize with the Customer

Once you have shown customers that you understand their frustration or upset, they are less likely to keep telling you how frustrated or upset they are.

Give the Customer Your Name Clearly and Confidently

Stating your name signals the customer that you are assuming responsibility for the call and for the customer's issue.

Overcome Speech Mannerisms That Sound Unassertive

Speaking too softly can sound weak to a customer who is concerned about control, so ensure your voice volume is adequate. Raising your voice at the end of a statement to make it sound like a question is a common speech habit that communicates uncertainty and may make the customer feel less confident in your ability to help. This can spur the customer to try to assume control of the call. This speech habit is the most common cause of poor call control, largely because people who have this habit also have the personality characteristics that draw them to jobs that involve interpersonal interaction (see the **Relater** personality type described in Chapters 8 and 9). This habit can be overcome by developing a consistent greeting with an appropriate tone. That way the habit is not part of the first impression. Since this habit is typically due to a lack of confidence, faking confidence can help overcome it. Listen to your calls, or have friends or coworkers assess your interactions to see if this is an issue for you.

Speaking in a hesitant way, in which your speech does not flow naturally, communicates uncertainty. When your speech sounds distracted or uncertain, the customer may feel you are ineffectual and will be encouraged to take control of the call. Again, the key is to use a well-practised greeting that flows smoothly and starts the conversation in the right way. Reps who speak hesitantly can practise finishing one sentence before pausing to consider the next one rather than pausing in the middle of a sentence to plan the next one.

Regaining Control: The "Wedge"

No matter how effective you are at establishing control, some customers will still take control of the call. Rather than give up or get into a power struggle with the customer, you need to know how to effectively regain control. The following are steps for regaining control.

IDENTIFY WHEN TO REGAIN CONTROL

Often upset customers contain themselves for the first few moments of the call and then gradually allow their upset to surface. If you can establish control through empathy and questions before the customer gets to the venting phase, you may be able to divert that reaction.

If the customer is already "blowing off steam" right from the beginning of the call, it is best to allow some venting rather than try to wrestle control from an upset customer. Once you sense that the customer is running out of steam, you will have a better chance of getting through and exercising control. While the customer is venting, listen to collect information that is relevant to the customer's situation. Don't "tune out" to minimize the effects of the customer's anger. If you don't return your attention to the call until the caller has calmed down, you may miss valuable information and further irritate the customer when you ask for information that has already been provided. Also, rather than staying absolutely quiet while the customer is venting, which may make the customer think you're not listening, interject listening responses such as "Yes," "Okay," and "I see." These give the impression that you are part of the conversation and are a useful entry point when it is time to regain control of the call.

Once you have collected enough information, look for an opportunity to regain control. This may come at a natural pause when the customer has finished her or his story or stops to think or look for information. The right time may be when the customer begins to repeat information because there are no new things to add. This is an opportunity for you to paraphrase or summarize, showing that you have understood and that there is no need for the customer to repeat the story. The right time to regain control may also be when you hear a fact or feeling from the customer that you can use to pull yourself back into the conversation—such a hook allows you to show the caller you understand the information or the emotion expressed.

INSERT THE WEDGE

Once you have identified that the timing is right, it is time to use the **wedge**. The wedge allows you to interject into the customer's monologue and positively redirect the call to make it productive. As Figure 7.1 illustrates, the wedge consists of three parts: the interjection, the connection, and the redirection.

Figure 7.1

The Wedge

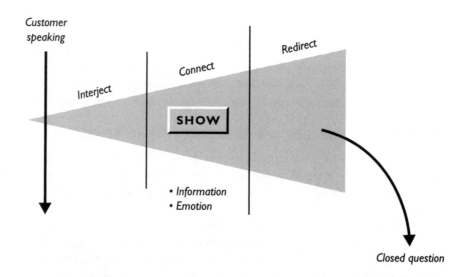

INTERJECTION

As the customer speaks, appropriately insert listening responses to show that you are with the customer. Then, when it seems an appropriate time to assume control, your listening response can become the tip of the wedge. The specific listening response you use should express an end to the customer's input, such as "Okay" (which says "Okay, you are finished") or "Good, then" (which offers the same message).

If you are having trouble getting in a response, then here are some other options to try, in the order you should consider them:

- Use the customer's name. When customers are so caught up in what they are saying that they are not listening to you, hearing their name will get their attention (see Chapter 5 for more on using the customer's name). Sometimes you will need to repeat the name for this to work.

- Interrupt with an apology for interrupting. Saying "Excuse me for interrupting" legitimizes the interruption, causing the customer to pause while you continue with the wedge. This is particularly effective when used along with the customer's name.

- Ask permission to speak. This is useful when the customer repeatedly speaks over you once you have begun the wedge: "Ms. Alfar, may I please take a quick moment to summarize my understanding of your concern?" Again, using the customer's name adds greater impact. Typically, the customer says yes. If she or he says no, then try adding a benefit of allowing you to speak: "Once I'm clear on what the concern is, we can get this resolved for you." If the customer still resists, move to the next option.

- Explain your need to speak. Help the customer see the negative impact of refusing to let you speak: "Ms. Alfar, I can only get this fixed for you once I'm sure I understand your concern. Please, allow me just a moment to confirm my understanding."

If you are not able to interject and the customer continues to speak, the problem may be that you are interjecting too early, while the customer still needs to vent. If so, continue listening for another opportunity to interject. If you find that the customer intrudes and resumes control during or after the connection phase, you need to assure the customer that you understand his or her emotion or the facts of the situation. Only then will the customer be able to let go and allow you to move the process past the information-collecting stage.

CONNECTION

Following immediately after the interjection, the connection phase justifies your assuming control of the conversation. It says to the customer, "See, I do understand your situation or your feelings," so the customer doesn't feel the need to continue describing either to you. Connect with either the information or the emotions. For example:

- Connect with the information: Paraphrase or summarize the customer's main points: "Mr. Doyama, I think I understand your situation. It's…." Then redirect with "Is that correct?"

- Connect with the emotion: Offer an empathy statement. Adjust the degree of emotion in your tone to fit the level of emotion of the caller: "I understand your frustration, Ms. Ng. You certainly should expect that your shipments will be accurate." Then redirect with "Let's get this sorted out for you. May I ask you a couple of questions?"

The connection phase is one of the most ineffectively handled in call control. Reps regularly omit this step in an effort to handle the call more quickly, with the result that the call takes longer because of the battle for control.

Often reps try to tell the customer they understand or empathize rather than show them. Showing you understand information requires that you repeat it back to the customer. Showing you understand the customer's feelings requires referring to the feeling and the situation and demonstrating empathy in your tone of voice. Telling is "Yes, right, I understand. Now here's what I'd like you to do…." or "I empathize. Now here's what I'd like you to do…." Telling does not prove you understand.

REDIRECTION

Once you have gained the customer's attention with the interjection and connection phases, you take over control by leading the conversation. Redirection typically takes the form of confirming the connection step: "Am I correct?" or gaining the customer's verbal permission for you to continue: "May I ask you a few questions?" or "May I make a suggestion?"

The first step in redirection is to ask a closed question. This encourages the customer to respond to you rather than taking the call back to its previous direction. Once the customer has verbally agreed with you, you are in a stronger position to continue with control, as long as the customer perceives your approach as being productive. This may require that you explain the reasons for your questions or explain the benefit to the customer of what you are proposing. Avoid using open-ended questions when trying to reestablish control of the call—the customer may take over the call again. Reintroduce open-ended questions gradually once a few closed questions have established your control of the call.

Learning Application Exercise

1. *Practise using the wedge to control conversations by role-playing with a partner. The partner role-plays a customer who is resisting control and trying to dominate a call.*

2. *Tape-record your role-playing or have a friend watch, and assess your effectiveness in establishing control and in using all parts of the wedge (see Table 7.1).*

3. *Where possible, tape some calls with customers and do the same.*

TABLE 7.1

Establishing Control

Score yourself on each achievement as follows:

0 = not used or ineffective
1 = used, but could be improved
2 = used effectively, no improvement necessary

Achievement	Self	Coworker 1	Coworker 2
– establishes control with effective tone of voice			
– uses the wedge at appropriate time			
– interjects effectively			
– connects effectively—shows understanding			
– redirects effectively—asks closed questions first			

Effective Use of "Hold"

The way in which call centre representatives use the telephone "hold" feature can affect the success of calls. See if the experience described in the Have You Ever? box sounds familiar to you.

The hold feature is regularly abused. Call centre reps often put someone on hold because

- They did not prepare for the call and have to search for needed customer information.

- Their work area is disorganized so resource information is not readily available.

- They want time to think about how to deal with the customer's situation.

- They want to continue chatting with a coworker.

- Their computer system is slow that day, so they put customers on hold while waiting for screens to appear.

Sometimes reps even put a customer on hold so they can finish a personal call, or use the "mute" feature so the customer can keep talking while the reps have a few words with a coworker.

None of these is an appropriate reason for putting a customer on hold, and these are only some of the abuses. Sometimes the reasons for the poor use of the hold feature are based in the call centre's system or are accepted company practice. See the On the Job box.

ON THE JOB

Corporate Use of the Hold Feature

Consultants made calls to a number of competitors in the same industry, asking the same questions of each. Some companies provided answers and rarely used the hold feature. Other companies used the feature several times, for long periods of time, on each call. An analysis yielded a range of reasons for the differences.

Some of the companies that used the hold feature less had excellent computer-based reference systems that allowed reps to quickly access information. Others had efficient, organization-wide, paper-based filing systems that achieved the same end. Many of the companies that used the hold feature a lot had haphazard systems, and usually left it to the reps to design and manage their own system.

In some companies, the reps kept up a dialogue with the customer while seeking information, often asking relevant questions about the client's relationship with the company. In other companies, the reps didn't bother to keep up a dialogue—it was part of the companies' cultures to automatically put the customer on hold for the slightest reason.

Some companies had large numbers of reps who were fairly new and who put customers on hold so they could seek answers from other staff. Other companies also had lots of new staff members, but they were well-trained in product knowledge, and also knew how to efficiently access their reference systems and maintain interaction while accessing information, so they used the hold feature less frequently.

The hold feature should be used only when you must leave the telephone during a call to handle the business of that call or to help with a priority business issue. For example, you may need to make another call for information to resolve the customer's issue, to get direction or information from a supervisor or coworker, or to deal with a coworker's high-priority need. In this latter case, interrupting your call is appropriate only if your coworker's issue is critical, and if you sense that your current call will be so long that your coworker cannot wait.

RULES FOR PUTTING CUSTOMERS ON HOLD

Use the Hold Feature

When you must leave your desk during a call, always use the hold feature. Never simply put a hand over the mouthpiece of your headset or put the receiver down on the desk. Either of these lets the customer hear background office noise and does not create a professional image.

Ask Permission to Put the Customer on Hold

Do not just say "Hold, please" and put the customer on hold without considering whether the customer has the time or the inclination to wait.

Give the customer a chance to respond to your request. "Hold, please (click)" and "Will you hold, please? (click)" do not give the customer this chance. Ask, wait a moment to give the customer the opportunity to respond, and then put the customer on hold (unless, of course, the response is "No").

Offer a Reason for Putting the Customer on Hold

Explain why you need to put the customer on hold: "I need to call the shipping department" or "I can confirm this with my supervisor." The reason must make sense to the customer and must sound like it is contributing to resolving the customer's issue. When the purpose of the hold is to deal with a coworker's urgent request, advise the customer that you have to leave the call for a moment, apologize, and indicate that you will be right back—then make sure you are. This type of situation should be rare.

Tell the Customer How Long to Expect to Be on Hold

If you expect the customer to be on hold longer than 30 seconds, offer the alternative to call him or her back. If customers know how long they can expect to wait, they are less likely to get restless and angry. Time on hold always feels longer than it really is.

Engage in Conversation Rather Than Use Hold

If you are not leaving your desk and do not have to use the telephone for another purpose, if the time on hold is expected to be less than 30 seconds, and if you do not have to do serious mental work like calculations while the customer is waiting, avoid the hold button altogether. Instead, talk to the customer: ask questions, verify information, or tell the customer what actions you are taking on his or her behalf.

When Desperate, Use Hold for Cooling Off Time

If the customer is hostile and you are having trouble keeping cool and professional, asking to put the customer on hold for a moment may give you both time to cool off. This should not be your first approach, however. It is much better to deal with the behaviour while keeping your cool, but putting someone on hold for a moment may be better than losing your patience.

Avoid Using the Word "Hold"

Some companies encourage their staff to use other terms for "hold" that they consider less offensive: "Can I ask you to give me a moment to…?" and, later, "Thank you for waiting."

Return to the Call during a Long Hold

If the hold is lasting longer than you originally promised because, for example, you are having trouble connecting with another information source, go back on the line and tell the customer the reason for the delay. Then apologize and give the customer the option to stay on hold or be called back.

When You Return to the Call, Say the Customer's Name

Saying the customer's name will help you avoid the situation where you get back to the call, start to give the customer the information you have collected, and, after a moment, the customer says. "I'm back." In other words, the customer has put you on hold while you had her or him on hold. When you answer multiple phone lines, saying the name also ensures that you have reconnected to the right person.

Apologize for the Wait

When you get back to the customer, offer a brief apology—then move the conversation on. Don't over-apologize, and don't pause after the apology to encourage the customer to respond.

IF THE CUSTOMER PUTS YOU ON HOLD

If a customer tries to put you on hold, interject if possible to see if you can call back instead or have the customer call back, whichever is most appropriate. If the customer has called you and then puts you on hold, unless it is critical from your perspective that you speak to the customer you may wish to allow 15 to 30 seconds and then disconnect. If it is critical that you wait, do some paperwork or organize your desk until the customer returns—don't waste the time.

Learning Application Exercise

Practise using the hold feature effectively on your business and personal calls. Assess your calls to see if you are using all the techniques for effectively using this feature.

Voice Mail

Voice mail has been considered a boon to organizations who want to cut costs. Rather than have a live person answering the telephone and taking messages, the voice-mail system captures this information, saving the costs of the extra staff and preventing lost calls. However, to many employees, voice mail is a major source of job frustration. Often, so many calls accumulate that they cannot all be returned (e-mail frustration is rapidly catching up, for similar reasons). When call centre representatives access their voice mail, they find that some customers leave inadequate information (such as no return telephone number or area code). Some messages require replaying the call several times to make sense of the mumbled words, and some are long and rambling.

The problems continue when reps have to use other people's voice-mail systems. Many people use their voice mail as a call-screening device, leaving it on all the time and picking up only those calls they feel are important enough to warrant their attention. Others never return voice-mail messages, and still others have dated messages that have callers wondering if these people are even in the office.

Used appropriately, voice mail can facilitate effective communication and even eliminate the frustration of telephone tag (see page 139).

Managing Your Own Voice Mail

Here are some tips for using your own voice-mail system effectively.

Speak Clearly

If you speak clearly and pace yourself, the customer is more likely to mirror your style and do the same. If you speak in a rush or mumble your words, the customer will likely copy this behaviour as well.

Sound Personable

Most people sound mechanical in their voice-mail messages, even if they are naturally personable people. This can give customers a negative image of the rep and the company. Try to sound human and warm, and friendly yet professional in your message.

Avoid Being Cute

Not all business contacts appreciate a cute message, and it may make you sound unprofessional. Aim to sound businesslike and friendly.

Be Concise

A message that is too long keeps busy customers waiting to leave their message, and it may encourage naturally talkative customers to be even more wordy.

Tell Callers What Information to Leave

Ask callers to leave their name, company name, telephone number with area code, and a brief description of the purpose of their call if that's the information you need. Don't set yourself up for disappointment because someone didn't leave information you didn't ask for.

Update Your Message

If you leave a dated message ("This is Monday, June 2nd") make sure you update it every day, whether you are in the office or not.

Leave Availability Information

If you are not in the office that morning, day, or week, say so in your voice mail so callers don't leave messages and then get frustrated when they are not returned quickly. Give this information early in your message rather than at the end. Some callers have learned how to fast-forward through a message to get to the beep and may miss the information that you are away for the month if it isn't given at the beginning.

Check Voice Mail Regularly

Set a schedule if you don't have a system that advises when you have calls in your voice-mail box. Return calls quickly. Some organizations require call centre reps to return all calls within three hours. While it is okay to inform people in your voice-mail message that you check your messages regularly, it is not advisable to tell them you'll return all messages within three hours, even if this is company policy. If something interferes and customers' calls are not returned until later, they'll feel slighted.

Call Everyone Back

Don't call back only those customers you deem worthy of your attention—everyone deserves a response.

Don't Save Old Messages

If necessary, write down relevant information and delete each message. It is frustrating for callers to find they cannot leave an important message because your mailbox is full of undeleted calls.

Allow Enough Time for a Detailed Message

If a person is leaving necessary detail rather than a simple "call me" message, it is annoying to be cut off by the system. When message time is limited, tell people in your message how much time they have and ensure that the actual time allotted is reasonable.

Provide Alternatives to Leaving a Message

If you are unavailable to take calls but don't want to have important calls delayed in your mailbox, tell callers in your message how to get an immediate contact, either with you (perhaps through your pager) or a coworker.

HANDLING OTHER PEOPLE'S VOICE MAIL

Speak Slowly and Clearly

Speak particularly slowly when you are providing your name and telephone number, since the person receiving the message will likely be writing down this information as he or she hears it.

Leave an Organized Message

Leave information on the machine that you would have provided in person (being sensitive to any confidentiality concerns) rather than a "call me" message that sets up telephone tag. When you don't have time for conversation but need to get someone information, calling during off-hours and leaving a detailed message is more efficient.

Be Prepared for Voice Mail

If you are unprepared to leave a concise, clear message when you connect to someone's voice mail, hang up before the beep, plan what you want to say, and call back.

Leave Your Telephone Number Again at the End of the Call

Leaving your phone number twice assures people that they have written down the number correctly.

Dealing with People Who Misuse Voice Mail

If someone doesn't return her or his calls,

- Call the main line (if you're calling a business) rather than the person's direct line, and have the receptionist connect you. Or, speak to someone whose desk is near your target person's to arrange a connection.

- Try the #, *, or 0 buttons on your telephone keypad to get out of the person's voice-mail box and connect to someone who can help you track down your target person.

- When you do get in touch with the person, ask how he or she prefers to be contacted in the future. If the person says voice mail, suggest that there may be a problem with the voice-mail system, and you're not sure if your messages are getting through.

Here are some ways to deal with problem message-leavers you know you will be talking to in the future. These might include people who repeatedly leave you "call me" messages when they can give the information you need, who consistently speak too quickly or mumble, or who leave long, rambling messages.

- When you connect with these people, advise them, in a friendly and helpful tone, that you can get back to them more promptly and you'll be able to work more effectively if they leave a detailed message, speak a little more slowly or clearly, or just leave you the key points.

- Take responsibility rather than accusing: "Just so you know, my voice mail is confidential, so it's okay to leave information," "My old ears just can't pick out the words when they come too quickly," or "Often I'm just quickly checking in to pick up messages on my way to a meeting and I can't wait through a longer message."

- Provide a benefit for the caller in accepting your request: "I can get back to you much more quickly if you give me just the key facts" or "I can act on your information right away rather than waiting to connect with you in person."

- If you are concerned about being too direct with such a request, position it with: "I wonder if I could ask you a favour...."

Using E-Mail Effectively

Most organizations use either e-mail or an e-mail–like internal system to communicate within the organization and with customers. Many normally very professional call centre reps demonstrate less than professional habits in using e-mail. Here are some basic rules for using e-mail in a business environment:

- Use sentences, upper- and lowercase spelling, and grammar as you would in writing a letter.

- Check your spelling—it's easy to get spoiled by the spell-check features word-processing packages use that e-mail software doesn't have.

- Start with "Dear ...," leave out the recipient's address, and end with your name, title, company name, and e-mail address.

- Many e-mail software packages lack the wrap-around feature that word-processing software uses to take you to the next line, so you must end each line of text yourself.

- To respond to an e-mail message, don't start a new e-mail. Instead, use the "Reply" feature so the reader can more easily understand the context of your response.

- Keep your e-mail message concise and put the key information in the first sentences so a reader who skims through her or his e-mail won't miss your core message.

- Not all e-mail users are familiar with the abbreviations that many people use, so it's best to avoid these.

- Don't assume e-mail will be read immediately. Use the telephone for immediate attention or if your message requires a quick response.

- Assume no privacy or confidentiality in e-mail messages. Treat the content more as you would a written letter (which it is) than as a telephone conversation.

- If your computer doesn't automatically notify you, check for new e-mail messages regularly.

- Don't save all e-mail messages, and don't print them all out.

- Don't read all e-mail messages in detail. Assess how closely you need to read based on the sender and the first few lines, and develop your ability to scan messages that don't require detailed reading.

Learning Application Exercise

1. Apply the rules for handling voice mail to your own and others' voice mail or answering machine or service. Assess your calls to see if you have incorporated all of the elements of effective use of voice mail.

2. Repeat this exercise to assess your use of e-mail.

Minimizing "Telephone Tag"

Some call centre representatives have voice mail and may receive calls on a direct line—a separate line, not the queue line that will be picked up by another if one rep's phone is busy. For these reps, **telephone tag** can become an issue. Telephone tag occurs when a customer calls the rep's direct line when the rep is on another call. The customer gets voice mail (or a coworker) and leaves a message for the rep to call back. The customer has "tagged" the rep, and now the rep is "it" and must try to catch the customer, much like the children's game of tag. The rep calls back when the customer is on another call or unavailable to take the call, so the rep leaves a message—the customer is now "it" again and must try to catch the rep. This game can go on for days, especially if both parties are away from their desks or on their phones often. Telephone tag can be a significant waste of a rep's time. Fortunately, it can be minimized.

When the person you are calling is not available, leave a detailed message that gives the customer the information you want her or him to have (taking confidentiality needs into consideration). If you leave a message with another person, confirm that this person has recorded the details accurately and has a plan for passing the message on to your target recipient by asking, "When do you expect Ms. Jacobson will be receiving this message?" You create the mental image of handing that message to its intended recipient—an image that is refreshed when the message-taker sees the recipient, making it more likely that the message will be passed on rather than forgotten. If your call is to collect information from the customer, leave a message outlining the information you need (again respecting confidentiality) and how to communicate that information to you. Let the customer know, in your message, that if he or she calls and gets your voice mail or one of your coworkers, that the customer should provide the information you have requested. If you must speak to the customer personally,

- Advise the customer of a time range when you will be most available to receive a return call.

- Ask the customer to leave a message telling you when she or he will be available for you to call back—and make sure you arrange to call then.

- Suggest some alternative callback times, and ask the customer to call and leave you a message confirming which will be most convenient—then make sure you arrange to call then.

When you are speaking to a customer who will have to call you back, advise the customer of your poor availability to personally answer his or her call due to your ongoing phone responsibilities. Provide specific instructions as to how the customer is to leave a message should you be unavailable:

- what information to leave you in a message

- which coworker to speak to (then update the coworker so she or he can deal with the situation)

Reconfirm your name (first and last) and telephone number for the customer who may need to call you back. Recognize that customers may assume they must speak with you. If all call centre staff have access to each customer's file, let customers know that anyone who answers the telephone will be able to help them.

When speaking to a customer you will have to call back, set an appointment if you know when you'll be ready to call. Otherwise, confirm what times and telephone numbers are best. Ask for another person or voice-mail box where you can leave a message if you are unable to connect with the customer.

Learning Application Exercise

Apply the techniques for minimizing telephone tag to your business and personal telephone calls. Assess your calls to see if you are incorporating all of these techniques.

Transferring Calls Effectively

When customers must repeat the purpose of their call each time they are transferred to another employee, they are left feeling that they are dealing with an uncaring bureaucracy. Such an experience can turn otherwise pleasant customers into frustrated and angry people by the time they finally do get to the person who can help them—if they have the patience to wait that long.

This problem of multiple transfers has led many organizations to establish "one-stop shopping" call centres. These companies have moved away from multiple access points and specialized groups to a call centre staff that is trained and provided with the resources to resolve a range of customer issues. But even in these call centres, some calls may have to be transferred.

To effectively transfer calls, follow these steps:

1. Question the customer and actively listen to ensure you understand the reason for the call. Confirm that you cannot resolve the customer's issue or are restricted from doing so.

2. Where possible and appropriate, arrange to get the information the customer needs, and either have the customer wait for it or call the customer back.

3. If the call absolutely must be transferred, advise the customer that you will be doing so and give a positive reason that benefits the customer ("I'm going to connect you with our expert in this area" or "Jesse will be able to help you resolve this" rather than "I don't know the answer").

4. Ask the customer to wait while you connect with the other person (the target recipient), and advise the customer that you will pass on the information she or he has already provided.

5. Connect with the target recipient, give this person the information you have collected and the reason for the transfer, confirm that this person can resolve the customer's issue, and let the person know you have advised the customer that you are passing on the information.

6. If the customer has refused to give you information or time did not permit you to collect it, inform the target recipient of this. If the customer asks for a specific person, ask "May I tell her what this is regarding?" to try to get some information for the person receiving the call.

7. If the person you planned to transfer the call to is not the appropriate person to resolve this issue, solicit her or his help in identifying who might be more appropriate, or call someone else who might help you determine this, and repeat step 5.

8. If the target recipient is unavailable, inform the customer of this and ask if you can put the call through to voice mail. Give the customer a name and a direct phone number for the appropriate person in case the customer needs to call back.

   a. If the customer agrees to go to voice mail, advise him or her about what information to leave.

   b. If the customer resists going to voice mail, offer to forward a message personally.

   c. If the customer does not want to leave the phone, seek an alternative contact for the customer to speak to, such as a coworker or supervisor of your target recipient.

9. Once you have given the information to the target recipient, get the customer back on the line and introduce the two, again restating that you have passed on the customer's information: "Mr. Leiderman, I have Joan Woo on the line. I have given Joan all the information you gave me. Goodbye."

10. If the customer had already been transferred before you received the call and now must be transferred again, reassure her or him that you will confirm that the target recipient can help, or, if the customer resists being transferred, offer to get the information yourself or to have the person with the information call the customer back.

On a reception desk, time may not permit this thorough a transfer. This can result in inappropriate transfers and frustrated customers, as well as annoyed staff who receive these wrong calls. To minimize mistakes, develop a quick reference of who is responsible for what types of issues. When you encounter a new issue, ask for guidance and add that to your reference information. Create questions to clarify customer requests that are easily misdirected. For example, if the customer asks for marketing, but most customers with this request want a catalogue, ask, "Are you calling about a catalogue?" to know whether to direct the call to distribution instead. To avoid callers going into long explanations, end your greeting with "How may I direct your call?" instead of "How may I help you?" so the caller knows that this is reception and expects to be put on hold or transferred. Arrange for a person in each department to receive calls when you don't know where to send them. Get feedback on calls you forward to these people so you can increase your call-forwarding accuracy.

When you receive a transferred call,

1. Thank the person who is transferring the call for the information the customer has provided. If the person does not provide information, ask for it. If you are the wrong person to receive the call, advise the person and help identify the appropriate recipient.

2. As appropriate, access any available information on the customer so you can have it in front of you as you speak to the customer.

3. Greet the transferred customer by name, introduce yourself, and confirm the information you have received ("Hello, Mrs. Robinson. This is Danielle speaking. I understand you're calling about...."). Don't make the customer repeat information she or he has already provided.

Escalating a Call

It is usually in the customer's and the organization's best interests for call centre representatives to deal with customer issues rather than transfer them to a supervisor. This is usually more time-efficient. Also, because reps have the responsibility and authority to make most decisions regarding caller concerns and they—unlike the supervisor—spend most of the day making these decisions, reps can usually handle calls most effectively. In some cases, however, it is necessary to **escalate the call**, so the rep must be prepared to escalate appropriately. Handling escalated calls is one of the supervisor's roles; the supervisor is there to support the rep. It is also a customer's right to speak to someone more senior in the organization if he or she so wishes.

When a customer calls and asks to speak to the supervisor, the rep can say, "Certainly. May I ask what this is regarding?" If the purpose of the call falls into the rep's area of responsibility, the rep can advise the customer of this: "Oh, actually, I can help you with that." If the customer has asked for the supervisor by name or if the issue is one the supervisor should handle, the rep should either get the customer's number and have the supervisor call the customer back, or transfer the call appropriately as discussed earlier in this chapter. If the customer refuses to state the purpose of the call, the rep can say, "I do have the responsibility and authority to deal with customer issues. I would like the opportunity to help you" to try to intercede. If the customer is still adamant, indicates that this is a personal call, or says that the supervisor asked the customer to speak to her or him directly, the rep should transfer the call and tell the supervisor the customer's comments.

Learning Application Exercise

Apply the techniques for transferring and escalating calls, as appropriate, in your calls. Assess your calls to determine if you are using all the appropriate techniques.

Saying "No" to Customers

Most call centre representatives are not comfortable with saying no to customers. The job would be so much easier if we were always able to say yes and avoid conflict. Unfortunately, we cannot always do this. A customer request may be impossible from a time perspective ("I want to liquidate my holdings. Could I pick up my cheque in an hour?") or illegal or against strict company policy ("Could I have my husband's account balance please?") or what the customer believes to be the case may simply not be so ("I know I'm at my credit limit, but I understand you can extend my card limit if I request it. I'd like you to put through this $9000 charge to my travel company").

Often, instead of saying no or telling the customer what you cannot do, you can avoid the issue by telling the customer what you can do: "I can put a rush on your transaction and have your cheque ready for pick-up tomorrow at noon," "If I can speak to your husband and get his verbal authorization, I'd be happy to give you that information," or "I can arrange an appointment with the manager at your local bank branch so you can discuss a credit increase with her." If, however, the customer is insistent, you will have to advise her or him that you cannot comply with the request.

We often unconsciously undermine the effectiveness of our no's and sabotage the customer's receptiveness. By following seven simple steps for effectively saying no, we can significantly increase the customer's acceptance and avoid much of the conflict.

SEVEN STEPS TO SAYING NO

1. Ensure You Understand the Customer's Position

Ask questions, paraphrase, summarize, confirm—make sure you are clear on the customer's position and that saying no is justified. Use positive phrasing to redirect the customer and satisfy yourself that the customer is not responsive to this approach. Confirm in your mind that the customer needs to hear "no."

2. Verify the Key Facts with the Customer

Review the key facts, and get the customer's agreement that this is the sum of his or her position. This verification

- Confirms that you have all the relevant information so that you don't say no only to have the customer add new information that changes your decision. This step represents the final opportunity for the customer to amend the information.

- Lets the customer know the basis for your decision so that, when the customer agrees that those are the facts, he or she is in effect saying, "I rest my case."

- Reconfirms in your own mind that you have made the right decision.

3. Empathize Where Appropriate

If appropriate, empathize with the customer's real reasons for wanting a yes. For example, the customer may be arguing the basic unfairness of having so short a warranty on a particular part when the real issue is the cost to have it repaired because it is no longer under warranty. You might say, "Mr. Warren, I know it's frustrating to be faced with these repair costs on a three-year-old car. Most of us don't tend to budget for those types of expense." Identifying, in an empathic way, what you know to be the real issue for the customer helps him or her know that you understand what's really driving the argument. The real issue is evident for both of you to see, weakening the strength of the customer's argument and her or his commitment to it.

4. Provide the Rationale for Your Decision Pleasantly but Firmly

Because most reps are not comfortable saying no, many become so apologetic about it that the customer may not even hear the no. Or, the customer may believe that a rep is being so apologetic because he or she is not really convinced this should be a no. This may make the customer feel that pushing a bit may change the decision. By sounding indecisive, reps set themselves up for an argument.

Other call centre reps take a deep breath, steel themselves for the no, and then beat the customer up with it. These reps become almost aggressive with the no. If the customer is bullied into going along with the decision, she or he leaves the call with a negative feeling about the rep and the company. If the customer refuses to be bullied and responds with aggressive behaviour, the rep ends up having to deal with a conflict.

If you understand that a no is justified, then you don't need to over-apologize for it—it is the right decision, and it is your responsibility to make. A Relater personality type, many of whom are drawn to call centre positions (see Chapters 8 and 9), is likely to become over-apologetic when stressed. If you empathize with customers and understand the underlying reasons for their wanting a yes, you don't have to be angry with them for it. In most cases customers have convinced themselves that their request is justified. There is no reason to be hostile with customers who are attempting to get a decision in their favour. It's important to realize that if you are feeling hostile, it is because you are not comfortable saying no, you are anxious about the customer's reaction, and this is your way of compensating for your own discomfort.

Aim for a balance between being pleasant with the customer while being firm as you provide your rationale for saying no.

5. Clearly State Your Position or Say No

Some call centre representatives who are uncomfortable with saying no give their reasons (usually with many apologies) but never actually say no. Again, this can leave the customer confused or ready for a fight. It's fair to let customers know where they stand.

6. Offer an Alternative

Customers do not go to the time and trouble of planning their arguments and making their calls only to hear a no and then meekly go away. In addition, many customers believe that if they complain enough they'll get their way, so they don't want to give up too easily. Customers want to feel that they have gained something with their call. They will be more likely to accept the no if they feel they have achieved something. For example,

- While they do not get the time commitment they want, they do get their request fast-tracked or made a priority.

- While they do not get what they want, their request does get a sympathetic ear, and the appropriate department is advised of a glitch in the process.

- While they do not get a full refund, they do get a coupon for a discount on future services (take care with how you present such coupons presented to the customer—they should not be construed as a "payoff" for complaining).

- While they do not get satisfaction from the organization, they are directed to another way to overcome their problem. For example, we couldn't automatically raise their credit limit given their circumstances, but we did set them up with the branch manager who has the authority to do so.

- While they do not get full coverage for an out-of-warranty repair, they do get partial coverage so the repair won't cost them as much.

- While they do not get what they want, at least they pushed the issue as far as it could go. For example, we took their case to our review committee and called them back (after initially lowering their expectations with our prediction that it would not be accepted).

7. Move the Conversation on to Another Topic or to Closure

The most common problem of call centre reps when they have to say no or give customers an answer they don't want to hear is that they deliver the news, then pause. When you pause it's like challenging the person to argue: "I've made my case. Now it's time for your rebuttal." People are not comfortable with silence, and they often feel obliged to fill it. Customers will fill it with why they don't think your answer is right, fair, or well-considered, or they'll say you haven't understood their point of view, or they'll want to talk to someone who might make a different decision. These are all responses you wish to avoid, yet you set yourself up for them by pausing—and almost everyone has the pause habit when they say no. If you believe the no is correct, there is nothing to gain by encouraging the customer to argue.

Instead, move the conversation to another topic or to closure right after saying no. This ensures that the customer is not encouraged to argue, and is more likely to accept the position and let it go. It is not being unfair to the customer—if he or she really wants to debate the decision, the customer can interrupt and bring the conversation back to his or her point. Just don't encourage this reaction.

These steps to saying no will not always work. However, by using this formula the rate of acceptance of your no's will increase. For customers who continue to argue, you may want to use one of the following techniques:

- Escalate the call to a supervisor or a senior rep. Although this won't likely change the decision, it will satisfy the customer that he or she has taken the issue as far is it can go.

- Offer an appeal system. This may be a department or committee to which the customer can present a verbal or written appeal.

- Offer to personally champion the customer's issue through an internal appeal system.

Learning Application Exercise

Role-play saying no with a friend or coworker in a situation in which you cannot comply with the customer's request. Tape your role-playing or have another friend watch, and assess the effectiveness with which you used each of the seven steps to saying no (see Table 7.2). Use this process in other personal or business situations.

TABLE 7.2
Saying No

Score yourself on each achievement as follows:

0 = not used or ineffective
1 = used, but could be improved
2 = used effectively, no improvement necessary

Achievement	Self	Coworker 1	Coworker 2
– questions to ensure understanding			
– verifies key facts			
– empathizes with underlying reasons			
– provides rationale pleasantly but firmly			
– states position clearly			
– offers an alternative			
– moves the conversation along without pausing			

Summary

Managing calls is important for call centre reps to quickly and efficiently resolve customer concerns. While control is less of an issue if the customer provides information that is relevant to the issue, it still benefits the rep to assume an image of positive control.

To establish control at the beginning of the call, sound confident, and initiate the information-collecting process. Reassure the customer that you will help, and empathize with customers as appropriate. Give your name, and sound assertive.

You can use the wedge to regain control of a call. Once you have identified the appropriate time in a conversation to regain control, interject, connect, and redirect the conversation.

Many call centre representatives abuse the telephone "hold" feature. Remember to use it when you must leave the conversation during a call—don't just put your hand over the mouthpiece or set the receiver on your desk. Ask the customer's permission to be put on hold, offer a reason for the hold and advise how long the customer can expect to wait, then give the customer a chance to respond before you put her or him on hold. You may want to avoid the term "hold" and ask the customer to wait, since many people have a negative reaction to being put on hold. Better still, avoid using the hold feature at all—continue talking to the customer as you access information or do something else.

Return to a call periodically during a long hold. Say the customer's name when you get on the line, and always thank the customer for waiting. Although it's best to avoid putting someone on hold, if both of you are losing patience with each other, putting the customer on hold so you can both cool off is preferable to expressing your frustration.

Voice mail also needs to be managed. Use these tips for your voice-mail message:

- Speak clearly.
- Sound personable.
- Don't be cute.
- Be concise.
- Tell customers what information you need.
- Keep your message up-to-date.
- Leave information on your availability.
- Regularly check for messages.
- Call everyone back.
- Delete old messages.
- Make sure callers have time to leave detailed messages.
- Provide callers with alternatives to leaving a message.

When you leave messages for others, speak slowly and clearly. Leave an organized message by preparing for voice mail before you call. Leave your telephone number twice—once at the beginning of your message, and again at the end.

To minimize telephone tag:

- Leave a detailed message.
- Confirm with the message-taker the process for getting your message to your target recipient.
- In your message, request specific action.

- Provide callback alternatives.

- Use messages to plan how to connect personally.

When customers will have to call back, advise them what to expect regarding your availability. Provide instructions and alternatives. Help customers understand how to use the call centre effectively.

To effectively transfer calls, question the caller and listen to understand the issue and whom to transfer to. Alternately, get this information for the customer. Explain why you need to transfer the caller in a way that expresses a benefit for the caller. Advise the customer that you will pass on the information you have collected, then do so (if no information has been provided, pass this on too), confirming that you have transferred to the appropriate recipient. Get help from that person if you need to transfer to someone else. If the call will be put on hold, explain this to the customer and offer another option, such as giving her or him the name and phone number of the person to call back. Introduce the customer to the transfer recipient before leaving the line. If a customer has been transferred several times, take responsibility for helping him or her get to the right person.

A reception desk doesn't usually have time to manage transfers in such detail. Develop a quick reference system for finding the people who handle certain types of issues. Ask the customer clarifying questions when the request is ambiguous and the call could be mistakenly transferred to the wrong person or department. Finally, arrange for certain people to take "destination unknown" calls.

When you receive a transferred call, thank the person who transferred it, collect any customer information he or she has, and access the customer file. Then greet the customer by name, introduce yourself, and confirm the information.

Attempt to intercede and resolve calls before escalating them to a supervisor, but respect the customer's need to escalate if necessary. When escalating, use the call transfer rules.

The call centre job sometimes requires reps to say no or to give an answer the customer does not want. In these situations, follow these steps:

1. Ensure you understand the customer's position.

2. Verify key facts.

3. Empathize with any underlying reasons for the customer's position.

4. Pleasantly but firmly provide reasons for your decision.

5. Clearly state your position or say no.

6. Offer an alternative.

7. Move the call along.

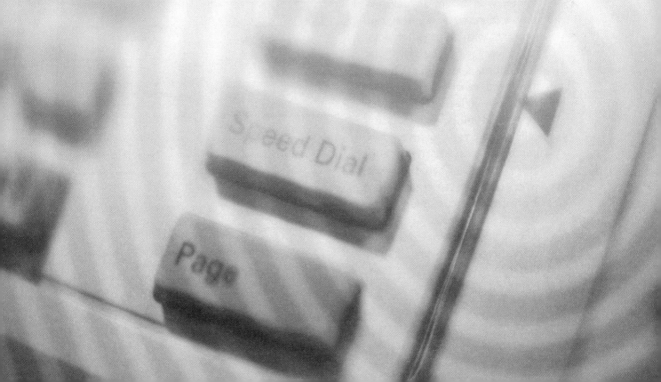

CHAPTER 8
Style Flexibility

Learning Outcomes

After successfully completing Chapter 8, you will be able to:

- Discuss why interaction style flexibility is important to a call centre representative's success.

- Assess and understand different interaction styles.

- Better understand and accept different people.

- Effectively adjust your style to connect with each customer.

- Better understand yourself and your reactions to others.

Why Is Style Flexibility Important?

Critical to success in a call centre position is an ability to connect with each customer, to adapt one's personal interaction style to fit each customer. This style flexibility enhances communication with customers and the rep's ability to manage calls.

Though we each have the ability to adapt our personal style, some people are more naturally flexible than others. For most of us, the adjustment is automatic and unconscious. For example, if a customer is friendly and empathic, we become more friendly and empathic toward the customer. If the customer is more formal and detail-oriented, we adjust our style in this direction.

This natural flexibility may be reduced when, for example, we have just had a difficult call with a customer and are feeling the effects of stress, or when we are at the end of a long and tiring day. None of us is as flexible when feeling the effects of stress or when physically, mentally, or emotionally exhausted. When we lose our flexibility, we revert to communicating in the style that is most comfortable for us—and we interact that way with every customer, whether it is a fit for that customer or not.

Even the rep who is less flexible and who consistently uses the same interaction style ("I treat everyone exactly the same, I'm very fair that way") will connect well with a customer who has the same dominant style. So, the low-empathy rep will connect satisfactorily with a customer who has low-empathy needs, while the very businesslike rep who is uncomfortable with humour will connect well with the customer with a similar personality. When, however, the rep interacts with a customer who has a very different style, the connection is less effective and may even cause conflict. As a rep's style inflexibility leads to more and more unsuccessful calls, the call centre job becomes less satisfying and more stressful. Then the rep's stress reaction can create even more negative customer interactions, leading to even greater inflexibility, and so on—an ever-worsening downward spiral that can lead to burnout (see Figure 8.1).

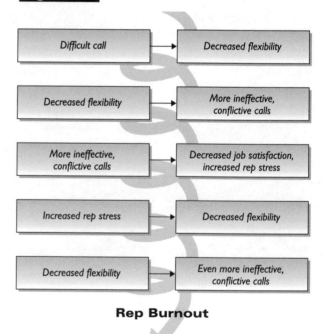

Figure 8.1

Difficult call	→	Decreased flexibility
Decreased flexibility	→	More ineffective, conflictive calls
More ineffective, conflictive calls	→	Decreased job satisfaction, increased rep stress
Increased rep stress	→	Decreased flexibility
Decreased flexibility	→	Even more ineffective, conflictive calls

Rep Burnout

This type of situation can be overcome. When our natural flexibility fails us, we can still mentally assess each customer's preferred interaction style and consciously adapt ours to fit. This is easier if we have an assessment tool that helps us understand the customer's style.

An assessment tool also benefits those reps who have no difficulty in adapting their style. People—their personalities and their behaviours—are complex. The more support we have in understanding them and connecting with them, the better off we are as communicators.

This chapter will introduce a simple yet effective style assessment tool for understanding and identifying different interaction styles. This tool will enhance reps' ability to connect with customers even when feeling the effects of stress or fatigue.

An Interaction Style Assessment Tool

The interaction style assessment tool presented here is based on a personality model. A "model" explains something that is complex (in this case, personality) in a simplified way that makes it more understandable and predictable. This chapter will present an interpretation of Dr. Taibi Kahler's **Process Communication** Model.[1] Dr. Kahler's model is theoretically sound and well-researched, and is in turn based on Dr. Eric Berne's Transactional Analysis theory. The description here will not explain all the details of the model, but will focus on those elements that will help call centre representatives to do their job better. Using this model can enhance your ability to effectively interact with different types of customers. As an added benefit, this model will give you insight into your interactions with coworkers, friends, and family members.

Two aspects of this model make it particularly useful for our purposes. First, the model is predictive. It recognizes that each person is unique, but also that groups of people share similarities. The model identifies similarities that tend to occur together, and these "packages" of similarities are called "personality types." For example, if a person exhibits three personality traits and it's known that these traits are part of a package that includes a number of other traits, we can predict that that person will have other traits in that package (see Figure 8.2).

This knowledge gives us more options when we are attempting to build rapport with another person. We can connect with that person by "mirroring" back those characteristics we observe, or we can connect with some of the other characteristics we don't notice but can predict to be part of the person's

Figure 8.2

"Personality Type" Package

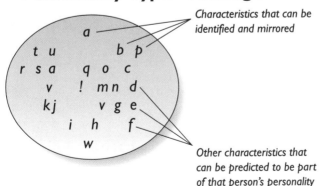

Characteristics that can be identified and mirrored

Other characteristics that can be predicted to be part of that person's personality

personality. For example, when speaking to a customer who has a soft, personable, empathic tone of voice who apologizes for taking up our time, it is possible to predict that this person will feel comfortable if we use her or his name, share personal information, engage briefly in some small talk before getting to the business of the call, and show an interest in the person's feelings.

While a predictive model is useful, it is important that it not oversimplify the human personality. Some of the more simplistic personality models tend to stereotype or "pigeon-hole" people into categories. Dr. Kahler's model, rather than typecasting people as fitting neatly into one or another **personality type**, recognizes that people are a rich combination of all the types, with one personality type simply being more dominant in a person while others are less of an influence.

The second useful aspect of this model is that it is observational. Many of the characteristics in a personality type can be observed from the manner or content of the customer's conversation.

This model identifies six personality types, or packages of characteristics. We are all combinations of these six types, but each of us is dominant in one type. We all, then, have at least one type that is a "strong suit" for us. "Strong suit" means we have a lot of a specific type in our personality, while "weak suit" means we have very little of a specific personality type. Many of us have more than one strong suit, and we typically have one or more weak suits.

It is important to realize that none of these personality types is better than any of the others. None is the "right" or "wrong" way to be—they are just different. By understanding, accepting, and adapting to these differences, we can increase our interpersonal effectiveness.

Table 8.1 names the six personality types.

Everyone has at least some of each personality type. If we were to quantify the relative strength of each personality type in a person on a scale of zero to 100, represent each type as a bar, and lay these bars on top of one another from the strongest suit personality type to the weakest suit, we would end up with a bar graph with a structure that looks something like a pyramid (or at least half of one), as in Figure 8.3. Pyramids vary, both in the order of the personality types and the strength of each type.

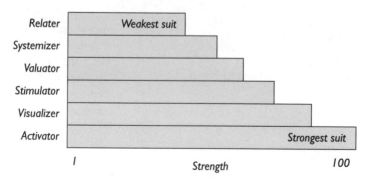

Figure 8.3

Personality Bar Graph

The order and relative strength of these personality types are established, through some combination of heredity and early social conditioning, by the time we are about five years old. That doesn't mean that we don't change after the age of five, because we certainly do—or at least many of us do. Personality type

TABLE 8.1

Personality Types

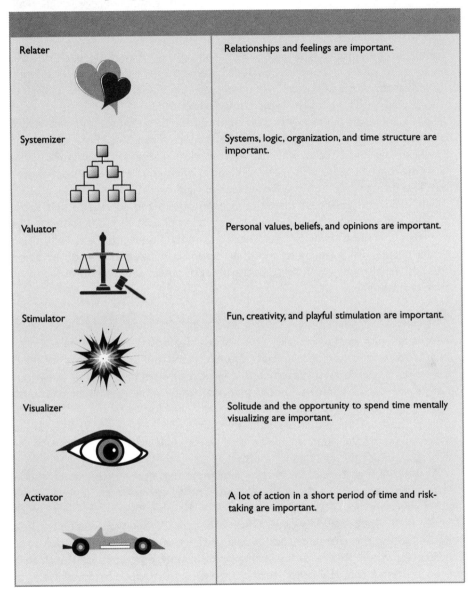

Relater	Relationships and feelings are important.
Systemizer	Systems, logic, organization, and time structure are important.
Valuator	Personal values, beliefs, and opinions are important.
Stimulator	Fun, creativity, and playful stimulation are important.
Visualizer	Solitude and the opportunity to spend time mentally visualizing are important.
Activator	A lot of action in a short period of time and risk-taking are important.

change is accomplished not by changing the order, which is permanently set, but by enhancing our ability to communicate from a type that is less strong for us or increasing our strength in a type—that is, by becoming more flexible. We can, for example, develop more strength or comfort in one of our less dominant personality types so that we can relate more effectively with people for whom that type is dominant. We can improve our ability to move around in our pyramid to tap into and use the various parts of our personality. In addition, some of us may experience **phase change**, where we move one step up in our pyramid and the next type becomes dominant for us. Phase change will be examined later in this chapter.

TYPE CHAUVINISM

Though no personality type is the "right" or "wrong" way to be, each of us has a natural tendency to view our dominant personality type more favourably than the others. We tend to look at the world as if there were two types of people: people who are like us, and those who should be! This is called **type chauvinism**.

For example, the person whose strongest type is **Systemizer** and is therefore very logic-oriented may view a strong Relater, who is more feelings-oriented, as less than effective. Likewise, the Systemizer, who is very work-oriented and structured, may view the **Stimulator**, who is very play-oriented and spontaneous, as being inappropriate or ineffective. The Relater may view the Systemizer as rigid or shallow.

It is important to accept the differences in others and appreciate that each of the personality types has strengths and needs. Accepting people with different strong suit personality types is critical to being effective in our interactions with them.

This chapter will examine each of the personality types and their observable characteristics. We will also explore how to deal with each personality type in order to relate to customers more effectively.

DEFINITION OF PSYCHOLOGICAL NEEDS

Associated with each personality type are **psychological needs**. One element of effective interaction with others is the ability to understand and offer support for their psychological needs. Satisfaction of these needs is what motivates many of our behaviours. If we are not getting our psychological needs met in a positive way, we will unconsciously try to get them met in a way that has negative consequences for us or for people we interact with (this is the basis for the stress behaviour discussed in Chapter 9). We can communicate more effectively and often reduce stress if we can help satisfy the customer's dominant psychological needs during telephone calls.

As we review each personality type, remember that everyone is a combination of the various types. Although we may refer to someone as, for example, "a Relater," we would be more precise to say a "strong suit Relater," as the label Relater implies he or she has none of the other five personality types, which is not true. When we examine the Relater, we will be looking at the characteristics in that package and discussing how to connect with a person for whom Relater is the strong suit. Although a person may have a strong suit that is so dominant that the other personality types seem weak by comparison, most people demonstrate some characteristics from each type.

Learning Application Exercise

As you read through each type, identify someone you know for whom that type is the strong suit. Remember, we are all a combination of these types, so the person may not have all the characteristics identified as being part of that package.

Six Personality Types

RELATER

People with a strong Relater suit are naturally caring, sensitive people. They tend to be compassionate and demonstrate personal warmth toward others. Roughly 30 percent of the total population in North America consists of strong suit Relaters, including 45 percent of women. This is an important statistic. The Relater is the stereotypical woman, yet this statistic shows that if we were to treat all women as Relaters we would miss connecting with over half. To be effective communicators and interact appropriately with all customers, we must look for more than one cue to their dominant personality type and resist the temptation to stereotype. It is also important to appreciate that 15 percent of all North American men are strong suit Relaters, which represents a substantial percentage.

Relaters are nurturing people who are naturally empathic and caring. They are comfortable to be around. They tend to like people, and it's comfortable to be around someone who likes you.

Environment is important to Relaters. For example, these are the people who will spend weeks looking for just the right piece of furniture to create just the right feeling in a room of their home. The Relater's work area will have plants, family pictures, knickknacks, and other personal touches. These "nesting" people tend to personalize their homes as well with mementos that each have a personal memory attached.

There are visual cues that identify someone as a strong suit Relater. Relaters care about their appearance. They tend to colour-coordinate their clothing tastefully and dress stylishly. Their hair and makeup are conscientiously attended to. Relaters have a warm and easy smile, are comfortable with eye contact, and have a tendency to touch the other person during a conversation. With people they know, Relaters are often "huggy."

These are "people" people. Relaters are usually drawn to jobs that involve interacting with people. They are comfortable in groups and are natural team players. Relaters are sensitive to the needs of others, they strive to please others, and they do not like to offend. They are natural peacemakers who can feel bad if they are unable to help others feel better. Relaters have a psychological need to be appreciated as whole people, not just as people who do well on or off the job. The messages they need to hear are "I care about you," "You're important to me," and "I like you just the way you are." They also need sensory satisfaction. Food can satisfy this sensory need with its tastes, smells, and textures. These, plus the good feeling Relaters get from helping others and giving to others, often mean Relater strong suits like to cook or give food to others. Relaters are the type most drawn to fragrances, they like melodic music, and they have trouble adjusting room and car temperatures to be just right for them.

A strong suit Relater who feels cared about as a person and who is working in a comfortable work environment with a friendly and supportive team brings a strong customer service orientation to the call centre job. As call centre representatives, Relaters nurture others and are naturally empathic, caring, and helpful.

Relater Customers

Customers who are strong suit Relaters can often be recognized by their soft tone of voice. They tend to make the contact personal, even in a business interaction, talking *to* instead of *at* you. Relaters personalize the interaction by using your name, sharing personal information, and taking a particular interest in any personal information you share with them. If you tell a Relater customer in one conversation that you are feeling ill, in the next conversation she or he will ask if you are feeling better. Relaters take a personal interest in others and remember personal information about them, and they like you to do the same in return. They prefer to begin an interaction with some small talk so they can feel connected to you.

Relaters are comfortable with sharing their feelings. It is important for them to get along with others and to have others like them. They feel comfortable offering empathy and do so naturally.

The winning approach for the Relater customer communicates "This is an organization that truly cares for its customers" and "I am a caring person who genuinely likes you and wants to help you." To connect with a strong suit Relater, engage in small talk early in the call, show empathy, and soften your tone of voice. As appropriate, share personal information with the Relater. Make sure to use the customer's name to help personalize the interaction. Picture the Relater customer in your mind as a nice person you would like to help. Demonstrate in tone and words that you like the customer.

Learning Application Exercise

1. *Who do you know (customer, coworker, or friend) who is a strong suit Relater?*

2. *Why do you feel that person is a strong suit Relater? Discuss your assessment and reasons with a peer.*

SYSTEMIZER

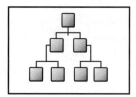

The person whose strong suit is Systemizer is naturally very logical, analytical, and orderly. This is the second-largest personality type in North America at 25 percent of the population. Most Systemizers are male (37.5 percent of the male population), therefore the stereotypical male is a Systemizer just as the stereotypical female is a Relater. However, this stereotype includes less than half of the male population, and, since a significant number of females are strong suit Systemizers (12.5 percent), such stereotyping can be very inaccurate and, if acted upon, can lead to communication breakdowns.

Systemizers strive to be perfect, and as a consequence they tend to behave in a responsible way. Strong suit Systemizers like to feel in control of their own destiny and have input in decisions that affect them. They work well with clear policies, objectives, and expectations. Systemizers like structure and systems, and will organize their environment to make their lives easier. They like to set and achieve short-term goals.

Systemizers' sense of organization and need to build systems can be apparent in small signs, such as their clothes closet being organized by type of clothing, CDs organized by type of music and artist, sock drawer organized by colour, and so on.

Systemizers are overrepresented in supervisory and management positions compared with other personality types. Because they are logical, organized, responsible, and goal- and achievement-oriented, they are drawn to these positions. They approach life's problems and understand their environment through thinking and analyzing.

Visually, strong suit Systemizers are neat in appearance, and it is common to see horizontal creases across their foreheads that become more obvious when they are concentrating or when they are stressed or tired.

The psychological needs for Systemizers are positive feedback for their work, thoughts, and accomplishments, and the sense that they have a structure to their time and how it is filled. They work well with personal organizers, schedules, to-do lists, and agendas. Systemizers need positive feedback more than any other personality type, and this feedback must be specific. "You're doing a great job" is less meaningful to the strong suit Systemizer than "That was an excellent report, very thorough and complete." Their time consciousness results in their concern with not wasting time—they dislike being late, waiting in line, and, typically, shopping. Systemizers like to plan their time and use it effectively.

ON THE JOB

The Systemizer

Following is an illustration of a Systemizer working at home and displaying the need that Systemizers have to structure their time.

Josef is a strong suit Systemizer. One evening as he is working at home on his computer, his wife, Sue, a strong suit Relater, comes into the room and says, "Honey, can we talk?" Josef responds, "Sure, I should be finished here at about 10:00 o'clock. How about we get together then?" After Sue has made her appointment, she leaves the office and Josef gets back to work. At 10:00 exactly, Josef saves what is on his computer and goes into the kitchen to meet with his wife.

Sue is sitting at the kitchen table with her cup of tea. Josef sits down and asks, "Well, honey, what is it you want to talk about?" Sue, comfortable in her chair and cupping her warm cup in her hands, responds, "Oh, nothing specific. I just wanted to talk." Josef, his mind still back in his office where his partially completed work lies, replies, "Well, I can understand that, but I've got an awful lot of things I could be doing back there in the office right now. Tell you what. I'll go back to my computer, you figure out what it is you want to talk about, and when you do, just come and let me know and I'll be glad to sit down and talk with you."

As Josef rises from his chair to return to his home office, Sue, in a gentle and reasonable tone, responds to his suggestion with "Remember how before we got married we'd spend evenings just sitting and visiting and talking about nothing?" Josef, a confused expression on his face, replies, "Yes, of course I do." Sue, still quietly and reasonably, says, "Well, that was really important to me." Josef, sounding a bit confused, replies, "Yes, I know that." Sue's voice firms up, and in a determined tone of voice she states, "Well, it's still very important to me."

Josef receives the message loud and clear. There is no more computer work that evening.

Systemizers do well in a "management-by-objectives" system, in which objectives and the time frames for achieving them are set. As call centre representatives, Systemizers are good at setting objectives with time frames and then meeting them. When their psychological needs are met, they can apply their productivity-enhancing skills to the job.

Systemizer Customers

Customers with a Systemizer strong suit are typically organized and logical, and want to get right to business. These customers may have an agenda of items they want to resolve or points they want to address during the call. Typically they prepare for the call and know what they're talking about. Systemizer customers are very professional in their tone, and their speaking style is articulate. They often demonstrate a good vocabulary.

Systemizers want to know the "why" behind something, and will ask questions to enhance their understanding. They like detail, but the relevance of information they're given—rather than "information dumping"—is critical.

The winning approach for the Systemizer customer communicates "We'll supply you with the information and some choices so you can make a decision" and "We are a responsible organization, and I am an organized person." It's important to meet time commitments with a Systemizer. Diagramming your calls will help you present yourself as organized to the Systemizer.

Use the active listening techniques of summarizing and paraphrasing to show you are listening and to confirm your understanding. With Systemizer customers, present arguments logically, and work from an agenda—plan your outbound calls. Be prepared to provide additional information to these customers, as they have an inquiring mind.

Since Systemizers need feedback that they are doing a good job, one excellent way to fulfill this psychological need is to ask them questions. By asking for input, you are telling them their thoughts are important to you.

Communicate respect for the Systemizer's time. When you provide a time frame, stick to it. Call back when you said you would. Don't be late. Listen for and respond to cues that the Systemizer may be in a hurry.

To support the Systemizer's need to be in control of decisions, provide alternatives for her or him to choose from. Involve the Systemizer in decision-making, since this personality type likes to problem-solve and have her or his input heard.

Lean toward professionalism with a Systemizer customer, demonstrating greater formality in language, use of the customer's surname, and so on.

Learning Application Exercise

1. *Who do you know (customer, coworker, friend) who is a strong suit Systemizer?*

2. *Why do you feel that person is a strong suit Systemizer? Discuss your assessment and reasons with a peer.*

VALUATOR

People whose strong suit is Valuator tend to have strong personal values. They are dedicated, observant, and conscientious. Valuators make up about 10 percent of the total North American population—12 percent of men and 8 percent of women. They are conservative like Systemizers but with a little more flare. Typically, honesty, integrity, reliability, and quality or value for the dollar are all very important to Valuators. They have usually sorted out the role of religion in their lives. Valuators have opinions on everything and are usually willing to share their opinions, whether the listener wants to hear them or not! They have theories to explain everything, and a "theory B" to explain anything their original theory misses.

Valuators are able to commit to long-range objectives or goals. Then they stay focused and dedicate themselves to accomplishing those objectives. Valuators have a very strong sense of fairness and right and wrong. They make good mentors, as they like to help other people develop.

Trust can be an issue for strong suit Valuators. It can take time for them to trust someone, and that trust may be very fragile, being withdrawn at the slightest sign that the other person is unworthy. If Valuators commit to a job or a relationship, then as long as the trust is intact they can be very committed and loyal. They are often viewed as being very intense.

One visual cue that you are dealing with a Valuator is his or her eyes. Valuators often have either piercing or "bulging" eyes (eyes that get rounder when the Valuator communicates something very important to his or her value set), and most have vertical creases between the eyes that get deeper when they are concentrating or when they get a little stressed or tired. Valuators often have erect posture as well, and typically dress conservatively.

Recognition for their work, input, ideas, values, and opinions is a psychological need for Valuators. The need here is not just to have those opinions and share them, but to get some recognition that those opinions are valued and worthy of respect.

As a call centre representative, the strong suit Valuator, when feeling respected, is very committed to the organization and customers, and to effective customer service.

Valuator Customers

Customers with a Valuator strong suit are typically opinionated and value-driven and behave somewhat formally. These customers express their opinions, beliefs, and theories, and they love to debate. They will talk about current events or politics, and they want to talk on the "big picture" and conceptual level as opposed to the details. The strong suit Valuator uses phrases like "in my opinion" and "I believe," and uses a vocabulary with many value-laden words.

The winning approach for the Valuator customer communicates "We value and respect our customers" and "We are an ethical organization, and I am a fair and honest person." When interacting with a Valuator customer, communicate your honesty and demonstrate your reliability. Your tone of voice, choice of words, and suggested actions must demonstrate your integrity and ingrained values, which in turn are seen to reflect those of your company.

It may take time to build trust with the Valuator, and even once it is built, that trust remains fragile and must be consistently reinforced. Give honest, positive feedback on values and opinions as well as on ideas and accomplishments.

In words and tone of voice, communicate respect for the Valuator and his or her opinions and values. Even if you do not agree with these opinions, take care not to show disrespect for them or to try to prove the Valuator wrong. In part, respect is communicated by showing that what the Valuator has to say is important to you ("Thank you for bringing this to our attention") or that her or his issue will be treated as a priority.

Rather than prove the Valuator wrong (yes, the customer is not always right!),

- Identify an element of rightness in what the Valuator has said. When the customer has given a series of opinions, respond to one or more of them with "When you say…I couldn't agree with you more. In fact…." and pursue that line of reasoning.

- Help the Valuator make a new decision based on new information, such as "What you are saying is, I believe, exactly right given this set of parameters….Might I suggest though that in this situation, these are the parameters….And that would mean that the most appropriate way to go is…."

Learning Application Exercise

1. *Who do you know (customer, coworker, friend) who is a strong suit Valuator?*

2. *Why do you feel that person is a strong suit Valuator? Discuss your assessment and reasons with a peer.*

STIMULATOR

Strong suit Stimulators need playfulness, spontaneity, creativity, and fun in their lives. In North America, 20 percent of the population are strong suit Stimulators—24 percent of females and 16 percent of males. In addition, over 60 percent of people for whom Relater is the strongest suit have Stimulator as their next strongest suit. There are, then, many more female Stimulators than male.

Stimulators are fun to be around. They get real joy out of living and enjoy each moment in life as it is experienced—often with the wonderment and enthusiasm (and even behaviour) of a child. Stimulators like to have fun things in their environment and enjoy "toys."

Stimulators are polarized people. They make quick decisions about whether they love or hate something—there is little room for grey areas. Likewise, the whole world tends to know when Stimulators are in a good mood and when they are in a bad mood, because they "wear" their moods obviously.

Stimulators often have a high energy level. These people like to be moving and have trouble sitting still for any length of time. They are usually physical and often musical, either playing a musical instrument, enjoying dancing, or owning a really good sound system. They often enjoy fun, high-energy music.

Stimulators often dress for fun and for effect. Even in a business environment, Stimulators dress with a flare that sets them apart. They have an easy smile and an open, genuine laugh. As they age, they typically develop laugh lines around their eyes.

Fun or playful stimulation is the Stimulator's psychological need. Strong suit Stimulators must play before they can work, often through joking around and light bantering.

ON THE JOB

The Stimulator

Tomas is a strong suit Stimulator. He managed to get an MBA degree, even though he spent much of his time down at the dean's office trying to argue his way back into the program. Tomas loved to party and to be the centre of attention. People at parties either loved his zany sense of humour or they hated it.

He eventually graduated and got a job in an advertising firm. However, his job was not on the creative side but on the "suit and tie" side, dealing with the firm's clients and acting as liaison between the conservative clients and the firm's creative staff.

Although Tomas wore the required three-piece pinstripe suit, he still walked with the relaxed, fluid body motion that Stimulators tend to have, and in the centre of his tie he sported a large Mickey Mouse tie pin. He was expressing his individuality, trying to get a reaction.

The advertising firm's management was perceptive. Within a year, Tomas was moved to a creative job, where his business education and creativity led him to success and a senior management position.

As call centre representatives, once Stimulators have had their "fix" of play, they can focus their attention on business. Stimulators who have enough play in their lives help to energize their environment and encourage others to avoid taking things too seriously.

Stimulator Customers

Customers with a Stimulator strong suit are energetic and playful, injecting humour into their interactions. These customers will take every opportunity to talk about fun things, especially nonwork things. They are relaxed and informal, sometimes to the point of over-familiarity. Reps must be careful to resist following the Stimulator across the line between professionalism and over-familiarity, especially if a rep is a strong suit Stimulator as well.

The winning approach for the Stimulator customer communicates "We are a fun, relaxed organization, and I am a fun person with a good sense of humour." Pump up your energy level and increase your voice inflection with a strong suit Stimulator customer. Act excited about what you do; show you are having fun and enjoying your job.

When interacting with the Stimulator, communicate playfully. At the very least, if you are not comfortable in this role, be aware of when the Stimulator is playing with you. The Stimulator will either like you and want to do business with you, or, in very short order, not like you and not want to do business with you. It is much better to start off on the "like" side.

Your style should be less formal and more familiar with Stimulators. Be careful not to seem unprofessional, however. Be aware of the Stimulator's tendency to wander off-topic and talk about fun things. As necessary, pull the conversation back on course in a playful way. Enjoy the Stimulator—be a good audience—but don't try to out-stimulate her or him.

Learning Application Exercise

1. *Who do you know (customer, coworker, friend) who is a strong suit Stimulator?*

2. *Why do you feel that person is a strong suit Stimulator? Discuss your assessment and reasons with a peer.*

VISUALIZER

A strong suit **Visualizer** is calm, quiet, and introspective. Visualizers make up 10 percent of the North American population—12 percent of females and 8 percent of males. Visualizers are stable, relaxed, "laid back," and "centred." They are comfortable in their own company and typically enjoy time on their own in which their minds can free-flow or drift. Visualizers often enjoy meditation or gardening, or may be the marathon runner whose mind can free-flow while she or he is running.

Visualizers have the ability to stay with repetitive tasks that bore other people. While their hands perform the task, their minds are free to think about what they want. Visualizers are usually not interested in interacting with others, and when they must interact, they are shy and reserved and do not volunteer much information. These are private people whose psychological need is for personal space or solitude. Visualizers do not show much enthusiasm.

Visualizers often don't show the lines and wrinkles of aging because they tend to use the facial muscles less. Outward appearance is unimportant to them, and they may appear untidy, with items of clothing that don't match one another or the occasion.

The Visualizer personality type is one of the most common weak suits (the other is the Activator). We tend to react most negatively to our weak suit personality type. We tend to be uncomfortable with or criticize those whose strong suit is our weak suit personality type. It is important to understand which type is your own weak suit so you can recognize the source of your negative response to someone for whom that type is a strong suit and be able to overcome or minimize your reaction.

ON THE JOB

The Visualizer

Phillip, who is a strong suit Systemizer but a weak suit Visualizer, had a great working relationship with his Visualizer colleague Leah. They were working on a project together one afternoon when Leah decided to take a short break in the park next to their office. A short while later, Phillip came out to join her.

As Phillip approached Leah sitting on the park bench, he thought he saw a look of deep concentration on her face. He asked, "What are you thinking about?" For a Systemizer like Phillip, if you are awake, you are thinking. Leah answered, "Oh, nothing really."

Phillip persisted with his interrogation: "No really. You can tell me. What were you thinking about?" Leah reflected for a moment and answered, "Well, if you must know, at the moment you joined me I was looking at the pattern the light was making as it came through the trees, and thinking of absolutely nothing." Phillip just shook his head and took a seat beside her on the bench. "I'll accept that but I sure don't understand it."

Visualizer call centre reps have a stabilizing influence. They seem to take issues in their stride and manage times of stress without all the flurry of emotion and energy that characterizes other personality types.

Visualizer Customers

Customers with a Visualizer strong suit are recognizable by their low inflection and paced or even hesitant speaking style. These customers are also likely to say as little as possible, so you need to use focused questions to get the required information from them.

Visualizer customers give you few cues as to their level of interest or comprehension of what you are saying. They provide few listening responses. Be sensitive to the Visualizer's cues and minimize the amount of interaction. Visualizers can be uncomfortable with face-to-face or telephone interaction, especially if you are very friendly and try to pull them out of their "shell."

The winning approach for the Visualizer customer communicates "I will make this interaction as brief and trouble-free as possible," "I will respect your need for personal space," and "We do it all for you."

Speak more slowly—match the tone and pace of Visualizers. Allow these customers opportunities to pause and collect their thoughts before responding. Don't try to force small talk on Visualizers, or attempt to draw them into conversation. Respect their need for personal space. Keep your call as short as possible—offer clear directions on how the customer's problem can be resolved, be specific, and focus your questions.

Learning Application Exercise

1. *Who do you know (customer, coworker, friend) who is a strong suit Visualizer?*

2. *Why do you feel that person is a strong suit Visualizer? Discuss your assessment and reasons with a peer.*

ACTIVATOR

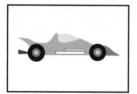

A strong suit **Activator** is adaptable, persuasive, and charming, with a natural flexibility that enables him or her to fit in with just about every other personality type. Strong suit

Activators are the smallest personality type at only 5 percent of the North American population—approximately 7.5 percent of males and 2.5 percent of females.

Activators are typically very direct and to the point. They need to cut through the "red tape" and detail and get right to "How can I use it?" "What can I do with it?" and "How much will it cost me?" People with this strong suit tend to be very energetic, good at taking control and running with something, good at "thinking on their feet," and generally seem very "up." They are naturally optimistic and can see opportunity everywhere.

Activators have an "If you've got it, flaunt it" philosophy; they understand the importance of the first impression. Often, they dress expensively and enjoy wearing a lot of jewellery.

Strong suit Activators have a psychological need for action in their lives—getting a lot of excitement in a short period of time. They are gamblers, and the Activator part of each of us is that action-oriented, risk-taking part. If you are very risk-averse, you likely are a weak suit Activator.

The Activator action orientation is a crucial and often missing part of organizations. Organizations that have a predominantly Systemizer approach to business may defer action until they have done extensive analysis. These are the organizations described by Tom Peters and Robet H. Waterman, Jr. as "ready, aim, aim, aim, aim, aim…."[2] who plan in detail before a major launch. The Activator does not work well in that style but is the "ready, fire, aim" type: "Let's try it out, fix it, try it again, and when we have it right, launch it on a grander scale."

As call centre representatives, Activators exude confidence, natural flexibility, and an action orientation. This may make them a strong, charismatic influence when cast in a role where these attributes can be positively exercised and the results immediately recognized.

Activator Customers

Customers who are strong suit Activators can be very charming and familiar on the telephone. They typically use a lot of slang expressions. These customers never respond to "How are you today?" with "Fine," "Not bad," or "Okay," but with "Super!" "Fantastic!" or some other superlative. Activators always seem positive, "up," and winners in life.

These customers are direct and to the point on the telephone, interested in the bottom line, and impatient with small talk. They sound confident and comfortable.

The winning approach for the Activator customer communicates "We are an action-oriented organization that gets things done," "I am confident and good at what I do," "Consider it done," and "I'll take care of it." When dealing with Activators, behave in a confident, positive, and upbeat manner.

Activators need to get the message that you are action-oriented, are going to make things happen, are very "do"-oriented in a very "do"-oriented organization, and are good and professional at your job. Avoid flowery compliments and long explanations—get to the point. Mirror the Activator customer's use of slang expressions, but only if you understand them.

Learning Application Exercise

1. *Who do you know (customer, coworker, friend) who is a strong suit Activator?*

2. *Why do you feel that person is a strong suit Activator? Discuss your assessment and reasons with a peer.*

Phase Change

Each of us, then, is a combination of the six personality types, although one type is generally dominant. While a person's dominant personality type may be consistent throughout his or her life, it can also change.

As mentioned at the beginning of this chapter, we all have a foundation in our pyramid (see Figure 8.3). About one-third of the population stays in that foundation and has the same dominant personality type for their entire lives. About two-thirds move at some point in their lives from this base to another dominant personality type. Some will move through two, three, four, or even five phases. These moves are called "phase changes."

When a person experiences a phase change, she or he begins to view the world through the new dominant type. The person's psychological needs change as well. He or she is able to draw on different character strengths and reacts in new ways to everyday stressors. A phase change is typically preceded by a long period of stress or a short period of intense stress. A phase change is a long-term, permanent change that ends only if another phase change occurs. Often there is a period of adjustment as a person accepts the changes in her- or himself and learns to cope with the new phase. We've all seen a phase change in others or experienced one ourselves. You may know people who are very different now than they were 5 or 10 years ago.

See if you know the following people.

SYSTEMIZER TO RELATER PHASE CHANGE

Doug was a hard-driving businessman, a national sales manager. He travelled so much he hardly knew his sons or his wife, and when he was home, all he thought about was work. He reached a point in his life where he found himself reexamining what was really important to him. He realized that his list of important things no longer included work, to which he had been dedicated almost exclusively for the past 20 years. At this point in his life, Doug determined that what was really important was his family. As a result, he decided to leave his high-powered management position to become a supervisor in a greenhouse. Although this didn't have the same pay or prestige as his previous position, it was near his home and it did have regular hours, allowing him to spend time with his family. This allowed Doug to focus on reestablishing his family relationship and better meet his changed psychological needs. Doug, who had been a Systemizer his whole life, had moved to a Relater phase.

The stressor that preceded this change was likely the fact that, after an initial period of rapid career growth, Doug had "plateaued"—reached a point at which he was unlikely to advance further. As a result, the positive reinforcement he had been receiving from the promotion was removed. Work was no longer rewarding, and recognition and positive feedback became rare, leading to that period of stress necessary for phase change to occur.

VALUATOR TO STIMULATOR PHASE CHANGE

Danna had strong personal values, opinions, and beliefs about how things should be done. She shared these opinions with everyone whether they wanted to hear them or not. Her stress had increased to the point that she was very critical of others and was driven to tell everyone how they should do their jobs, raise their children, and run their lives. Danna was very hard on herself and on those around her. Then, at a particularly stressful point in her life, Danna moved from a Valuator to a Stimulator phase in which she "lightened up" on herself and others. Now, after a period of adjustment, she is able to balance work with play and have fun in her life. Her focus now is on enjoying her job and her life. Though Danna moved from a Valuator base to a Stimulator phase, she has still retained the positive elements of the Valuator, as is the case with any phase change. The period of adjustment for Danna involved balancing these elements with the new Stimulator characteristics.

Learning Application Exercise

1. *Given what you know about the six personality types, which do you think is your strong suit? Which is your weak suit? Provide reasons for your selections.*

2. *Assess a number of your taped calls, or role-play calls or face-to-face interactions with a peer. Are you able to adjust your style to others' dominant personality types?*

3. *Observe peers, family members, television shows, and so on, and practise looking for cues as to personality strong suits. Record your observations.*

4. *Complete Table 8.2, then confirm your answers by reviewing this chapter.*

Summary

Effectiveness in a customer service role requires a flexible interaction style. Professional call centre representatives appreciate that customers have different personalities, and adapt their style to connect with each customer.

While we each have an interaction style that is most comfortable for us, we naturally adjust our style to connect with others. This is most effective when we are

- conscious of the need to be flexible, accepting that another person's style may be different from ours
- not experiencing stress

When we are unable to adjust our style to fit the customer, we don't connect with the customer as effectively.

If customers are experiencing stress, they are more likely to show its symptoms when they are not feeling a rapport with us, and they are less likely to show stress symptoms when they do feel a rapport. It is harder to be angry with someone with whom you feel connected. It is therefore in the customer's best interest and our best interest to accept differences in personality and communication style, and to be flexible in style as we work with customers.

Endnotes

1. Dr. Taibi Kahler, *The Mastery of Management* (Little Rock, AR: Kahler Communications, 1992).

2. Tom Peters and Robert H. Waterman, Jr., *In Search of Excellence* (New York: Harper and Row, 1982), 119, 142.

TABLE 8.2

Personality Type Review

	Strengths	How to Recognize on the Phone	How to Connect with
Relater			
Systemizer			
Valuator			
Stimulator			
Visualizer			
Activator			

Managing Stress and Handling Difficult Customers

Learning Outcomes

After successfully completing Chapter 9, you will be able to:

- *Recognize personality types based on individual stress reactions.*

- *Manage the stress reactions of others by responding constructively to each stressed behaviour.*

- *Minimize your tendency to personally respond to others' stress reactions by:*
  - *understanding the root causes of difficult behaviour;*
  - *recognizing and managing your own stress reactions.*

- *Create a personal strategy for reducing your susceptibility to stress.*

Stress on the Job

THE ROLE OF STRESS

Dealing with stress is a major part of the call centre job—the stress of the customers who call as well as the stress of the reps themselves. Call centre representatives regularly deal with customers who are upset, anxious, or angry when they call. Also, reps must cope with high workloads and a constant queue of customers on the telephone. The ability to handle the stress of others and to manage one's own stress is key to call centre job satisfaction and ultimately to success in the job.

Have you ever gone to work and, for some reason, your workday seems insane? Everything goes wrong, everyone is upset, all the customers seem hostile, yet you somehow take it all in stride. You confidently deal with the problems and crises of the day with little apparent effort. You are calm and manage to keep your patience while everyone else seems to be losing theirs. Yet on another day, you go to work feeling fine, but for some reason every little thing seems to irritate you. After about two hours the cumulative effect of these little annoyances makes you wonder how you'll make it through the day!

It isn't the external stressors that cause one day to be worse for you than another—it's how you handle and react to those stressors. More than that, something within you leads you to be better or worse at handling those daily stressors. If you can learn what that something is, you can create more good days and fewer bad days. The personality model we explored in Chapter 8 can help.

None of us is as effective at work when we are experiencing the negative effects of stress. Under stress, we lose our natural style flexibility and revert to our strongest personality type (see Chapter 8), communicating to the customer only from that type whether that is appropriate or not. Even worse, we may give each customer our strongest type's stress reaction, which, depending on our personality and stress level, can range from being mildly inappropriate to offensive. Most of us are not particularly nice to be around when we are feeling the effects of stress. If we can avoid feeling stressed and exhibiting our **stress reactions**, we are better at connecting with customers and consequently are more effective in our jobs.

Learning Application Exercise

1. *What happens to you when you are stressed?*

2. *Think of a time when you lost patience—and maybe control—at home or at work because of stress. What caused this reaction? How did you behave? What were you thinking at the time?*

CONTROLLING THE STRESS REACTION

How we react to stress is part of our strong suit personality type, but how often and how easily we experience that stress reaction is the result of many factors. One of them is conditioning. Many of us have spent a lifetime responding with our own reaction when we are confronted with someone else's stress reaction. The other person's stress reaction is like an invitation for us to respond with our own. If, for example, we are verbally attacked by someone, we may automatically attack right back. This might work outside of the job. But then, on the job, a reaction we have spent our whole life practising (and incorporating into our interpersonal style) is wrong. Attack behaviour is only one way to react to stress. Your own stress reaction may include feeling like a victim, blaming others, and so on.

If we react to stress by, for example, verbally attacking a customer, we risk losing the customer and even our job. Even if the stress reaction just comes out as a negative tone of voice, we become less and less effective as call centre reps. We also carry around inwardly turned stress that we may take home with us and take out on family or friends.

The following model can help call centre reps find a better way of dealing with job stress.

Professional Distancing

The key to preventing stress is to recognize the other person's behaviour as a stress reaction, to visualize it as a "hook." We can either "take the bait and swallow the hook," lose our control over the situation, and respond with our own stress reaction, or we can recognize the other person's stress and professionally distance ourselves from it.

The term **professional distancing** comes from the counselling field. When people in therapy begin to make a breakthrough in dealing with their problems, often a phenomenon called "transference" occurs. The emotion attached to the person or situation that is a source of the patient's problem is transferred from its true source to the counsellor. The patient may become verbally abusive toward the counsellor, venting, for example, anger felt toward an abusive parent. As well, the verbal attack may be very personalized, sounding as if the patient is upset with the counsellor.

A professional counsellor is not offended by such attacks since they represent a positive step in the counselling process. The counsellor empathizes with and appreciates the client's pain, but takes a step back and does not take the attack personally.

This concept works well in the call centre role. If you can recognize that a customer's difficult behaviour is a result of stress, then you can professionally distance yourself from the customer and handle the situation appropriately.

For many of us, particularly those for whom the stress reaction is close to the surface, developing the ability to professionally distance takes practice. Developing this skill typically involves the following steps:

- inappropriately reacting to the stress behaviour of another person without realizing what you have done, but feeling justified in your reaction

- recognizing after the fact that you went for the hook

- recognizing while you are reacting that you have gone for the hook

- recognizing just before you do it that you are going for the hook but, unable to stop yourself, going for it anyway

- recognizing the customer's behaviour as stress-induced and controlling your response before it can escalate to your stress reaction

- finally, recognizing the customer's behaviour as stress-induced and having no corresponding stress reaction yourself, but rather handling it as a professional

STRESS AND PSYCHOLOGICAL NEEDS

Each personality type has associated psychological needs (see Chapter 8). When these needs are met in a positive way, we are less susceptible to stressors and the stress reactions of others. When we do not take care of our psychological needs positively, we are more vulnerable to the stressors.

When psychological needs are not met, we consciously or unconsciously seek to have them met in ways that have negative consequences for us. These ways are our stress reactions.

Table 9.1 lists the psychological needs associated with each personality type.

Example: Relater

Linh is a strong suit Relater. Her psychological needs are for appreciation, connection with people, and sensory pampering. Linh's relationship with her husband is currently at a low ebb. She is feeling unloved—her husband is a Systemizer who is spending too much time at work and too little time with Linh. If her psychological needs are not met in a positive way, Linh will unconsciously arrange to get those needs met in a way that has negative ramifications for her. She may, for example, become unassertive or over-accommodating, catering to her husband and children, doting on them, and making everything in her life revolve around them. She will do for them to such an extent that she denies herself. In doing so, she is unconsciously seeking appreciation.

Alternately, Linh may swing in the opposite direction and spend excessive amounts of time and money on shopping for nice things for herself. Unconsciously, she is striving to pamper her senses—to look nice and feel appreciated. The negative consequence of this spending may mean financial or relationship problems. Or, again through negatively satisfying the need for sensory pampering, Linh may start to overeat and consequently put on weight. Then, because appearance is important to Relaters, she will feel bad about herself and exhibit even more stress.

Example: Systemizer

Jeremy is a strong suit Systemizer. His psychological needs are positive feedback on his thoughts, ideas, and accomplishments, as well as time structure. He is not getting enough positive feedback at work. This is not unusual, since Jeremy is a good, solid worker and his supervisor is focusing on those who are not doing as well. Because Jeremy needs positive feedback, he starts working even harder. Initially he receives positive recognition from his boss, but after a while, Jeremy's hard work is expected and the feedback stops. So Jeremy starts working more hours (he can't work any harder). If he continues to work as hard for these longer hours, he will start to exhibit health problems. Typically, Systemizers will lower the intensity of their work over the longer workday. Jeremy is the employee who is in the office at 7:00 in the morning and doesn't leave until 10:00 at night, yet he doesn't seem to get much more work done. When he tells everyone about his long hours, he is really crying

TABLE 9.1

Psychological Needs

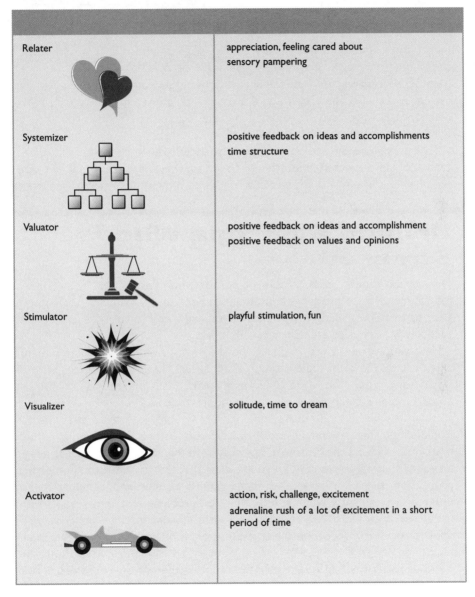

Relater	appreciation, feeling cared about
	sensory pampering
Systemizer	positive feedback on ideas and accomplishments
	time structure
Valuator	positive feedback on ideas and accomplishment
	positive feedback on values and opinions
Stimulator	playful stimulation, fun
Visualizer	solitude, time to dream
Activator	action, risk, challenge, excitement
	adrenaline rush of a lot of excitement in a short period of time

out for positive reinforcement. Unfortunately, when he gets it at this stage, it just encourages his dysfunctional behaviour.

The problem is multiplied if Jeremy happens to be married to Linh, the strong suit Relater, whose psychological need for appreciation is met by Jeremy spending time with her. A downward spiral occurs: Jeremy works more hours to get his needs met, Linh accommodates to gain appreciation ("Call me when you're leaving the office, and I'll have a nice hot meal ready for you when you get home"). Jeremy wrongly interprets this as understanding that he's working all these long hours for her and the kids, and continues the long hours. Linh endures for a while, then eventually either seeks to get her psychological needs met elsewhere or begins to make mistakes around the home (usually a lack of orderliness or cleanliness, mishandling of money, or not thinking clearly will get attention from a Systemizer) while eating and putting on weight. Jeremy then gets angry or rejecting, Linh feels like a victim, and all because of stress reactions and the unconscious negative striving to meet psychological needs. Systemizers and Relaters are often drawn to each other, and the mutually reinforcing stress reactions described here are common in these relationships. Perhaps you know a couple who are at some stage in this downward spiral.

As we examine the stress reactions associated with each personality type, notice how each is simply a subconscious attempt to get psychological needs met. The stress reactions occur when these needs are met in a way that produces negative consequences.

Helping Someone Who Is Stressed

One person cannot make another person become "unstressed." Sometimes a call centre rep can do all the right things and the customer will still exhibit stress. Too often reps feel a sense of failure, taking it personally if they are unable to make customers feel better, particularly if the reps are strong suit Relaters.

Have you ever dealt with a customer who seems overly upset about a minor issue? And when you fix the issue, the customer is still upset? Have you wondered why?

For many people, the world is a stressful place. Many people have relationship problems, health problems, family problems, and financial problems. These stressors are all big, and they all seem beyond the individual's control. They typically lead to an overwhelming feeling of helplessness. Then something more specific goes wrong. Perhaps your company makes a mistake that affects the customer. The customer then feels she or he has a legitimate place to put all that pent-up stress. So your feeling that the amount of customer upset is out of proportion to the small issue it is focused on is justified, and it's understandable why this upset doesn't go away when you fix the little problem. That little problem is not the real issue. The customer's overreaction is usually an unconscious behaviour. The customer doesn't necessarily recognize the true cause of his or her stress, and feels totally justified in his or her reaction.

Though you may feel responsible for reducing the customer's stress, it is important to recognize that this may not be possible. You should not take it as a personal failure if some customers leave the call without being totally satisfied. While call centre reps should attempt to meet the caller's psychological needs and try to calm the stress reaction, they must recognize that the right behaviours will not always lead to the desired results for the customer. It is like throwing a struggling swimmer a lifeline—all the would-be rescuer can do is throw it. For the lifeline to be effective, the swimmer must grab hold of it. Likewise, all reps can do is offer the most appropriate response to the customer's stress reaction. The customer may be too overwhelmed by stress to be able to grab the lifeline. The customer's potential inability to grab the lifeline does not mean we shouldn't throw it—in some cases it may help, and in all cases it doesn't hurt.

Handling Different Types of Customers

Now let's review the stress reactions of each personality type, and examine ways in which we can offer a lifeline to each.

THE STRESSED RELATER

On a subconscious level, Relaters want to meet the psychological needs of pleasing and being appreciated. In doing so, stressed Relaters can become unassertive and over-accommodating—anything to please the other person. Signs of early Relater stress include a meek, unconfident tone of voice and the use of words like "eh" or "you know" at the end of sentences (essentially saying, "You do agree with me, don't you?"). Stressed Relaters may raise their voice at the end of a statement, turning it into a question, or may demonstrate a lack of self-confidence by asking questions indirectly: "Do you think you could look at my account?" or "Maybe we could go out tonight?" rather than asking directly and risking a negative response. Stressed Relaters become overapologetic over minor things or when they are not even at fault. They may even apologize for apologizing too much!

As strong suit Relaters get more stressed, their tone of voice can sound whiny. They may start to feel and act like victims. While readily volunteering to do for others, the Relater may wonder "Why do I always have to be the one to do this?" or can even drift into the **martyr syndrome** that is unfortunately common in abusive or alcoholic relationships.

Stressed Relaters may feel unappreciated even though they are trying very hard to please others. They are trying to get their psychological needs met in a way that undermines their own sense of self-worth. As Relaters start to feel more stressed, they become less and less assertive, and may start to make mistakes. These will be obvious mistakes, ones that will be noticed and reacted to by Systemizers. The Relaters will get negative attention for their behaviour to substitute for the positive attention that is missing.

Relaters may also become self-deprecating and say things like, "Boy, was I ever stupid" or "How could I be so dumb?", or they may discount themselves in front of others. If someone agrees with the Relater ("Yes, that was kind of a dumb thing to do"), the Relater's sense of being a victim is reinforced ("How could you speak to me like that?").

Stressed Relaters may also feel and express confusion or a sense of being overwhelmed. This can interfere with their ability to think or problem-solve.

The Relater personality type is naturally more feelings-oriented. Stressed Relaters may talk about their feelings of depression. They may also become upset and even be moved to tears.

Relaters may try to make up for the sensed lack of appreciation by pampering their senses, thus meeting their sensory needs. They may pamper themselves with food, overeating and gaining weight, or they may go on inappropriate spending sprees for new clothes or other things.

Example: The Stressed Relater

At work, Linh was typically a very caring and personable call centre rep. When stressed and confronted by an angry caller, she found her feelings were hurt more easily and she took the caller's verbal attacks more personally. Her coworkers noticed that Linh's tone became less confident, she sounded unsure of what she was saying even though she was one of the most knowledgeable reps in her department, and she spent much of her call apologizing for what she couldn't do or didn't know. When she was stressed, she ended up with a greater number of attacking callers and more callers demanding to speak to her supervisor, and Linh felt emotionally drained by the end of her shift.

Dealing with the Stressed Relater Customer

To deal with a stressed Relater customer, soften your tone of voice, personalize your inter-action, and use the other techniques discussed in Chapter 8 for connecting with the Relater personality type.

Be prepared to demonstrate empathy when it is appropriate—refer to the customer's emotion, paraphrase the feeling, and use an empathic tone of voice. Remember that a stressed Relater who is offered a sympathetic ear may launch into a long description of per-sonal problems. In this situation, don't ignore the personal issues, but rather acknowledge each with a brief empathic statement, then use questioning to direct the conversation back to the reason for the call.

When appropriate, share relevant personal feelings or information with the stressed Relater ("I understand how you must feel—I have a baby at home myself"). This helps the Relater feel less alone and personalizes the interaction, helping the Relater to connect per-sonally with you. Ensure that the information you share is appropriate to the professional nature of the call.

It is counterproductive to try to solve stressed Relaters' problems if you haven't first taken care of their emotions. They need to express their feelings and be heard. Relaters can focus on fixing the problem only after they feel fully understood or appreciated. It is common for Systemizers to misread this need to experience the feelings and respond to the Relater's problem by immediately offering ideas to fix it.

Relaters may need your reassurance that their confusion or upset is understandable and okay. They need to know that you will be able to resolve the issue, that you want to help and are able to do so, and that there is a "light at the end of the tunnel."

THE STRESSED SYSTEMIZER

In the early stages of stress, Systemizers use big words when little words will do. This comes from trying to be perfect—simpler words just don't convey the Systemizer's message as appro-priately as more complicated words. The problem is, the listener may not understand. So, while trying to clarify a point, the slightly stressed Systemizer may actually confuse the issue.

Stressed Systemizers may also insert qualifying clauses in their sentences. They know there is no black and white answer to anything, so they use qualifiers to try to communi-cate the appropriate shade of grey: "I'm no expert, but...." or "This may be a little off topic, however...."

Because of the need to be perfect, the stressed Systemizer may also give too much detail in an attempt to create a picture in the other person's mind. Systemizers need to make themselves perfectly understood.

Systemizers' psychological needs are positive feedback and time structure. To get positive feedback, they may take on more projects (saying no would be admitting they can't handle more), work longer hours, and resist delegating appropriately (because "if you want to be sure it's done right, best do it yourself").

Because Systemizers take on such a large workload, time becomes an issue. They can become overly concerned about making every minute productive, ignoring the need for downtime, family time, leisure time, and so on, which provides less opportunity for accomplishment and positive feedback. Stressed workaholic Systemizers cut back on sleep and take less personal time.

Stressed Systemizer customers are impatient and hurried. They speak quickly and get angry with perceived poor thinking. Their anger may lead to them to verbally attack others. When they do so, Systemizers tend to generalize and personalize.

If a stressed Systemizer customer calls to complain about a specific mistake, quickly fixing the problem just leaves the customer still angry and with nothing to serve as the focus for the anger. So Systemizers learn unconsciously to generalize their complaints: "You people don't know what you are doing there!"

With most attacks, you can simply acknowledge the customer's frustration but professionally distance yourself from it. For example, if the customer says, "You big companies drive me crazy!" you might respond with "I can understand your frustration." If the customer says, "Your department doesn't know what it's doing!" you might respond with "I can appreciate your concern." Systemizers have learned that, to get a reaction from others, the attack needs to be personal. If the customer says, "You are a total idiot!" your own stress reaction is more likely to be triggered, and the Systemizer has a better chance of getting a response—hence the tendency to personalize the attack.

Example: The Stressed Systemizer

Jeremy becomes impatient when he is experiencing stress. He is impatient with coworkers and family members when they don't think clearly, make mistakes, or are not orderly. He gets angry about inefficiencies: a tool not returned to its proper place or a messy kitchen. Jeremy is also very hard on himself if he makes a mistake. He is so concerned with being perfect that he proofreads a report he's written over and over before handing it in, even then feeling he could have done better if only he had given it more time. He is his own worst critic.

Dealing with the Stressed Systemizer Customer

Dealing with a stressed Systemizer customer begins with using the positive connecting techniques presented in Chapter 8. If you can connect with the Systemizer and meet her or his psychological needs in a positive way before she or he is too stressed, you may divert a more serious stress reaction.

Dealing with personal attacks is a challenge for any rep. Focus on specifics in order to understand and deal with the issue, and avoid taking the attack personally. Your response to a personal attack may be something like "I understand you are angry. What specifically are you upset about?" This acknowledges the upset and adds a focusing question. Your tone of voice should be positive and professional.

The key is to get stressed Systemizers out of the complaint mode and into the problem-solving mode by asking questions to clarify the issue, and then inviting them to join you in resolving the problem. Questioning also gives Systemizers positive feedback, showing them that what they have to say is important to you.

If the customer needs to vent, it's best to allow the venting and then use the wedge (discussed in Chapter 7) to regain control at an appropriate point in the call.

Learning Application Exercise

1. *Consider the people you identified as Systemizers and Relaters in Chapter 8. List the stress reactions that you have seen each of those people display.*

2. *Identify constructive ways of dealing with/responding to these stress reactions.*

THE STRESSED VALUATOR

People with a Valuator strong suit strive to help other people be perfect. When not stressed, this makes them good mentors and teachers. When feeling stressed, this leads Valuators to see others' imperfections—and point them out—and become critical of others' thinking, values, or opinions. Stressed Valuators see what's wrong, not what's right.

Similar to Systemizers, stressed Valuators use big words, complicated questions, and complicated sentence structures. However, while Systemizers try to be perfect themselves, Valuators aim to identify other people's imperfections or try to help them to be perfect by asking a question that points out the fact that they aren't so perfect after all.

Stressed Valuators can also become "preachy" and try to push their opinions and ideas on other people when they are feeling stressed. Their tone of voice may become demanding or condescending.

Although stressed Valuators are critical of others, they are overly sensitive to negative feedback themselves, even to the point of reading neutral remarks as negative. "How are you today?" may meet with "What do you mean by that?" or "Why? Don't I seem happy to you?" Trust is an issue for Valuators at the best of times; when stressed, they are even more sensitive to causes for distrust. They may become suspicious of friends, coworkers, or family members.

Like Systemizers, stressed Valuators will verbally attack people. These attacks are more likely to focus on opinions, values, morals, or beliefs (whereas Systemizers are more likely to focus on thinking and doing ability). Stressed Valuators have also learned to generalize and personalize the attacks.

Valuators may be prejudiced, but for the "right" reasons. They'll devise rationalizations to justify their prejudices.

Under stress, Valuators may become argumentative, reflecting their need for feedback, even if it is negative, for their beliefs and values. They can argue over anything and everything, and may justify their negativity by saying they are "playing the devil's advocate."

Stressed Valuators often offer unsolicited advice on how others should do their job, raise their children, or run their life.

Example: The Stressed Valuator

Jasmine's supervisory job is frustrating. Her company is doing poorly, and everyone fears for their job, so the environment is chaotic. Jasmine often receives directions that conflict with those of the previous day or even the previous hour. She is suspicious that her boss is intentionally trying to undermine her to make her look bad. She feels she gets no respect for her commitment to the company. Jasmine is very hard on the people who report to her. She is condescending and constantly critical. At the beginning of a staff meeting, when one staff member mentioned casually that his daughter was refusing to go to ballet class, Jasmine lectured him for five minutes in front of the others on the proper way to parent his daughter. The lecture was out of place and so bizarre that the others were glancing at each other in amazement, trying to make sense of her behaviour.

Dealing with the Stressed Valuator Customer

To deal with stressed Valuator customers, use all the positive connecting techniques discussed in Chapter 8, including professionalism, respect, and positive reinforcement for their values and opinions. If they have become angry, allow them to vent.

Even though these customers may be very critical of you, you should never, in words or tone, be critical back, or you may see an increase in the Valuators' stress. Again, the key is to avoid the hook and maintain professional distance. It is often more difficult to do this when attacks are personal. Communicate respect for stressed Valuators, no matter how disrespectfully they may be speaking to you. Throughout the call, demonstrate a sense of urgency and show respect for the customer's concern while presenting a professional, responsible image.

Never try to prove stressed Valuators wrong. Instead, help them make a new decision based on new information, or identify and build on an element of rightness in what they have said (see Chapter 8). If you can identify points of honest agreement with their opinions, do so. If you cannot agree with anything they've said, at least communicate respect for their opinions. Also, ensure that your agreement does not compromise your professional relationship with the Valuator.

Learning Application Exercise

1. *Consider the people you identified as Valuators and Stimulators in Chapter 8. List the stress reactions you have seen each of these people display.*

2. *Identify constructive ways of dealing with/responding to these stress reactions.*

THE STRESSED STIMULATOR

As with every other personality type, the Stimulator's reaction to stress is simply an attempt to get psychological needs met. Stimulators needs playful stimulation and to get a reaction from people—either in a positive way or a negative way. Early stages of stress for Stimulators may involve negative attention-seeking.

In the early stages of stress, Stimulators get confused. They will try hard, but will be unable to understand, as though their brain has simply shut down. An example is the Stimulator child trying to do math homework. The Systemizer father explains it again and again until he starts to get frustrated, while the child, who may usually do well in school, just can't seem to get it. The root of the problem here is the child's need to play before moving to logical thinking.

Stimulators need stimulation! They may work on something with the radio or TV on in the background, while conducting a conversation on the phone. Unlike Systemizers, who get satisfaction from work and the accomplishment of completing it, Stimulators need to have fun before they can work.

Stressed Stimulators can be negative and complaining, and it's always somebody else's fault. They are more interested in finding someone else to blame than they are in trying to solve the problem. They resist being part of the solution, because that makes it harder to blame someone else for the situation. Stimulators see themselves as the heroes of their own story—things will work out for them. They don't feel the need to take action on their own to ensure a positive outcome, leaving it for someone or something else to make it right. And if not, then it certainly isn't the Stimulator's fault!

Stimulators in the early stages of stress may become bored very quickly. This may be interpreted as a short attention span. They have a high energy level and need to be doing and moving, and if they can't, they get bored and then seek negative attention. Again, it is someone else's responsibility to relieve their boredom. You've probably seen this at work or school, when someone constantly complains about the company or the manager or the teacher, but nothing any of these do seems to satisfy the stressed Stimulator.

When stressed and having no playful outlet for this stress, Stimulators may act silly or outrageous in a serious or tense situation. Their tendency to live for the moment often results in Stimulators not anticipating the consequences of their behaviour.

Stimulators are spontaneous, outspoken, and like to get a reaction from people. When stressed, they may suffer from "foot in mouth" disease, in which they speak before considering the ramifications of their comments. And if others are hurt or upset by the comments, Stimulators will blame them for their reaction: "Can't they see I'm just kidding around?"

Stimulators' tendency toward polarized behaviour means their moods are either very up or very down, and neither will be subtle—everyone else will know about it ("Don't talk to me today, I'm in a bad mood"). Similarly, Stimulators either love something or hate it—there is no in-between.

Stressed Stimulators can also shirk their responsibilities: "I need my break time. They shouldn't expect me to stay here to help with this crisis. After all, it's the company's fault they don't have enough staff scheduled."

Example: The Stressed Stimulator

Juanita has her friends thinking she has had a series of supervisors who hate her. She doesn't review the daily updates she receives or otherwise prepare herself to deal well with the problems at work, such as handling difficult customer issues. The consequences are dissatisfied customers and frustrated coworkers who must deal with Juanita's mistakes. Then when she gets a poor performance assessment, it's the supervisor's fault and evidence that the supervisor doesn't like her. Juanita truly believes this, to the extent that she quit her last company to go to a new one where the supervisors wouldn't be against her. She is doing poorly at her new company, which convinces her that her new supervisor has heard from her old company!

Juanita is known to be very moody. She can slip from being very "up" and entertaining to very negative and complaining, at which times she complains to anyone and everyone about the current source of her annoyance. Coworkers are either in her good books, where they can do no wrong, or she hates them. Juanita's tendencies to be spontaneous and complaining, combined with her lack of consideration for the consequences of her behaviour, turn her into a "loose cannon," speaking before ensuring that what she is saying is appropriate. She has been overheard telling customers negative things about managers and even being purposefully rude to customers she has taken a dislike to when she is in one of her "moods."

Dealing with the Stressed Stimulator Customer

To deal with the stressed Stimulator customer, use the techniques discussed in Chapter 8 for connecting with Stimulators.

Resist the temptation to respond to Stimulators' blaming. Avoid, minimize, or defer the blame, and avoid the word "blame": "Let's first get this problem fixed for you, then we can try to sort out what happened in the first place." Not going for the hook may also mean that you don't react to the stressed Stimulator's inappropriate use of humour.

Use subtle humour to tap into the Stimulator's natural ability to see the light side of anything: "My goodness, you've had quite a day!"

THE STRESSED VISUALIZER

When stressed, Visualizers, who have a psychological need for personal space, withdraw and cut off the rest of the world, creating a personal space inappropriately. Stressed Visualizers may start missing work, not meeting or calling friends, or missing social obligations to satisfy their psychological need for solitude. When at work, they may mentally separate from others. They go through the physical motions of a task, but are not driven to finish it and are easily diverted to another, leaving the first incomplete. Stressed Visualizers mentally drift off at meetings or during discussions in order to meet their need for mental space.

Stressed Visualizers are very uncommunicative and unresponsive and resist sharing personal information. They generally avoid interacting with other people.

Example: The Stressed Visualizer

Sandy is a strong suit Visualizer who is generally friendly with coworkers though she rarely lunches with others, preferring to find a corner of the lunchroom by herself to read while she eats. She enjoyed the travel that was a big part of her work, even though it kept her from her young family at least two or three days each week. On these travel days, Sandy appreciated the personal time spent driving with the radio off and spending evenings by herself in a hotel room. These opportunities for personal space met Sandy's psychological need for solitude, allowing her to be flexible and effective in her interactions with customers.

Then Sandy was promoted, and problems started to appear. In her new job, she doesn't travel and is required to interact with people all day long. Sandy's need for solitude is no longer satisfied by her job, and she has started to create her own personal space. She has withdrawn from her family and spends time by herself at home—her husband thinks she is angry with him about something. She misses important meetings only to be discovered in her office working alone. She has begun to miss work with a variety of illnesses that require her to be alone in her home, in her room. With the travel—her source of psychological need satisfaction—gone, and nothing to replace it, Sandy is showing symptoms of Visualizer stress.

Dealing with the Stressed Visualizer Customer

Dealing with stressed Visualizer customers requires adjusting your style as described in Chapter 8. With these customers, it is necessary to take control of the conversation and the problem-solving process. Be specific with questions and instructions. Keep calls short, and collect and give only the information you need to resolve the customer's issue.

Lower your energy level so Visualizers don't feel overwhelmed. As much as possible, respect their need for personal space—do not try to get them to open up.

Ideally, follow-up with stressed Visualizers will be in the form of fax or e-mail, rather than a phone call, which is a more personal interaction.

Expect that interactions with these customers may be slower paced and take longer. Try not to get impatient with the pace.

THE STRESSED ACTIVATOR

Activators who are not getting their action needs met may experience stress. Their need for action can cause Activators to be impatient and to act impulsively—action for the sake of action, with little regard for whether it is appropriate. The negative consequences of these actions can cause them to feel cornered, and the only way they can see out of it is through manipulation, either by bending or breaking the rules themselves or trying to persuade others to do so.

Stressed Activators feel blameless when they are being manipulative or are experiencing the consequences of their risk-taking. A symptom of this is their use of "you" or "it" when they mean "I": "You know what it's like when you're just about to close a deal, when you've got them eating right out of your hand. You know the rush that gives you?" when they mean "Do I ever like the feeling when a deal is about to close!"

Their need for risk and action may cause stressed Activators to do things in which they run a risk of being caught, failing, losing, or being found out. Stressed Activators may take risks that expose them to a big "downside" with little chance of an "upside." The psychological need for the adrenaline "rush" the risk gives them prevents them from reasonably assessing the appropriateness of the gamble (for example, gambling with this month's rent money).

In an office environment, the action-deprived Activator may set up inter-staff conflicts to get others fighting. Activators may lose some of their natural flexibility and charm when stressed, and their tendency to be direct and to tell others what to do may be even more obvious. Coworkers may find these employees offensive, bossy, or pushy.

Activators tend to be "I can take care of myself" sorts of people. When stressed, they may expect the same of others and will not provide sufficient instructions when assigning a task, expecting subordinates to fend for themselves and "land on their own two feet."

Example: The Stressed Activator

Carlos is the co-owner of a small company. He loves to "wheel 'n' deal," and he has been responsible for bringing in most of the company's larger clients. Although Carlos owns the largest portion of the company, his partner, Frank, who is responsible for ongoing operations, insists Carlos should focus on selling and even prefers that Carlos stay away from the office. With Carlos' shoot-from-the-hip, action-focused style, he tends to create a whirlwind when he's in the office, in effect uprooting and scrambling everyone.

Today is Friday. It's the low season for business, and deals have been rare. Carlos is feeling a little restless. He has made all the connections he can for this week. There's nothing more he can do but wait—but Carlos hates waiting. So, he decides to spend the day in his office getting caught up with telephone calls. As he sits down to his desk he remembers, "That darn administration manager was supposed to get me a direct line—I'll just whip down to her office and find out where it is." On his way, Carlos passes through client services and order processing (both of whom report to the administration manager, Su Mei). Several employees are standing together talking. They don't look like they're working.

Carlos is a little stressed because of the current lack of action, so diplomacy takes a back seat to action and directness. He slams his hand down on a desk and bellows, "Doesn't anybody work here anymore? Get back to work!" The administration manager is standing in the door of her office when Carlos arrives. Once inside her office, she says, "Carlos, just because people are talking doesn't mean they aren't working. No wonder some of the staff are afraid of you." Carlos responds with, "Maybe they should be a little afraid of me. And, while I'm here, where's my private line?" On the way back to his office, Carlos wonders, "What's wrong with Su Mei today? I'll ask Frank what he thinks her problem is."

Dealing with the Stressed Activator Customer

In dealing with stressed Activators apply all the Activator connecting techniques discussed in Chapter 8. You can ease the stress reaction by presenting yourself as action-oriented, emulating the customer's own style and even using some of the expressions the customer uses. It is critical to appear confident and good at what you do, offering Activators "respect among equals."

As a call centre rep, it is usually not appropriate to create an incident that will meet the Activator's need for action. Often, the most you can do is to protect yourself from manipulation.

Stressed Activators may try to persuade you to bend or break the rules because of the their "unique" circumstances and only "this one time." They may use words in a convincing way to make their position appear reasonable. During these manipulations, Activators feel superior.

It is important to know what you can and cannot do. Often, paraphrasing the customer's request will help you put it into perspective so you can establish whether it falls in or out of your "can do" area.

When dealing with a stressed Activator who is not providing adequate information, ask questions to get what you need. Be direct, focused, and confident in your questioning.

Learning Application Exercise

1. Consider the people you identified as Visualizers and Activators in Chapter 8. List the stress reactions that you have seen each of these people display.

2. Identify constructive ways of dealing with/responding to these stress reactions.

Protecting Yourself from Stress

If you do not take care of yourself first, you may be unable to take care of customers. Since stress can make us less effective with customers, it is important to manage ourselves so as to minimize our reaction to the stressors in our environment. We do this by consciously arranging to take care of our own psychological needs, those needs associated with our strong suits (see Table 9.1). When these are taken care of, we are less susceptible to stressors and are better able to take care of customers' psychological needs so they, in turn, are less stressed. While many people unconsciously take care of these psychological needs, if you are aware of your needs you can better ensure that they are satisfied. Your resistance to stress is assured rather than a "hit and miss" proposition.

TABLE 9.2

Personality Types: Summary

Everyone has some of each, but one or two will dominate.

	Relater	**Systemizer**	**Valuator**
Characteristics	– caring, warm, nurturing – wants to please others, feels responsible for others' feelings – likes people and to be around others – home and work environment important	– analytical, logical, organized – ideas, thoughts, and achievements are very important – orderliness important at home and work – strives for perfection	– strong personal values, opinions – will commit self to something believed in – loves to teach, mentor, coach others
Psychological needs	– to feel appreciated by others – sensory pampering	– positive feedback on thoughts, ideas, and accomplishments – time structure	– positive feedback on thoughts, ideas, accomplishments, opinions, and values
Cues	– "I feel ... appreciate ... share ... care ... comfortable ... special" – personalizes conversations – soft, nurturing tone	– "I think ... does that mean ... logical ... realistic ... practical ... sensible ... facts ... options ... makes sense" – uses numbers and time frames	– "In my opinion ... trust ... investment ... fair ... value ... I believe ... dependability ... quality ... appropriate ... integrity ... right/wrong" – talks politics and current events
How to connect	– empathize, soft tone – remember personal info – use feeling words and expressions	– be organized, provide detail and information – ask for input, provide positive feedback – find points of agreement regarding ideas	– respect values and opinions – demonstrate personal integrity – find points of agreement regarding opinions and ideas
Stress	– unassertive, raises voice at end of statement – "You know" or "eh" at the end of each sentence, tries to please – over-accommodating and over-apologetic – makes mistakes, feels confused or overwhelmed, self-deprecating – emotional, upset, teary	– uses big words – uses complex sentence structures with qualifying words and clauses – strives to be perfect, over-detailed, gives unnecessary specifics – overly concerned with time waste and use, workaholic – anger with those who don't think clearly or do their jobs well – verbally attacks, over-controls, shows frustration – impatient – personalizes and generalizes attacks	– uses big words – uses excessive and complex questions – accusing, negative, picky – pushes beliefs and opinions – critical, verbally attacks – overly sensitive to negative feedback – argumentative – personalizes and generalizes attacks

TABLE 9.2

Personality Types: Summary (continued)

	Stimulator	Visualizer	Activator
How to handle	− empathize, nurture, soften tone, legitimize feelings, encourage − help to see light at end of tunnel	− allow venting, keep cool − provide time frames, sound responsible and organized − focus on specifics	− be honest, consistent − connect with values and opinions − demonstrate that concern is important − allow venting, keep cool − show respect, don't criticize
Characteristics	− lives for today − animated − play now, work later	− introspective, imaginative, quiet, enjoys being alone − not interested in appearance of self, home, or workstation − good with hands at repetitive tasks, looks to others for direction	− charming, adaptable, quick to make a decision − likes expensive and showy jewellery and clothing − very direct, loves to negotiate a deal
Psychological needs	− fun − play	− personal space − solitude	− action, doing − risk
Cues	− "I like ... dislike ... want ... don't want ... fun ... hoot ... blast" − talks of fun activities − uses lots of inflection − is playful and humorous	− terse, monotone voice − may speak slowly or sound tired or distracted − may need to be prompted to speak or provide information	− uses slang − has high energy and enthusiasm − uses superlatives: "fantastic," "tremendous"
How to connect	− be playful, don't take work or self too seriously − recognize when they are kidding	− speak slowly − be specific, direct − minimize rapport-building − allow space	− be direct, avoid excessive detail − seem action-oriented − exhibit assertiveness and control of what you are doing
Stress	− doesn't ask or answer questions directly: "huh?" "I don't know" − fidgety, inappropriate use of humour − complaining and negative − blames others − shirks responsibility	− extra quiet, uninvolved − passive, avoids interaction, withdrawn − mind wanders − feels shy	− uses "you" or "it" instead of "I" − runs ahead of conversation, impatient with talk − pushes to move to action − manipulates others − blameless, ignores or breaks rules, impulsive − expects others to fend for themselves, takes unnecessary risks − tries to get others to ignore/break rules
How to handle	− allow venting, keep cool − avoid issue of blame − use low-key humour	− take control, be specific with instructions − "flatten" style − be direct, give space	− maintain control − appear action-oriented

Learning Application Exercise

1. What is your dominant personality type?

2. What psychological needs are associated with your dominant personality type?

3. What can you do to satisfy your psychological needs? What do you currently do? What could you do?

4. What stress reaction of another personality type is your strongest "hot button"—the one most likely to get a reaction from you? Why do you think that is?

5. How do you (or your friends, family, or coworkers) know when you are feeling the effects of stress?

6. How does your level of stress affect the quality of your customer service?

7. How does stress change the way you interact with people?

8. What can you do to help yourself cope when you start to feel the effects of stress?

Summary

Each of the six personality types has its own unique way of "being" in the world. Each type has its own psychological needs—needs that, when unmet, may cause people to act in negative ways.

It is important to recognize that, as customer service professionals, we cannot make someone "unstressed," much as we'd like to. What we can do, however, is appreciate the stress reaction for what it is and respond with understanding. We can learn how to recognize the signs of stress in order to deal with customers effectively. At a minimum, we must learn not to take a customer's difficult behaviour personally, but to professionally distance ourselves from this behaviour, redirecting the customer back to the point of his or her call.

We must deal with our own stress to be able to handle others' stress reactions appropriately. Knowing your personality type and psychological needs can help you recognize the sources of stress in your life. When you meet your psychological needs, you are less likely to experience stress and you will know better how to deal with it when it occurs.

CHAPTER 10
Telephone Sales

Learning Outcomes

After successfully completing Chapter 10, you will be able to:

- Discuss the role of sales in the call centre.

- Describe why believing in your product or service is key to effectiveness in sales.

- Adapt the right attitude for sales.

- Execute the six steps of the selling process.

- Apply the techniques for making successful outbound calls.

- Implement the eight tips for success in sales.

The Role of Sales in the Call Centre

Traditionally, in call centres that have both customer service and **sales** functions, telephone sales is a separate department or at least a separate group within the call centre. Call centre staff either sell or they don't, and customer service staff usually put themselves in the "don't" category. Telephone customer service is seen as very different from telephone sales. Customer service is more often viewed as a cost centre, sales as a profit centre.

An example of this attitude was encountered by a consultant who was dealing with a company that was considering either creating a separate sales function within its call centre or introducing a sales element to the customer service role. Each of the customer service reps the consultant spoke to about this potential change was very adamant in protesting "I don't sell!" These reps implicitly yet forcefully warned the consultant not to even try to recommend this change. A few staff members even admitted they were thinking of quitting their jobs simply because of the rumour that the customer service representatives might be forced to sell.

The perception that selling is very different from customer service, with customer service somehow being the nobler or "nicer" of the two, is all too common among call centre customer service staff. Yet telephone sales staff consider themselves to be "nice" people and don't see that as being at odds with their selling role. In fact, being a nice person is a positive influence on one's success in the telephone sales role. Relationship building with the customer is at least as critical in the telephone sales role as it is in customer service.

Yet the perception persists that sales and customer service are incompatible, as if being better in one means you are less effective in the other. In Figure 10.1a, the continuum shows how it is perceived that more sales-oriented people are less service-oriented, and vice versa. Instead, sales and customer service should be considered to exist on separate dimensions, as seen in Figure 10.1b. As this figure shows, a rep can be good in one and not the other (points X and Y), good in both (point Z) or good at neither (point W).

Figure 10.1a

It is commonly believed that being too sales-oriented means customer service will necessarily suffer, and vice versa, because of an incorrect belief that they exist as a single-dimensional continuum.

Figure 10.1b

Instead, customer service and sales should be thought of as existing on separate dimensions. A person can be good at one or the other (X or Y), both (Z), or neither (W).

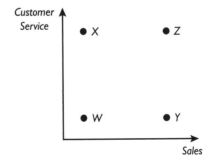

The weighting of sales and customer service skills required of the salesperson varies depending on the following factors:

- Type of customer. Who is the salesperson selling to? For example, is the customer a small business owner, a homeowner, a buyer for a large organization, a retired person, or a young parent?

- Type of product or service. Is this a "big ticket" item or a regularly purchased small-value item? An emotional purchase item or one that is subject to a more rational decision? A commonly understood product or service or an unusual or complex one? A single product or a "solution" involving numerous products and services?

- Company's relationship with the customer. Does the customer currently buy this product from this company, buy other products or services from this company, or deal with a competitor? Will the customer know about the company and its products? Is the ongoing relationship with the company more critical than the individual sale?

- Rep's relationship with the customer. Will the rep have spoken with this customer before? Does the rep deal with the customer on other issues or for other products?

- Nature of the contact. Does the customer call the company to express interest in this product, to purchase another product, or because of a question or problem? Does the rep call the customer to offer a product or service based on his or her status as a valued customer, because this customer has stopped purchasing from the company, or because the customer is a likely user with a potential need for the product or service?

- Nature of the sale. Is the rep looking to introduce the customer to an additional product or service that will likely be of interest due to other products she or he has ordered? Is this a long **sell cycle** during which the rep will make numerous contacts with the customer, or is this expected to be a one-call close? Is the rep calling to arrange an appointment with a sales representative, selling the product, or simply trying to build awareness? Is this a **hard sell** (in which the salesperson applies techniques to encourage a buy decision now) or a **suggestive** or **soft sell** (encouraging the person to buy but using low pressure for a decision now)? Is this a **relationship sell** (in which the relationship with the company is of the highest importance and must be maintained whether there is a sale or not) or a **"one-shot" sale** (the company is unlikely to be calling back and does not intend an ongoing relationship, so this call needs to work)? Is the company **"cherry-picking"** (looking to identify customers with a perceived need for its product or service) or helping to create the customer's awareness of his or her need?

Telephone sales, then, is multidimensional. With all of these factors affecting the sales role, no two call centre sales roles will be exactly the same. Also, because of the many dimensions, "sales" may not always look like what we traditionally think of as selling.

Selling can be defined as "that which positively influences the decision to exchange property or services for money or other valuable consideration." By this definition, everyone in the organization has some role in sales. Those who directly or personally interact with the customer have the largest potential for affecting individual buying decisions. Every time a call centre representative interacts with a customer, she or he is influencing the customer's attitude toward the organization and the customer's decision to buy or to buy again. So every contact is at least a "passive" sales call and potentially an "active" sales call. At the very least, the call centre rep should have a positive effect on the customer's attitude toward the company, a form of passive selling.

Furthermore, many companies are coming to believe that call centre reps, no matter what their job title, should assume responsibility for influencing the customer's buying decisions. Consequently, all reps need a basic understanding of the role of sales in their job and the skills that influence sales within the confines of their particular telephone role. If the call centre rep is not also a salesperson for his or her organization, the organization misses numerous sales opportunities every day from that rep alone. These missed or ignored opportunities may occur in companies who, at the same time, spend significant amounts of money on a designated sales staff. Many companies waste hundreds of sales opportunities every day by not preparing all their customer contact staff to adopt a sales consciousness and to develop their sales skills.

Those call centre representatives who develop their sales capability enhance their value to their organization and significantly increase their marketable skills. Every call centre representative, whether or not the job title includes the word "sales," needs to understand telephone selling.

Basics of Effective Telephone Sales

Success in sales results from a combination of attitude and skills. A positive sales attitude begins with a belief in the company's product or service.

BELIEF IN THE PRODUCT OR SERVICE

The "natural" salesperson is very rare. This is the person who can sell anything to anybody anytime. Most of us do not fall into this category. For most of us, effectiveness in the sales role requires that we believe in our company's product or service.

ON THE JOB

"I Don't Sell"

A woman being interviewed for a telephone sales role saw herself as a people person who enjoyed interpersonal interactions, but was adamant that she was not a salesperson.

During the course of the interview, the woman demonstrated remarkable interpersonal skills and became increasingly enthusiastic as the company's services and values were explained to her. She asked very astute questions to enhance her understanding of the company and verbally presented herself very well. At the end of the conversation, she again repeated her conviction that she did not sell.

She got the job, and the job title of Customer Service Coordinator, with no mention of the word "sales" with relation to her job function. Her job, it was explained, was to call companies who might have a need for her employer's services, introduce herself, explore whether or not the services she could offer might be a fit for them, and, if so, set up an appointment for them to meet with a consultant. Her supervisor believed that she had the skills to be effective in the job and that she was able to personally buy into the company's services to such an extent that she could infect the customers with her excitement. She didn't have to "sell," merely to be an advocate of what her company could offer to customers.

If you truly believe in the product or service your organization offers its customers, you want to share it with others and you become an enthusiastic advocate for your organization's products. This is the core ingredient for success in sales.

To become a believer in your company's products or services, you must

- Know your product's/service's features and benefits.

- Know what benefits are relevant to which types of customers.

- Believe in your product/service over the alternatives.

Features are attributes of the product. Benefits are what the customer gains from the features. People buy the benefits of a product or service, not its features. A feature of a product might be its high-quality casing that is vacuum-sealed. A benefit to customers may be that the product will require less maintenance, and this will save them money over the life of the product.

Some benefits mean different things to different people. For example, money saved may represent to one customer the security of knowing that there will be one less drain on future cash flow. Another customer may value the things that can be bought with that extra money. Before a product's features are meaningful to customers, they must translate the features into their corresponding benefits or values. We are better able to believe in our product or service if we can view it in terms of these benefits and values to the customer. Viewing the product or service from the customer's perspective, and getting excited about what that product or service can do for the customer, is the first big step toward effectiveness in telephone sales.

Know what benefits are relevant to which types of customers. As well, be aware that the features and benefits that might excite you if you were the customer won't necessarily appeal to every customer.

Each benefit does not equally appeal to every customer. The fact that a product will save time is less relevant to customers who enjoy the time spent using the product or have few other demands on their time (for example, the retired person who enjoys puttering around in the garden may not see a benefit in the time-saving feature of a lawncare service). If you understand the range of benefits your product provides and then identify which ones apply to a specific customer, you will be more inclined to encourage the customer to buy.

The only way to determine which (if any) benefits of your product appeal to a specific customer is to care enough to ask questions. If you don't ask the questions and don't identify which product benefits will address that customer's needs, then you may be denying the customer an opportunity to benefit from your product. Selling is an extension of good service. Failing to sell is poor service.

You must also believe your product is better than the alternatives, which include doing nothing, buying from a competitor, or meeting the customer need in some other manner (for example, alternatives to buying your company's bicycle include buying no bicycle and continuing to travel on foot, buying a competitor's bicycle, or buying a bus pass). If you believe there is an alternative to your product that is better for a client, you will not feel comfortable advocating your product to the customer. If, however, you feel that your product is best for the customer, then you will feel you are doing the customer a disservice if you do not offer your product.

Learning Application Exercise

1. *For a product or service offered by your company or school, develop a list of features with corresponding benefits and, as appropriate, values.*

2. *Determine which benefits fit which customer situations. Review your list with a peer.*

The Selling Process

Selling is not magic—it is a set of skills that can be learned. Some of these skills are the same as those necessary for effective customer service. These, in fact, are the more complex of the selling skills and the more difficult to acquire. Skills that are more closely associated with selling, such as closing the sale and handling objections, are simply sets of techniques that become easier with practice.

There are six basic steps in the selling process:

1. building rapport
2. questioning
3. confirming understanding of the need
4. closing: asking for the sale
5. handling objections
6. ending the sale: moving to the next sale

1. BUILDING RAPPORT

Customers are much more likely to buy from someone with whom they feel comfortable. The decision to buy something can be stressful: it typically involves spending money (which is stressful for many of us), it involves making a decision (what if it is the wrong or less than the best decision?), and it involves change (most of us aren't good with change). If customers feel comfortable with us, they feel less stress in making the buy decision, and if we know the buy decision is in customers' best interest, then we will want to help them overcome that stress and make that decision. Connecting and rapport building involve numerous skills (as discussed in Chapters 1 to 9 of this book), skills that are as critical to success in sales as they are to success in the customer service role and in virtually any call centre role.

2. QUESTIONING

To be able to sell, the rep needs to understand which benefits of the product or service are a fit for the customer. While, in some cases, customers may volunteer information that makes their needs obvious, in most cases the rep must question customers to understand these needs. Questioning uncovers, explores, and confirms sales opportunities. And, while collecting needed information, the rep also enhances the relationship with the customer by showing interest in the customer's situation.

The questions must have a direction. Each question should take the rep a step closer to understanding how the customer can benefit from the product or service. Ideally, the rep should have a mental picture of the various customer situations that represent sales opportunities, situations that might indicate a customer need for the product or service. For example, if the rep wants to explore whether a customer would benefit from a laptop computer, he or she would, before the call, create a list of the possible customer situations for which this product might be appropriate, including customers who need to use their computer at several locations.

The rep then plans questions that will determine which potential need is relevant for this particular customer. Initially, it is best to create a checklist of the potential opportunities associated with each product, along with questions that are scripted for easy reference to guide the rep in the process. In our laptop example, one question might be: "Do you ever encounter the situation, say while waiting at an airport or at your cottage, when you would like to be able to access your computer, but none is available?"

Note that this question is "closed" to confirm whether there is an opportunity or a customer need that the product benefits might satisfy. Questions can also be open-ended to encourage the customer to provide information that might identify a need: "People use their computers in different ways, and their lifestyle or how they work can affect what computer system will be best for them. Will you talk to me about your working style—when, how, and where you like to get your work done?"

Be aware that asking too many closed questions can make customers feel like they are being interrogated. A mix is usually best: open-ended questions are often used to get the information into the open, while closed questions are used to confirm that the customer has a specific need.

Questions should be clearly structured so as not to sound vague or ambiguous. Questions that are vague can give the impression to the customer that you are asking questions for no better purpose than to hear yourself talk, that you don't know what you are doing. Questions like "How's the widgit business these days?" is unfocused, whereas "Mr. James, how has this recent surge in offshore widget imports affected your pricing?" sounds like you know what you're talking about and also focuses the customer on confirming the problem of tighter profit margins, opening the benefit of your cost-cutting solution.

Questions should not appear self-serving or intrusive. Our purpose in questioning is to determine whether the customer has a need that one of the benefits of our product or service can satisfy. Our purpose is to help the customer. Therefore, we don't want to undermine ourselves by giving the impression that we want to sell regardless of the customer's needs or that we are insensitive to these needs. We appear self-serving or intrusive when we ask for information that may be perceived as confidential or personal without first establishing credibility, or showing the customer that we have her or his interests at heart. To prematurely ask personal questions can reverse the positive effect we intend. When you want to ask a question that may be perceived as personal, your tone of voice must show concern for the customer or at least be matter-of-fact (implying that your request is nothing out of the ordinary) rather than apologetic or manipulative. Asking for permission—"May I ask…"—can make your questioning less intrusive.

The questions must be answerable by the customer. "What are your company's strategic plans for the new millennium?" may not be a question the office supplies coordinator can answer. Instead, you might ask, "What have you seen that might indicate a change in the nature of office supplies you will be needing over the next year or two?" If you suspect your questions may be outside the person's scope, soften it, legitimize the fact that the customer might not have the information. Words like "What's your sense/take/feeling…," "ballpark," and "approximately/roughly" are useful to show customers you neither expect nor need the specifics—and if they do happen to have the specifics, that make them feel positive that they have surpassed your expectations.

Questioning should not be interspersed with closing attempts. In most types of selling, if we ask a question, get a little information, and then attempt to close the sale, customers will view our questions as self-serving and be less inclined to offer information. If, instead, we ask a series of questions and collect all our information before closing, we are more likely to be successful. For example, suppose you were attempting to sell computer training and one of your first questions was "What computer training do you currently offer your staff?" to which the customer responded "None." A natural inclination might be to explain the types of training your company offers and ask the customer to identify what he or she would like. This would be mixing the closing phase in with the information-collecting phase and is less likely to be successful. Instead, ask more exploratory questions to help you and the customer to more clearly identify the need. Your questions may include "What software do your employees currently use?" "Are all of your employees equally proficient in each of these software packages?" "Would you say that some people take longer to do the same piece of work because they are less proficient with a particular software package?" "Roughly how long does it take your newer staff to reach full proficiency with your software?" "How do they currently increase their skill level with the software?" and "Do you have the sense that there are some more sophisticated things your staff could be doing with the software you currently use?" Then, once you have a fuller understanding of the need and can fit those product benefits to the need, and you have increased the customer's awareness of this need, then you can proceed with the selling process with more likelihood of success.

Learning Application Exercise

1. *Create a list of questions that can open or explore opportunities associated with the product or service you identified in the previous exercise.*

2. *Review this list with a peer, giving each other input on your questions.*

3. CONFIRMING UNDERSTANDING OF THE NEED

After collecting customer information and assessing the customer's needs, effective telephone salespeople will confirm their understanding of the customer's situation rather than move immediately to close the sale. This is typically done by summarizing those elements of information the customer has provided that constitute needs for which the company's product or service can offer a benefit. Introduce the confirming step with a statement such as, "Then, if I understand your situation correctly...." or "So, basically, your situation is this...." Then offer your summary.

Summarizing or paraphrasing shows customers that you have listened and that you understand their situation, which will build trust and increase the likelihood of acceptance of your recommended solution. Ask customers to confirm your interpretation of their situation. If the customer doesn't agree with your summary, you can clarify your understanding before you close and thus avoid an objection later. If the customer agrees with your summary, the groundwork has been laid for a successful close.

Confirming is more effective when it is based on notes you have taken, since this allows you to provide more specifics. It is also beneficial to use reflective phrases such as "You said that...," or "You indicated that...," "As you said...," or "I believe you mentioned...," along with the specific expression or words used by the customer. This is a lot easier to do if you have effectively diagrammed the call (see Chapter 6), including the customer's needs and expressions.

When you outline your points, phrase them in such a way that the link with your product benefit is clear. If, for example, you work for a temporary help agency, you might include in your summary: "You suggested that, with your three key design people all married to people in the education field, March break is a yearly 'bone of contention' for vacation scheduling. You'd love to be able to let them all have the same week, but none of your other staff have the expertise to cover for them. Have I understood that correctly?"

4. CLOSING: ASKING FOR THE SALE

If the rep has done the first three steps in the selling process effectively, the rest of the sales process should flow smoothly. By this point, the customer will feel comfortable with the rep, trust that the rep has the customer's best interests at heart, know that the rep understands the customer's situation, and recognize that he or she has a need. The next step is logical—offering to fulfill that need by asking for the sale.

Many reps do poorly at **closing**. They do all the other steps well, then fail to ask for the business. They feel that asking for the sale may ruin the relationship with the customer or make the earlier steps seem insincere and manipulative. The "I don't sell" reps are usually fine with steps 1 to 3, but break down at step 4, the close. Even with dedicated telephone sales teams, a consistent manager complaint is "They need to close more." In many telephone sales calls, the rep completes call after call without once asking for the business. The rep only sells at all because some customers ask to buy! Reps don't close for a number of reasons:

- They don't want to seem pushy or intrusive. If you truly believe in your product or service and you have confirmed that it is a fit for the customer's needs, then you are doing the customer a disservice if you don't close. The close itself is not pushy. It is merely the impetus for the customer to move from a state in which they don't have but could use your product or service to one in which they have and can benefit from it. If the customer does react to your close like you are being too pushy, simply apologize: "I'm sorry. I didn't mean to rush you into a decision." Then reconfirm your understanding of the situation, question to understand the reason for the customer's discomfort (uncover the hidden objection), and describe the reason behind your enthusiasm: "It's just that I see this product as such a perfect solution in your situation."

- They don't know when to close. When reps are unsure about when to close, they often wait too long, so the customer almost has to say, "So can I buy one?" By waiting too long, you add unnecessarily to average call-handling time, you risk the customer losing interest, you communicate a lack of confidence in your product or service and its utility to this client, and you expose yourself to seeming less than proficient in your role, which can undermine the customer's trust in you.

  It is appropriate to close once customers have shown that they can see value in your product or service, when they understand how it will benefit them. Customers may have reached this point before calling a company, and the rep may simply be taking their orders. Or, customers may have had no intention to buy at the beginning of the call, but during the call they have recognized a needed benefit of the product or service. Buying signals, or cues that customers can see value for them in the product or service, include the following:

  - The customer agrees with the rep's summary of the customer's needs.

  - The customer acknowledges that a benefit the rep has identified is relevant to his or her needs.

  - The customer confirms that the rep has overcome her or his objection.

  - The customer offers an objection that is based on a misunderstanding about the company, product, or service, or expresses skepticism that what the rep has said is true. Both these types of objection are easily overcome and easily turned into a close.

  - The customer accepts the rep's **trial close** (see below).

- They fear rejection. When reps believe in their product or service, when they believe that it will benefit the customer, when they have built a relationship with the customer and shown them that they understand the customer's needs, and when they have then asked for the sale only to have the customer say "No," most tend to take it personally. Reps take it personally because they have made it personal— they genuinely have the customer's best interest at heart. So when the customer says no, the reps feel the customer is rejecting them, and that can undermine the reps' positive attitude. Often, for those who are new to selling, the sales process stops there and they back out of the call quietly. Hearing "no" can also cause reps to be less inclined to close with the next customer, because they do not like that feeling of rejection.

To overcome this problem, it is important to understand that

- There are many reasons a customer might say no to a close (we'll discuss some later in this chapter), and it is rare that the customer is rejecting the rep personally.

- A healthier mindset to adopt when customers say no is to feel bad for the customers—they have opted not to buy something that would have been in their best interest to buy, they have missed out on an opportunity (if you truly believe in your product or service, this mindset comes easily).

- No salesperson has 100 percent success. A percentage of customers will not accept the opportunity you present. It's a numbers game—track the percentage of your calls that result in sales, and learn to expect that the larger percentage of people will not buy. Knowing your "close rate" helps you to put the rejection into perspective and move on. As one seasoned sales rep put it, "If I know five out of six will say no, then each no moves me one call closer to the yes— so the more no's I hear the more motivated I get!"

- They don't know how to close. As mentioned earlier, the decision to buy can be stressful for customers. The effective close aims to reduce that stress and make the buy decision easier for the customers (usually by avoiding a "Yes I will buy or "No I won't" decision).

Customers are more likely to say no because that causes the least disruption in their lives. Our objective in closing is to help minimize this stress while helping customers acquire a product or service that we feel is in their best interest. That is *why* we close. The next section will address *how*.

Types of Close

There are many types of close—here are a few of the more common ones.

Trial Close

This is not a close in the true sense of the word because it does not ask for the sale, but it is particularly useful for assessing the customer's readiness to close. The trial close sets up the true close. The trial close can

- Test the customer's reaction to your summary, your benefit offer, or your recommendation, or confirm what you think was a buying signal: "How does that sound to you, Mrs. Schmidt?"

- Gain buyer commitment to buy if certain conditions are met. "If I can prove to you/convince you/show you how to … then would you buy?" If the customer says yes, then you can meet the condition and close.

- Uncover a buyer objection. If customers respond negatively to your trial close, you know there is something holding them back. You can question to uncover the objection—a surprised "Oh?" followed by "May I ask why not?" "Is there something you are uncomfortable with here?" or "Have I missed something important to you?" encourages the customer to express his or her objection. The worst kind of objection is one that is unstated. It interferes with the buy decision, you have no chance of overcoming it, and it prevents customers from making a buy decision that is in their best interest.

- Confirm a "true" objection. The trial close is also useful for identifying a true objection as opposed to a "smoke screen" objection. Sometimes customers offer an objection they think will let you down easy rather than tell you the truth, or they want to save face so they give you an objection that protects them. "I don't have the budget for it this year" may be a cover for "I'm not convinced there is enough benefit for me to justify the expenditure" or "I don't have the authority." To use the trial close here ask, "If it weren't for that objection, then would you buy?"

- Turn an objection into a buying signal. This is most effective when the customer objects based on a misunderstanding or skepticism that you know you can overcome. For example, suppose the customer says, "I need it in red, and all you have is blue and green." If you can get the item in red and the customer is just unaware of this, then the objection is based on a misunderstanding. You might say, "If I can find you one in red, do we have a deal?" Or the customer might be skeptical: "I don't see how you can provide the quality I expect at the price you've quoted me." If you have facts to back up your claims, you might say, "If I can prove to you that the quality is exactly what you need for the price I've quoted, do we have a deal?"

- Create a transition or turning point in the conversation. This can happen when customers have called with a problem that you have resolved to their satisfaction and you then want to close this part of the interaction and move to a sell. When you are talking to a newly pleased customer, you have a perfect sell opportunity. You might say, "Ms. McGowan, are you satisfied with this solution?" or "Can we anticipate that you'll continue to be a customer of ABC Widgets?" then, "If I can show you a way to save some money on your next order, to decrease your costs even further while ensuring the same quality product you currently use, would you be interested in discussing it with me?"

Assumptive Close

The purpose of the **assumptive close** is to reduce the stress caused when the customer must make a yes or no decision by assuming that the yes decision has already been made and simply deciding on the details. Instead of having to decide on whether to make the purchase, the customer just has to agree on the model that best meets his or her needs or the method of payment. For example: "We've discussed a few models. Are you still convinced that the 27G is the best for your needs?" or "On which account would you prefer us to set up the monthly withdrawal?"

The assumptive close simply makes the right decision easier. It does not coerce customers into a decision they don't want. If customers do not want to buy, they can simply say so during any close.

Contained Choice Close

The **contained choice close** is a variation of the assumptive close that makes it even easier for the customer, who simply selects one of the offered choices to complete the sale. As with the assumptive close, the decision to buy is implicit: "Would you like model 27G, or do you think the 58G is better for you, taking into account your potential future expansion?" or "Would you prefer the monthly withdrawal to be from your chequing account or applied monthly to your credit card?"

When you believe customers are leaning toward a specific choice, do not offer that choice and something less as the options, or they may take the lesser choice and not meet their needs as effectively. For example, if a customer is leaning toward a $50 per month investment in a savings plan, avoid saying "Would you like to start at $50 per month or $35?" Most will take the lesser amount. Instead, say, "Would you like to start at $50 per month, or do you want to try $75 and see how that works for you?"

ON THE JOB

Example of an Ineffective Close

A telephone sales department's calls were assessed to determine how sales could be improved. This department was part of a large retail chain that sold extended maintenance agreements. When the regular warranty on a product was about to expire, the sales reps called customers to offer an extension. When the extension was about to run out, they called to sell a further extension, essentially offering customers insurance against high or unexpected repair costs. These maintenance agreements were a large volume business for the company.

*The analysis of the calls uncovered many opportunities for improvement, but one minor adjustment promised a bigger impact on the department's income than all the other improvements combined. The department sold one- and two-year maintenance agreements. The two-year agreement cost twice as much as the one-year agreement, but protected buyers against a yearly increase in price and saved them having to make the decision again in a year. The department wanted to sell two-year agreements rather than one-year, but the reps' close was a contained choice: "Will that be one year or two?" Then, when the customer automatically chose one year, the reps were in the difficult position of having to **up-sell**. By changing the close to focus on the two-year agreement with a contained choice of payment methods, the company was able to increase the dollar value of each call, significantly improving income and profitability as the overwhelming number of customers chose the two-year option. The one-year option was used as a backup.*

Summary Close

The **summary close** works well in situations where you have identified a number of customer needs to which you can match benefits. Effectively diagramming the call (see

Chapter 6) makes the summary close even more powerful. With this close, you confirm the customer's needs (reflective phrasing helps ensure the customer "owns" this list), then you match the benefits of your recommended solution to this list of needs. For example:

> *Mr. Zwarych, you've told me you want a mobile phone that is simple to use, does not have a "whole bunch of features you can't figure out and will never use," and that is not going to cost you more to use than your current "line-based" phone. You also estimate that you spend no more than an hour a month on the phone in total. Is that correct?…In that case, I recommend our Alpha Plan. It comes with the Zignoid phone, which has all the features you requested. The monthly fee for this plan is only $25, including the phone, which is roughly equal to the cost of your current home line when you include the voice-mail feature. This fee gives you 100 free minutes of call time per month, which will allow for those months that do go a little higher than the 60-minute average. If you have a credit card handy, I can set that up for you right now, and you'll have your new phone within three business days.*

Puppy Dog or No Risk Close

Suppose a salesperson wants to sell you a puppy. You are having trouble making the decision whether to buy the dog or not. She offers to give you the dog for two weeks and take it back if you decide you don't want it. What could be more fair than that? You take her up on her offer because you have nothing to risk. Two weeks later, the salesperson shows up on your doorstep to retrieve the dog. By this time you have become attached to little Bowser, and you want to keep him. Or even better, the salesperson tells you to call her in two weeks if you want to bring the dog back. In this latter scenario, you have to go out of your way to bring the dog back. You have to be really dissatisfied to go to all that effort and are less likely to return the dog than if the salesperson showed up at your door. This is the **puppy dog** or **no risk close**, a "return if not completely satisfied" close. This close is very powerful, and if you believe your product is a fit for the customer, it is very fair: "Ms. Khan, may I suggest we try the $100 monthly withdrawal for a few months to see if that will work for you? If you find that leaves you a little tight financially, call us and we can reduce it to $75. How does that sound?"

Direct Close

The **direct close** is the most common close. It requires you to ask for the order. This close can produce the most stress for customers because it forces them to make a yes or no decision. Reps who use it exclusively tend not to be closers—they tend to have fewer sales because they close less often and later in the interaction, only after the customer has given very strong "buy" signals. People who close earlier open objections that they then have the opportunity to answer. Those who wait often don't hear these objections, the customer never gets to the point where she or he is ready to buy, and the sale is lost. This close is useful in some situations, but some forms of it are better than others.

- "Would you like me to process the order, then?" is the least sophisticated form of this close. It's like "So, would you like to buy one?" in its directness, but it makes it too easy for the customer to give the easy answer: "No."

- "Shall I have this transaction processed today, then?" is a subtle contained choice. The alternative if the customer says no is to arrange another day when the transaction will be processed. This close also creates a sense of urgency.

- "Okay, then, I'll put you down for $40." is still a direct close, but it is a little more assertive. It makes a statement rather than asks a question, and encourages customer agreement with your suggestion.

Closing Tips

Close believing the person will buy. If you have been effective in the previous steps, then you and the customer will both believe that this is the right product or service for the customer, so she or he should buy. Your tone of voice and words will transmit this assuredness, and the customer will be more inclined to accept your close.

Close expecting the customer to offer an objection. If you don't plan for the objection, it can take you by surprise and then you deal with it awkwardly and ineffectively. If you expect the objection, then you are more likely to plan a response that deals with it effectively and sounds more confident—which will encourage the customer to be more receptive to your response.

Throughout the conversation, be conscious of your purpose. Your purpose is to determine customer needs relative to your service or product, to confirm the fit of your product's benefits to the customer's needs, and to close the sale. Throughout the conversation, always be conscious of identifying sales opportunities and moving the call toward a sale. This is true whether your job is formally sales-focused or not.

Develop a repertoire of different closes. Since objections will occur, you can expect to have to close more than once. Also, particular closes may be more appropriate for different customer situations or products, so being comfortable with a variety of closes can increase your closing effectiveness.

After a close, stop talking. The customer may need a pause to consider the decision. If you continue to push the sale by offering more benefits, you cause the customer to feel pressured and the added stress may lead to a no decision. You can increase your close rate dramatically simply by allowing the silence and resisting the urge to keep selling. It is very common for reps to talk themselves out of the sale when they don't remember this simple rule.

Don't "feature dump." Remember, people don't buy features, they buy benefits. And people buy only those benefits that are relevant to their needs.

HAVE YOU EVER?

Have you ever been confronted with "feature dumping"? Here's a scenario that might sound familiar to you:

A representative for a computer company came to a customer's office to sell a computer system. The rep had sold the customer on the computer. The rep had identified the customer's needs and matched the appropriate benefits and features of the computer to those needs. The customer was ready to buy; the computer sounded perfect. The rep became excited at the prospect of a sale and started to tell the customer all the other reasons to buy it, listing a stream of additional features. As the customer heard these features that he couldn't visualize himself using, he started to think that he might be paying more for this computer than necessary, that the price likely included all these features for which he had no need. He therefore changed his mind and decided not to buy.

The objective of effective closing is to make it easy for the customer to say yes, to make the decision easier for the customer, and to help the customer acquire the product or service that you believe is beneficial for the customer with the minimum amount of stress.

Learning Application Exercise

1. *For the product or service for which you earlier developed a features/benefits list and questions, identify at least three closes that might be appropriate for different customer situations. Include at least one trial close.*

2. *Review your closes with a peer.*

5. HANDLING OBJECTIONS

Objections are part of the sales process. Saying no requires no change to what the customer is currently doing and therefore involves the least amount of stress, so it is the easy way out. Some objections come from customers who are convinced the product is right for them, but are uncomfortable making a yes decision. Other objections are genuine issues that make the customer feel uncomfortable going ahead with the purchase. In either case, if we believe it to be in the customer's best interest to acquire our product or service, we owe it to customers to try to help them feel comfortable with the decision and to get them past whatever stands in the way of making that decision.

There are four types of objection, and overcoming each requires a different approach.

Misunderstanding

In the **misunderstanding objection**, customers express a belief about your product that is incorrect and offer this as the basis for their reluctance to make a yes decision. This type of objection is relatively easy to overcome by simply identifying the misunderstanding. Take care not to prove the customer wrong or to belittle the customer. Your challenge is to turn the misunderstanding into a buy signal. You do this by responding with a trial close.

For example, suppose the customer wants your product in red, assumes you don't have it in red, and objects to your close. You know that you have only discussed blue and green options because that is all you currently have in stock. You can, however, place an order with the manufacturer to get red. If you simply respond with "That's not a problem, it is made in red as well," you fail to create a buying state of mind for the customer. If, instead, you say, "I understand why the colour is important to you. It's important to complement the rest of your decor. If you were able to get this product in red, would you be willing to place the order?" If the customer says yes, you advise her or him that you will contact the manufacturer to confirm that they have red in stock. If the customer indicates a reluctance to order even if you can get red, then there is another objection that must be dealt with, so you might follow up with "May I ask what's standing in the way of you making a decision to proceed at this time?"

The misunderstanding objection may simply be the customer's attempt to avoid telling you the real reason for not wanting to proceed—it is an attempt to take the easy way out. The customer may be thinking, "I really don't want this product. I can't see how the amount of benefit it provides me is worth the price. This rep seems like a nice person though and I don't want her to feel bad, so I'll get out of this by telling her the colour is wrong." You would rather hear the real reason so that you have a chance to deal with it. If you know you haven't communicated the benefits in terms that the customer can understand or you haven't shown that the value of the product justifies the price, then you can attempt to remedy the problem. If you are unaware of the real reason for the customer's rejection of your close, you have no chance to deal with it and the customer may miss the opportunity to acquire a product that would truly benefit him or her. The steps in dealing with the misunderstanding objection are as follows:

- Confirm your understanding of the objection. Restate, paraphrase, or summarize your understanding of the customer's objection to ensure that you have interpreted the concern correctly.

- Agree with the importance of the customer's concern. Showing that you understand the importance of the issue makes it the main decision-making issue, which encourages the customer to accept your trial close.

- Offer the trial close. "If I can satisfy that condition, do we have a deal?" or "If that was not an issue, would we have a deal?"

- Overcome the objection.

- Close again. As appropriate, first confirm that the objection has been overcome.

Learning Application Exercise

1. *For the product or service you selected earlier, think of at least three potential misunderstanding objections, and develop an effective response for each.*

2. *Role-play the selling process you have planned in this chapter. Have a peer offer each of the misunderstanding objections you have identified, and provide your response to each.*

3. *Discuss the effectiveness of your execution of each step of the selling process, including your responses to the objections. Develop plans for improvement.*

Skepticism

A skeptical customer doubts that your product or service will provide a benefit you claim it will. For example, suppose you have indicated the fit of your product's quality specifications with the customer's needs and advised the customer of the price. The customer, who may be currently paying more for the same quality product, responds with "I'm sorry, but I find it a little difficult to believe you can provide the quality I expect at that price." It would be easy to offer the customer independent lab tests that confirm the quality or an explanation of your cost-effective manufacturing process that allows you to pass the savings on to the customer. But if you just overcome the objection, you miss the opportunity to turn the skepticism objection into a buying signal. Instead, respond with "Yes, it does sound like an exceptional offer, doesn't it? Mr. Keene, if I can show you that the quality is exactly what you need for the price I've quoted, do we have a deal?" If the customer says yes, offer your evidence, confirm that you have held up your end of the bargain, and close. If the customer says no, you know that there is another objection that must be dealt with before the customer will feel comfortable buying, which can be brought out by saying "May I ask what's holding you back from making this decision?" The steps for overcoming the **skepticism objection** are as follows:

1. Confirm your understanding of the objection. Ensure that what you think you heard is what the customer meant.

2. Trial close. If the customer accepts the trial close, proceed. Otherwise, question to uncover the true reason the customer does not want to buy.

3. Overcome the objection using one or more of these techniques:

   a. Provide a more detailed explanation to support your claim.

   b. Provide statistics to support your claim. Give the source of the statistics to make them credible to the customer.

   c. Provide a third-party endorsement. This endorsement must be from someone or some organization that the customer is likely to consider credible.

   d. Tell a success story. Provide a case study that illustrates your point, one that parallels the customer's situation, so the customer is more likely to identify with the similarities in the case than dwell on the differences. The more the customer can identify with the principal character in the success story, the more the customer will be able to put him- or herself in the picture and see him- or herself sharing the success.

   e. Send product information. Avoid, if at all possible, deferring the rest of the discussion until the customer has received the information. If the customer insists on seeing information, fax or e-mail it if possible, and set up an appointment to talk when the customer has the information.

4. Confirm the objection has been overcome, and close again.

Learning Application Exercise

1. For the product/service/features/benefits list you developed earlier, identify those claims that could possibly result in a skepticism objection.

2. Plan a response to each possible objection that will create a "buying state of mind" for the customer.

3. Role-play the selling process you have planned in this chapter. Have a peer offer each of the skepticism objections you have identified, and provide your response to each.

4. Discuss the effectiveness of your execution of each step of the selling process, including your responses to the objections. Develop plans for improvement.

Stall

With the **stall objection**, the customer provides a reason for not making a decision now: "I'll think about it," "Can you send me some information?" "I need to talk it over with my spouse," " I need to investigate all my options before making a decision." If you have no way to overcome this objection, you may simply take it at face value and end the call, either suggesting the customer call back when a decision has been made or planning a follow-up call. The reason provided for the stall may be legitimate, or it may simply be the customer's way to avoid dealing with the stress of making a decision. The stall may also be the customer's attempt to get out of the call politely (without hurting your feelings) when she or he hasn't been sold on the benefits of the product or service.

The stall increases the customer's stress by stretching out the decision-making process, usually with no compensating benefit. If you can help the customer make a decision now, you save customers that additional stress and help them to acquire a product or service that is in their best interest. These are the motivators behind the various responses to the stall objection. Your response to a stall objection should include the following steps:

1. Verbally Accept the Stall

When you accept the stall, the customer is less defensive, less combative, and less closed to continuing the discussion. Your response may be "Fine," "Sure, I can do that," "Okay," "I'll be happy to send you some information," or "I understand. This is an important decision."

2. Question or Trial Close to Understand the True Reason for the Stall

The key is to keep the stall from ending the conversation. For example: "May I ask, are you comfortable with what we have talked about?" "Is there anything at all that you are uncomfortable with?" "If it weren't for ... would you be willing to go ahead with the plan we've discussed?" "Mr. Lee, I get the feeling you aren't totally comfortable making this decision." You want to make customers feel safe in voicing any misgivings they may have. You want to get the true objection on the table so you have a chance of dealing with it.

If another objection is uncovered, deal with it. If you find out the customer has not seen the value in your product or service, or has not seen enough benefit to justify acquiring it, then question further to identify additional needs.

3. Deal with the Stall in a Way That Doesn't Make It a "Deal Stopper"

If the customers really want to think about the decision, help them with the thinking process, work with them to sort out the pros and cons of the decision, and help them overcome the cons that are identified.

If customers really do want to discuss the decision with their spouse, or business associates, or advisers,

- Ensure that they are convinced that this is the right decision: "Do you have any misgivings at all?" or "What is there that's still not totally comfortable for you?"

- Try to intercede in the process on the customer's behalf. Offer to speak to the spouse, business associates, or advisers, providing a benefit to doing so: "If she asks any question that we haven't discussed, I'll be able to answer it for her."

- Assume the role of the customer's ally in the selling process. Help prepare the customer's case with the spouse, business associates, or advisers or help the customer to be successful in selling the idea to these people: "You were interested in these aspects of the product. Are those the same things your husband will be interested in, or do you think he might have other concerns?"

- Make a follow-up appointment that provides a benefit to the customer: "Can I make a suggestion? As you and your spouse discuss this decision, have a pen and paper handy, and as you encounter any points of confusion or concern, write them down. I can then call you in two days at this same time, and we can go through each of the concerns to ensure you have all the information you need to make your decision."

If the customer is in the process of "shopping around," or investigating alternatives before making a decision,

1. Reinforce the decision: "It makes sense to investigate your options. This is a big decision. In fact, many of our customers have done just that before making their decision."

2. Determine where the customer is in the shopping process: "Are you just beginning the information-collecting process, or have you had a chance to speak to other companies already?"

3. Offer to help the customer create a shopping list: "Have you had the chance to establish the criteria upon which you will base your comparison of the various options so you are comparing apples with apples? May I suggest some of the things you might want to consider that other customers have found to be important?" Then, as you discuss items for the shopping list, you are also exploring the customer's needs. You can also ensure that the shopping list includes areas in which your product or service has a competitive advantage.

4. Once the shopping list is agreed upon, provide information about how your company fares on each item. Provide more than just the data—let the customer know how your product or services compares with the competition: "We have the most inclusive warranty of anyone in the industry. We are in the top quartile on quality and the bottom quartile on price." Take care never to say anything disparaging about the competition; that only makes a bad impression on customers. Instead, explain how your company, product, or service is better.

5. Provide a benefit in making a decision now: "Interviewing each supplier can be a time-consuming process. If you're comfortable, based on the information I've provided you, that we can meet your needs, I can set up an account for you right now."

When Stall Objections Are Frequent

If the nature of your product, service, or customer base contributes to increased stalling, and if once the decision is put off your customers are difficult to recontact, difficult to close, or particularly vulnerable to competitors' offers, here are some ways to increase the rate of closes:

- Create a sense of urgency early in the call. A sense of urgency is created when product availability is limited or there is a special pricing offer for only a certain period of time. These can motivate customers to make a decision now, as they risk losing the opportunity if they do not. "Let me just check our inventory. I know that model has been very popular. Mr. Chilles, I'm looking at our inventory now and I can see that the number of units we have in stock for that model has dropped considerably even in the past few hours, but we do have a few units still available." Avoid trying to introduce the sense of urgency only after the customer has made a stall objection, since this has less impact and sounds manipulative.

- Use a puppy dog close. This is ideal if the reason for the stall is that the customer is unsure if he or she is making the right decision.

- Offer a customer benefit of closing now. Brainstorm a list of reasons why the customer should make a decision to buy your product or service now rather than wait, reasons that provide benefits to the customer. You can then access these quickly when you encounter a stall objection.

Learning Application Exercise

1. *For the product or service you identified earlier, develop a list of reasons that benefit the customer for making a decision to buy now as opposed to later. Review these with a peer.*

2. *Plan responses for at least three of the obvious reasons a customer may stall on making a decision to buy this product or service. Review these with a peer as well.*

3. *Role-play the selling process you have planned in this chapter. Have a peer offer each of the stall objections you have identified, and provide your response to each.*

4. *Discuss the effectiveness of your execution of each step of the selling process, including your responses to the objections. Develop plans for improvement.*

Drawback

The various types of objections have been dealt with here in ascending order of difficulty. The **drawback objection** is potentially the most difficult for reps to overcome, because the customer has identified an aspect of the product or service that is a competitive disadvantage or a legitimate shortcoming from the customer's perspective. The drawback objection is not the "kiss of death" many reps perceive it to be, although the chances of turning it around are somewhat less than with other objections. If, however, reps give up when they hear the drawback objection, they have no chance of turning it around.

The best way to deal with any objection is to plan for it ahead of time, and the drawback is no different. Typically, when a drawback is identified, the product also has a number of benefits. In dealing with a drawback, your objective should be to adjust the customer's perception of its importance by emphasizing the benefits, so the customer sees a small drawback against a long list of benefits. See Figure 10.2 for an illustration of this.

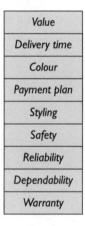

Figure 10.2

Drawbacks/Benefits

Using the example of a car purchase, the salesperson might be able to list these potential factors in determining the customer's final decision.

| Value |
| Delivery time |
| Colour |
| Payment plan |
| Styling |
| Safety |
| Reliability |
| Dependability |
| Warranty |

| Price |

Drawback "Pile"

Benefit "Pile"

Here are the steps for overcoming a drawback objection:

1. Acknowledge and then confirm the objection. Because we dread hearing drawbacks, we sometimes hear them even when the customer hasn't expressed them. So confirm by asking something like "Are you saying that you have a concern about the price?" to ensure that what you have heard truly is a drawback objection.

2. Question to understand. "And what is it about the pricing you do not feel comfortable with?" ensures that your understanding of the reason for the objection fits with the customer's. This line of questioning can help you determine the best response strategy and can also open up potential opportunities for compromise. A customer statement like "I don't know if what I'm getting justifies the higher price" will be handled differently from a statement like "We don't have the budget for that large an expenditure." A question from you such as "If it weren't for your concern

about price, would we have a deal?" determines whether this objection is the last barrier to resolution. "Let's sum up the situation. What are the things you like about the solution I've proposed?" starts the customer creating the list of benefits, which is more meaningful coming from the customer than from you.

3. Summarize the situation, or offer an alternative. In your summary, play down or minimize the drawback while bolstering the list of benefits. Or, offer an alternative: "I can understand if you don't have the budget for the solution I've proposed. We all have to work within our constraints. Let's look at the budget you have available and see if we can determine a solution that will work for you. What is your budget for this project?"

4. Confirm the objection has been overcome, and close again.

It's important to remember that in some cases the drawback is a legitimate condition that must be satisfied for the customer to buy. If the customer is adamant, recognize and respect her or his needs and look for an alternative way to satisfy these needs. You may opt for a partial sale as opposed to a full sale. For example, if the customer's business demands overnight courier delivery to a remote village and your company absolutely cannot provide such a service, your list of benefits cannot overcome this drawback. Instead, you might sell the customer on your company handling all of his or her courier business except this one location.

Learning Application Exercise

1. *For the product or service you identified earlier, identify at least three drawbacks. Develop a response to each. Review your drawback list and responses with a peer.*

2. *Role-play with a peer the sales process for your product or service. Include various objections in the role-play, including drawbacks. Conduct a number of role-plays using different customer roles, different needs, and different objections. Tape-record some of these.*

3. *Discuss each role-play. Focus on what was done well and what could have been done differently at each stage of the selling process.*

4. *Identify your own areas for improvement, and establish an action plan for improving your skills in each area.*

6. ENDING THE SALE: MOVING TO THE NEXT SALE

Once the customer has accepted the sale, work through the final arrangements of the deal, which may mean collecting delivery information, credit card information, confirming arrangements for a face-to-face appointment—the details will vary depending on the nature of your situation. Once the customer has accepted the close on the original deal, and before completing the paperwork, pursue **cross-sell** or up-sell opportunities.

Cross-Sell

Where the product the customer has bought is part of a family of products, check for a need for one of the other products. For example, if the customer has just bought a computer, he or she may also need a printer, cables, software, training, an extended warranty, or even a scanner. Good questions for introducing a cross-sell begin with "Are you aware…." or "May I suggest…." Creating lists of product families will help you remember to cross-sell.

Up-Sell

Once the sale has been confirmed with the customer, investigate opportunities to up-sell. An up-selling opportunity is present when there is a quantity discount for a product: "Ms. Delisle, you've indicated that you wanted three loads of #4 tubing. We currently have a special on. If you take a fourth load, the price difference means you get the fourth load at half price. Shall I put you down for four loads then?" Up-selling can also move a customer up to a higher-value product: "Mr. Jewison, I'm looking at a feature sheet for the computer that is one level up from the one you've decided to purchase—and it's amazing the additional features you get for just a 9 percent increase in price. You not only get a much faster processor and an extra 4 GB of RAM—you also get a high-speed modem. We can leave the order as is, or would you like to take a look at this other option?"

End the call by thanking the customer for her or his business and offering reassurance that the decision is a good one that the customer will be satisfied with (to minimize buyer's remorse—that sense of letdown or nervous feeling that people often get after making the decision to buy). As appropriate, leave your name and phone number, ask for a referral, or set up a follow-up call (a reason to call back that benefits the customer).

Learning Application Exercise

1. Identify a list of cross-sell opportunities (families of related products) and up-sell opportunities (quantity breaks or next steps in quality) for your product or service. Review these with a peer.

2. Develop statements for introducing each of the cross-sell and up-sell opportunities. Review these with a peer.

Outbound Calls

Call centres often have **outbound calls** as part of their mix. There are various purposes for outbound calls, and a major benefit to call centres is the greater staffing efficiencies that can be achieved by having staff who can handle outbound or inbound calls. Often call centres have a base of inbound call reps, a team of outbound call reps, and a group of "blended" reps who can move to outbound calls when call volumes are low and move to inbound calls when they are high. This allows the call centre to maintain its targeted service level, the average speed with which a call is answered by a rep. The purposes of outbound calls include the following:

- Outbound sales. "Cold calling" individuals who are not currently customers or who are dormant (inactive) customers.

- Surveys. Assessing customer satisfaction or collecting customer demographic or buying information.

- Follow-up. Returning customer calls or following up on customer issues.

- Customer retention or loyalty programs. Calling customers to show them that they are valued by the organization and to project a corporate personality to the customer.

There are a few basic rules for optimizing your effectiveness no matter what the type of outbound call. Apply all the techniques that make for effective inbound calls. Have a **reason to call** that benefits the customer—not the purpose of selling or collecting information, but a reason that encourages the customer to welcome and participate in the call. The reason to call may be to introduce customers to a special deal on a product they can benefit from, to collect their feedback so you can provide even better services to your customers, to provide them with information they have requested, or to offer a token of your appreciation for their patronage.

Script your opening statement. The first words out of your mouth shape the customer's receptiveness to your call, so these words must have impact and cannot be left to chance. Plan, rehearse, learn, and say them—don't read or recite them from memory, and don't be spontaneous and say whatever comes into your mind when you pick up the telephone. The opening statement must be clearly spoken, with good tone of voice and easy-to-understand pacing, and it must be brief. Ensure it includes a greeting, your name, your organization (and department, if appropriate), the reason for the call (a benefit or interest-grabbing statement), and a meaningful question—one that involves the customer in the conversation and provides you with information necessary for qualifying or understanding the needs of the customer. Make sure you are prepared for any customer response to your question and that you don't ask questions that might elicit a response that undermines the purpose of your call.

Plan some questions for opening opportunities or directing the conversation. Have a clear road map for the call—know what you want to achieve and how to get there. Also have a positive ending for the call—a call objective such as an appointment, sale, information, and so on.

Learning Application Exercise

1. *Identify three potential target market groups for your product or service.*

2. *Establish a reason to call for each group, and create an opening statement for each. Review these with a peer.*

Tips for Successful Sales Calls

Make sure you are knowledgeable about your products, your inventory, your product families, and your prices for different quantities. Plan a response for every conceivable objection or difficult question. Script these responses and learn them, but also have them organized in an easily accessible form.

Set objectives for yourself regarding the number and volume of sales for each week, day, and hour, then track your performance so you know how well you are doing. Recognize you are playing a numbers game and that a certain number of prospects are sure to say no. Track your close or "hit" rate so you know the percentage of no's to expect.

Celebrate your successes, and broaden your categories of success to include more than just "closed a sale." A call may be a success if the customer left it with a positive feeling for you and your organization, even if he or she did not buy, and a call in which you learned something that will help you improve as a salesperson may be considered a success even if you handled that call less than effectively.

Constantly remind yourself of the value your products or services give your client—believe in them yourself. Anticipate a positive, successful call. Attitude creates reality. If you believe you will fail, you are more likely to fail than if you believe you will be successful.

Recognize the customer will likely experience stress around the buy decision, and plan your approach to help minimize this stress.

Summary

Selling is essential for the success of any business. Anyone who comes in contact with customers as part of the job is in a selling role, either by passively selling the company's image and quality, or by actively promoting a product or service. Sales is not an either/or ability that you either have or you don't. We all "sell," and different sales styles fit different situations. Call centre roles and responsibilities are evolving in such a way that everyone must understand the sales process.

Success in the sales role depends on two factors:

- You must believe in your products or services and the real benefits they provide your customer.

- You must understand the sales process and develop the skills and tools that apply to each stage in the process. The steps in the sales process include

    - building rapport

    - questioning

    - confirming understanding of the need

    - closing: asking for the sale

    - handling objections

    - ending the sale: moving to the next sale

For outbound calls, apply these same sales techniques. Have a reason to call that benefits the customer. Script your opening statement, which should include a greeting, your name, the company and/or department's name, a benefit statement, and a meaningful question. The opening statement should be clear, pleasant, and brief. Plan some questions, and have a roadmap for the call.

For success in sales calls, know your products, plan for objections, and set objectives. Track your results and celebrate your successes. Believe in your products. Think positively, and help the customer overcome buying stress.

GLOSSARY

The definitions in this glossary describe each term in relation to how it is used in the text of this book and are not intended to serve as generic definitions.

Note: The number in parentheses at the end of each entry refers to the chapter in which the term first appears.

ACD
See "Automatic call distributor." (1)

Activator
One of six personality types based on Dr. Taibi Kahler's Process Communication Model. The Activator personality type seeks situations in which there is some element of risk, in which he or she can experience a lot of excitement in a short period of time. (8)

Active listening techniques
Techniques that make the listener an active part of the information-collecting process rather than a passive receiver of information. These techniques include paraphrasing, restating, summarizing, and focused questioning. (5)

Adherence to the staffing schedule
A measure of whether the staff in queue are ready to take calls during the period of time they are expected to do so.

AHT
See "average handling time." (1)

ANI
See "automatic number identification." (1)

ASA
See "average speed of answer." (1)

Assumptive close
A method of closing a sale that saves the customer the anxiety of making a "buy" or "don't buy" decision by assuming the customer has made the decision to buy. The salesperson sorts out the details of delivery or the payment process ("Would you like us to bring that around to your office next Tuesday?"). By confirming these details, customers implicitly agree to buy. (10)

ATT
See "average talk time." (1)

Attending mechanism
The part of our brain that constantly scans the environment to determine what elements are important to bring to our conscious attention. (5)

Automatic call distributor
The device that passes an incoming call to the next available (or most appropriate) call centre representative. (1)

Automatic number identification
Automated recognition of the telephone number a call is placed from, so the caller can be identified for the rep, the caller's file can be presented to the rep, or the call can be routed to the most appropriate rep. (1)

Average handling time
The average length of time it takes a rep to handle a call, including the amount of time taken on the call itself plus the amount of time spent on after-call work. (1)

Average hold time
The average length of time customers are placed on hold during a call. (1)

Average speed of answer
The average length of time callers wait before their call is answered by a call centre representative. (1)

Average talk time
The average length of time a representative spends on the telephone with the customer on each call. (1)

Average work time
The average length of time a call centre representative spends out of queue doing wrap-up work from calls. (1)

AWT
See "average work time." (1)

Baggage
The emotional damage left after a difficult call. Baggage from one call can result in a call centre representative

having a negative attitude or tone of voice in subsequent calls. Baggage is cumulative, so a series of difficult calls can increasingly negatively affect a rep and the people with whom the rep interacts. (3)

Batching

Collecting information into a computer system and then processing similar applications all at once (for example, updating similar files or preparing invoices or paycheques). (1)

Blended

A type of call centre representative who handles calls from customers (inbound calls) and also, when incoming call volumes are low, switches to initiating calls to customers or prospects (outbound calls). (1)

Breathy voice

A voice in which the speaker's breathing is so obvious it is distracting to the listener. (4)

Business centre

See "customer contact centre." (1)

Call centre

The mechanism through which an organization transacts business with an identified group of customers or potential customers, using the telephone as the primary method of communication. (1)

Call centre climate

What it feels like to work in a specific call centre. Each call centre develops its own personality or atmosphere that affects what it feels like to work there. (2)

Call monitoring

The practice whereby supervisors or coaches listen in on telephone calls between call centre representatives and customers for the purposes of evaluating, providing feedback, or coaching. (1)

Cherry picking

Choosing among customers to call or try to close a sale with, instead of dealing with all customers. Usually call centre representatives who "cherry pick" choose only customers they believe will be the easiest to deal with. (10)

Chronic interrupter

Someone who has a habit of repeatedly interrupting others while they are speaking. (6)

Chronic loudness

Consistently speaking too loudly. (4)

Closing

The step in the selling process when the call centre representative tries to help customers make the decision to buy. (10)

Closed questions

Questions that require a short, specific answer, such as "yes" or "no," a date, a name, or a number, and no additional elaboration. (6)

Cold call

A call initiated by a call centre representative to a person who currently does not do business with the company. In some organizations, cold calls include calls to anyone the rep has never dealt with before. (1)

Commands

Instructions written in a code or language that the computer can understand to tell the computer what processes to perform. (1)

Competencies

Those skills, abilities, or behaviours that contribute to success in the call centre job. Core competencies are those that are most strongly related to success in the call centre role in a specific organization. (1)

Computer–telephone integration

The linking of the information from the telephone system (such as the caller's telephone number) with the company's computer database (such as all the information in the customer's file) that can allow call routing to a specific representative or department based on customer information. (1)

Contact management software

The call centre computer system that stores customer background information and in which call centre representatives record and plan interactions with customers. The software allows any rep to access information on any customer, allowing whichever rep receives the call to deal with that customer effectively. (1)

Contained choice close

A type of close to a sale that saves the customer the anxiety of making a "buy" or "don't buy" decision by assuming the decision has been made. The sales representative offers the customer a choice between options in such areas as delivery (e.g., Tuesday or Thursday), payment (e.g., credit card or cheque), or product features (e.g., blue or red). By stating a preference, the customer implicitly agrees to buy. (10)

Contextual clues

Clues for interpreting a speaker's pronunciation, vocabulary, or expression that are based on the rest of what the person has said. (6)

Core competencies

Those observable behaviours that result in the rep meeting the job objectives and achieving the quantitative-performance standards.

Cross-sell

Sell a customer another product related to the one she or he has already decided to buy (for example, a printer with a computer). (10)

Cross-train

In call centres where different functions are handled by separate groups of reps (for example, telephone sales, collections, customer concerns, help desk), to train a representative with one area of specialty to handle one or more of the other functions. The rep can then be assigned to handle calls in whichever area has the greatest need. Cross-training helps call centres provide adequate staffing as the volume of calls in each area increases or decreases. (1)

CTI

See "computer–telephone integration." (1)

Customer care centre

See "customer contact centre." (1)

Customer contact centre

A term that is broader than "call centre" that encompasses a range of responsibilities that go beyond

handling telephone calls, such as handling mail and e-mail. (1)

Customer database

Information about a customer in a company's computer files. The database may include basic customer data such as name, address, and telephone number, and it may include information such as buying habits, approved credit level, and so on. (1)

Dead air

A period of silence in a conversation. Dead air is most damaging to rapport if it occurs after a customer has spoken and is waiting for the call centre representative to respond. (2)

Diagramming a call

Note-taking as a customer is speaking in a way that collects different types of information in different areas of the note page. Diagramming makes it easier for a call centre representative to access the information the customer has provided and to manage the call. (6)

Diaphragm breath

Also called a "stomach breath," this type of breathing uses the muscles of the diaphragm, below the rib cage, rather than the more shallow or laboured breathing that results from breathing from the upper chest. Diaphragm breathing can help a person feel and sound more relaxed and can add resonance to the voice. (3)

Diction

The clarity with which we speak. Mumbling, incorrectly pronouncing words, slurring words, or omitting sounds or syllables can cause unclear diction. (4)

Direct close

A type of close to a sale that involves directly asking the customer for the sale or telling the customer you will process the order. (10)

Display board

An electronic display linked to a computer (and usually the ACD) that updates call centre representatives on important information, such as how many calls are in queue, total sales to date, or whatever information it is programmed to display. (1)

Downtime

A period of time when call centre activity is stopped or at a low level. (2)

Drawback objection

A type of reason customers provide for not buying that is based on a legitimate shortcoming of the product or service being offered. (10)

Drive-by

A type of coaching or training of call centre representatives that consists of immediate feedback provided by a supervisor who overhears part of a rep's telephone interaction as he or she is passing by the rep's workstation. (1)

Economies of scale

Lower costs that are enjoyed when production or processing is done at a large facility rather than a number of smaller ones. Higher volume decreases the cost per unit produced or per call processed, making larger scale production more economical. (1)

E-mail

Electronic mail delivered from one user address to another via the Internet. (1)

Empathy

Acknowledging the feelings expressed by another person by referring to the emotion expressed, paraphrasing the situation that stimulated the emotion, and showing, with the appropriate tone of voice, that you care. (5)

Enunciation

Speech clarity (see also "diction"). (5)

Escalate the call

Transfer a call to a supervisor, manager, or someone else with broader decision-making authority who can more appropriately deal with a customer's issue. (7)

Exchange

The location at which telephone lines of callers are connected to the lines of those who receive the calls. (1)

Familiareze

Speech that is less formal—almost too friendly—than customers may be comfortable with. (5)

Fax

Transmit over a telephone line a document that is scanned by the sending fax machine, coded, and sent through the line. The message is decoded to create a "*facsimile*" of the original document by the fax machine on the other end of the line. (1)

Fields

Elements of information collected by a computer system, such as customer address or account status. (1)

Focused questioning

Questioning to clarify or further explore information a customer has provided. (5)

Forming phase

The first phase in team development, described in the Normative Model, in which team members look for reasons to feel good about the team and the other team members. During this "honeymoon" phase, differences or problems are minimized or overlooked, so the relationships are relatively superficial. (1)

Halo effect

When one good aspect of something makes other aspects seem good as well. For example, success and resulting confidence in one area of our lives, such as our job, may cause us to feel more successful and confident in other totally unrelated areas, such as our interpersonal relationships. (5)

Hard copy

A printed paper copy of information that is on the computer screen. (1)

Hard sell

A sales technique designed to coerce the customer to buy now. (10)

Help desk

A call centre whose function is to help callers troubleshoot a problem with equipment, software, technology, and so on. Typically customers call an

GLOSSARY

800 number when they have a technical problem, and the rep they connect with has the expertise to help them resolve the problem. (1)

Home-based agents

Call centre representatives who handle calls from their home, assisted by computer and phone systems that are linked to their company. These reps often have flexible work hours, staffing the telephones when the company is receiving the greatest volumes of calls. (1)

Humaneze

Speech that uses terms customers are likely to understand and feel comfortable with, which increases rapport with the call centre representative. (5)

Industrial age

The era that began with the Industrial Revolution of the mid-1700s, which was characterized by the development of production technology, mass production, and the assembly line. (1)

Inflection

Changes in pitch, volume, and emphasis on certain words or phrases that add variety to a person's speech and additional meaning to the words. (4)

Information age

Postindustrial age society in which we now live, in which information has become the most important source of wealth and national advantage, a result of the advancement in telecommunications and computing technology that began in the mid-1900s. (1)

Intellectualeze

Speech that uses a more complex vocabulary than the customer's. (5)

Interactive voice response

Equipment that provides the caller with information or directions via a tape-recorded voice. The specific taped message the customer hears may be determined by the customer's response to a previous taped message (e.g., "Press 1 for information on resorts, press 2 to hear about cruises"). (1)

Interactive Web site

A site on the Internet that, rather than being a passive information-only site, allows visitors to ask for additional information, provide input, or otherwise be involved. (1)

Internet

A system of linked computer networks that allows anyone to access all the information in those networks and to communicate with other users who have computer addresses in this environment. (1)

IVR

See "Interactive voice response." (1)

Job tiers

Job levels within a call centre that a representative can progress or be promoted through, typically based on clear job performance criteria. This provides a career path within the call centre that can increase rep job satisfaction and reduce reps' need to leave the call centre in order to advance in their careers. (1)

Keypad

The area of the telephone or computer that contains the keys with which numbers or letters are entered. (1)

Listening responses

Verbalizations by a listener that show he or she is paying attention to what the speaker is saying. Verbalizations include "yes," "okay," "I understand," "I see," and so on. (5)

Log on

Enter a code into a computer or telephone system that the system recognizes and that grants a person access to the system while tracking her or his activity. (1)

Mail order catalogue

A list of a company's products or services, typically accompanied by descriptions, prices, and pictures, that is sent to potential customers. Customers select the products or services they wish to purchase. Customers then fill in a supplied form describing the items they wish to purchase and mail their request to the company, which then mails the items to the customers. (1)

Martyr syndrome

A subconscious need to feel like and be seen as a victim or martyr. Very stressed people who are strong Relater personality types sometimes take on this victim role (can lead to involvement in relationships that are emotionally and even physically abusive). (9)

Minimalists

People whose work or performance level is just marginally acceptable. Minimalists do the minimum amount necessary to keep their jobs, but fall far short of their potential. (2)

Misunderstanding objection

A type of reason customers provide for not buying that is based on a misunderstanding of some aspect of the product or service (for example, refusing to buy because they think the product is not CSA approved when in fact it is CSA approved). (10)

Multitask

The ability to keep track of a number of projects, ongoing cases, or calls to be followed up on and not forget about these or let them get behind while giving full attention to the current customer. (1)

Mycompany-isms

Speech that uses terms, acronyms, identification numbers, or slang words that are peculiar to an organization used when speaking to a customer who is unlikely to understand them. (5)

Nasality

The voice quality that results when too much of the sound produced by the vocal cords is amplified by the nasal cavity (the nose and nasal passages) instead of the vocal cavity (the mouth). People with a nasal voice sound like they are "talking through their nose." (4)

No risk close

See puppy dog close.

Normative Model

A description of the phases of team development that includes forming, storming, norming, and performing. (2)

Norming

The third phase in team development, described in the Normative Model, in which team members begin to develop mature, realistic relationships with one another and their leader. The team begins to establish norms or rules of behaviour and a functional interdependency that allow it to work as a team. (2)

Objections

Reasons customers provide for saying "no" to buying a product or service. (10)

One-shot sale

A type of sale in which there is unlikely to be any further contact with the customer once the sale has been completed. (10)

One-stop shopping

A call centre that provides one-stop shopping cross-trains all of its reps to deal with any customer issue so customers do not have to call different numbers for different issues but can deal with only one rep. (1)

Open-ended questions

Questions that allow customer involvement in the conversation, encouraging customers to elaborate and share information. (6)

Outbound calls

Telephone calls to a customer that are initiated by the call centre representative. (10)

Outsourcing service

A company that specializes in being a call centre. This company contracts to be the call centre for another company (or, more typically, a number of client companies), taking or making those calls that an internal call centre would handle and responding to the customers as if they were the client company's internal call centre. (2)

Pacing

The speed of a person's speech. (5)

Paradigm shift

A paradigm is a set of fundamental mental rules about how something works or is done. The shift occurs when some event causes that set of mental rules to change (for example, between the 1500s and 1800s the paradigm that the world was flat and that the stars revolved around us—a paradigm supported by visual observation—was shifted to our current view of how the universe works). (1)

Paradigm-shift resisters

Those people whose belief in one paradigm, or mindset (see "paradigm shift"), is so entrenched that they have great difficulty accepting that their vision may not be the only way and so resist accepting an alternative paradigm. (1)

Paraphrasing

Restating something using different words, typically telling someone your interpretation of what he or she said. (5)

PBX

See "private branch exchange."

PC

See "personal computer." (1)

Performance standards

Measures of the performance results (e.g., how many calls a call centre rep is expected to handle on an average day) or behaviours (e.g., what the rep does to show respect for the customer) that lead to effectiveness on the job. (1)

Performing

The fourth phase of team development, described in the Normative Model, in which the team truly matures and becomes fully productive. Trust, interdependence, and productivity are at their optimum levels at this phase. (2)

Personal computer

A computer designed to be user-friendly that can be used by someone without computer programming expertise. (1)

Personality type

A package of characteristics that tend to occur together, so that if a person demonstrates two or three, one can predict that the person likely has some of the other characteristics in that same package. (8)

Phase change

Occurs when, after a period of stress, a person moves from the personality type that is most dominant for her or him into another. When this happens, the psychological needs, behaviours, and stress reactions for the new personality type become dominant. Phase change is a major life event that initiates long-term change. (8)

Phone jack

A device, either part of a telephone or separate, that splices into the call centre representative's line and allows someone to listen to both sides of a phone call. (1)

Physically challenged

A physical condition that may cause performance of some tasks to be more challenging for a person than they would be to someone without that physical condition (for example, paralysis or partial paralysis of some part of the body). (1)

Pitch

The highness or lowness that is a result of the frequency of sound waves produced by a person's voice. Most common is the problem of too high a pitch, which can make a person's voice sound childish. (4)

Positioned

A term used to describe the lead in to questions by explaining or stating the purpose for the questions first, thereby putting them into perspective.

Positive control

Control of a call by a call centre representative in a way that is acceptable to the customer in order to bring the call to a more rapid and effective resolution (which is in the best interests of both the customer and the rep). (7)

Preventive maintenance

A term borrowed from manufacturing that describes the ongoing care that is taken to prevent costly equipment breakdowns. (4)

Private branch exchange

A device that works like the telephone company's switch, allowing a company to have a limited number of telephone lines on which to handle the incoming or outgoing calls from a larger pool of staff. An outgoing call is switched to the next available telephone line, and an incoming call is transferred to the line of the employee for whom it is intended (a taped greeting asks the caller to enter the appropriate extension number). The private branch exchange also acts as an internal phone system that allows staff to talk to one another without using the telephone company's "outside" lines. (1)

Proactive customer retention

Steps taken by a company to ensure a customer's loyalty and satisfaction before the customer decides to end the business relationship. (5)

Process Communication

The name of Dr. Taibi Kahler's model that describes six personality types. (8)

Professional distancing

The ability to deal with a customer's stressed behaviour in a professional and empathic manner without taking the customer's behaviour or comments personally. (9)

Prospects

People or companies that are not currently customers of an organization but have the potential to be. (1)

Psychological needs

Needs associated with people's dominant personality types that subconsciously motivate many behaviours. Stress is our subconscious attempt to negatively address an unsatisfied psychological need. Examples of psychological needs include positive feedback, appreciation, and personal space. (8)

Puppy dog close

A method of closing a sale that helps the customer overcome the fear of making a wrong decision by providing a way to later reverse the decision if the customer wishes ("Try it and if you don't like it, just bring it back"). If the product is one the customer needs, he or she will not return it. (10)

Queue

The holding area for calls from which they are routed to reps based on established criteria, such as "first come, first served," prioritized by type of customer, and so on. (1)

Rapport

The customer's sense of feeling "connected" to the call centre representative and that the rep appreciates and understands the customer, a combination of customer respect for, empathy with, and liking the rep as a person. (5)

Real-time

Information is processed or acted upon as soon as it is entered into a computer system rather than collected and processed all in one "batch." For example, when a call centre representative can change a customer address in real-time, changing the permanent record as the information is entered, the next rep who accesses the file even a few moments later will see the new address. (1)

Reason to call

The call centre representative's stated reason for making an outbound call, one that offers a benefit to the customer. (10)

Reflective phrases

Phrases that a customer introduced earlier in the conversation and that a call centre representative uses later to show that he or she was listening. (6)

Relater

One of six personality types based on Dr. Taibi Kahler's Process Communication Model. Relaters are typically compassionate, want to create harmony, and are sensitive to their environment. (7)

Relationship sell

A sales technique in which the long-term relationship with the customer is of the greatest importance to the sales representative. The relationship may be the basis for the sales contact and perhaps for the final decision to buy, but the rep will not risk the relationship for the sake of this one sale. (10)

Remote monitoring

A system that is part of a company's telephone system that allows supervisors or coaches to listen to each call centre representative's calls from the supervisor's office or from a designated listening room. This is typically done as part of assessment, coaching, or feedback. (1)

GLOSSARY

Restricted-access Web site

A Web site that requires users to enter a code before they can participate in some parts or all of the site. Such a Web site may provide information or a service for a fee, such as a training site in which the learners are issued codes that allow them access to the training programs they have paid for. (1)

Retroactive customer retention

Steps taken by a company to try to win back customers who have discontinued some element of their business relationship with the company. (5)

Routing

Directing calls to the intended or appropriate destination. (1)

Sales

The activity or behaviour that positively influences customers' decision to buy a company's products or services. (10)

Satellite call centres

Smaller call centres that are linked to operate as one large call centre, typically located closer to the homes of the people who staff each centre, making their commute to work shorter. (1)

Screen pop

A computer–telephone integration application that uses caller identification to look up the caller's file in a database and have it appear as a screen at the call centre rep's terminal when the call is received. (1)

Scripts

Wording provided to call centre representatives, either in print form or on their computers, that is used to optimize their effectiveness in the specific situations for which the scripts are designed. (1)

Self-directed work teams

Teams of call centre representatives that, after being given clear objectives, assume responsibility for planning which role each team member will take in helping the team fulfill its mandate. (2)

Sell cycle

The time and process between an initial contact with a prospective customer and her or his decision to buy. (10)

Service level

The target average speed of answer (ASA) of an organization, typically stated as, for example, "We will answer 80 percent of calls within 10 seconds." (2)

Side-by-side coaching

Coaching in which the supervisor or coach sits at the call centre representative's workstation and listens to the rep's calls, typically by plugging into a separate jack on the rep's phone. (1)

Skepticism objection

A type of reason customers provide for not buying that is based on their not believing a claim made about a product or service. (10)

Soft sell

A sales technique in which the salesperson introduces the opportunity to buy, but does not try to pressure the customer into making an immediate decision. (10)

Stall objection

A type of reason customers provide for not buying in which customers give a reason to delay the decision to buy (for example, "I need to talk it over with my manager"). (10)

Stimulator

One of six personality types based on Dr. Taibi Kahler's Process Communication Model. Playful stimulation is important to the Stimulator, who tries to build fun into each interaction. (8)

Storming phase

The second phase in team development, described in the Normative Model, in which team members are in conflict with one another and their leader, accentuating their differences. Alternately called the adolescent phase, during this phase dissatisfaction and rebellion dominate and the team is largely dysfunctional. (1)

Stress reactions

Behaviour with negative personal ramifications that results from subconscious attempts to address unsatisfied psychological needs. (9)

Suggestive sell

A sales technique in which the salesperson offers a product or service for the customer to consider purchasing, but does not try to pressure the customer into making an immediate decision to buy. (10)

Summarizing

Collecting and then restating or paraphrasing the key points in what a speaker said. (5)

Summary close

A method of closing a sale that shows the customer that what he or she needs is exactly what the product or service provides, by summarizing and confirming the needs and matching each to a product feature and benefit. (10)

Switch

The mechanism in a telephone system that connects phone calls from callers to receivers. (1)

Switchboard operator

A person who answers incoming calls and switches them manually from the inbound line to the phone lines of staff members. (1)

Systemizer

One of six personality types based on Dr. Taibi Kahler's Process Communication Model. Systemizers are typically orderly and analytical. (8)

Techno-talk

Speech that uses terms related to computer systems, software, or technical aspects of a company's products when talking to a customer who is unlikely to understand them. (5)

Telecommunications

Communication over a distance with the help of some technological means, such as cable, telephone, or radio. (1)

Telegraph

A system for sending messages over a wire using a code that involves a series of electrical signals to represent each letter of the alphabet. The code is called Morse Code after the system's inventor. (1)

Telemarketing

Telephone sales, more commonly associated with outbound business-to-consumer sales, in which the call centre representative initiates the call. (1)

Telephone persona

The telephone voice that some call centre representatives use that is intended to sound like what they believe a person should sound like on the telephone rather than how they normally speak. The effect of a telephone persona on customer rapport is usually negative. (4)

Telephone tag

The situation where person A calls person B but is unable to connect in person and so leaves a message. Person B returns the call, is unable to connect in person with person A and so leaves a message. Person A then returns the call and the game of tag continues until the two people finally connect in person. (7)

Template

A generic version of a document, such as a letter or report, that is designed to allow information to be added at designated points to create a customized or personalized version. Time is saved since the creator of the final document starts with a partial version. (1)

Throat voice

The voice quality that results when too much of the sound is amplified from the throat rather than from a combination of the vocal and nasal cavities (mouth, nose, and nasal passages). The voice may sound husky or raspy, and the prolonged effect of throat voice may be hoarseness, loss of voice, or damage to the vocal cords. (4)

Tone

The nuances in the voice, primarily influenced by inflection, that add subtle meaning to the speaker's message that may be very different from that communicated by the words themselves. (4)

Trial close

A method of closing a sale that tests to see if the customer is ready to buy or proceed with the selling process, or to determine what objections might be keeping the customer from making a buy decision. The standard form of a trial close is "If this condition is met, then are you willing to buy?" (10)

Turnover

The number of staff who leave an organization or department, usually expressed as a percentage of the total number of staff and typically representing yearly activity. For example, if over a given year a total of 40 people leave a call centre of 200 people (quit, are promoted, are let go, etc.), the turnover is expressed as $40/200 \times 100\% = 20\%$. (2)

Type chauvinism

The natural tendency to view our own dominant personality type (and other people with that same dominant personality type) as the "right" or most desirable way to be, and to view personality types that are our weakest as if there is something wrong or lacking in them. (8)

Up-sell

To sell customers a higher-quality product than the one they seek to buy, or a greater number of products than they originally intended to buy (for example, the higher-end computer with more features, or four boxes of copy paper with an extra box for free when the customer has called to order two boxes). (10)

Valuator

One of six personality types based on Dr. Taibi Kahler's Process Communication Model. Valuators are characterized by strong personal values, beliefs, and opinions. (3)

Virtual agents

See "home-based agents." (1)

Virtual place

A place in the computer system that receives calls. The customers' perception of the place their call has reached may be their bank branch or a room with a representative who has their file on his or her desk. In reality, the call is received by a computer system that then makes a number of decisions based on the caller's telephone number, the number the customer dialled, and other information provided by the customer through the IVR. The call may be routed to the IVR or to a rep anywhere in the world in any of a range of environments that do not necessarily fit the customer's mental image of the "place" she or he has called. (1)

Visualizer

One of six personality types based on Dr. Taibi Kahler's Process Communication Model. Visualizers are typically calm and introspective. (8)

Voice mail

Technology that allows a caller to leave a tape-recorded message for someone. In a call centre, the representatives can access their voice mail later, listen to the taped messages, and take whatever action is appropriate. (7)

Voice quality

The sound of a person's voice and the effect the voice has on the listener, including nasality, throat voice, breathy voice, and high pitch. (4)

Web site

An Internet location at which a person or company provides information or otherwise interacts with visitors to that site. (1)

Wedge

A method for regaining control of a call from the customer by interjecting into the customer's dialogue, connecting with what the customer was communicating, and redirecting the call to a productive resolution. (7)

Wireless phones

Phones that don't require telephone line hookups. (1)

Workstation

An employee's work space. A call centre representative's workstation typically consists of two to four soundproofed partial walls that are movable and free-standing, a desk, a computer, a telephone, and a cupboard or shelves. (1)

INDEX

To the owner of this book

We hope that you have enjoyed *Contact: A Guide to Effective Call Centre Skills,* by Jack A. Green (ISBN 0-17-616797-8), and we would like to know as much about your experiences with this text as you would care to offer. Only through your comments and those of others can we learn how to make this a better text for future readers.

School _____ Your instructor's name _____

Course _____ Was the text required? _____ Recommended? _____

1. What did you like the most about *Contact?*

_____

_____

_____

2. How useful was this text for your course?

_____

_____

_____

3. Do you have any recommendations for ways to improve the next edition of this text?

_____

_____

_____

4. In the space below or in a separate letter, please write any other comments you have about the book. (For example, please feel free to comment on reading level, writing style, terminology, design features, and learning aids.)

_____

_____

_____

_____

Optional

Your name _____ Date

_____

May Nelson Thomson Learning quote you, either in promotion for *Contact,* or in future publishing ventures?

Yes _____ No _____

PLEASE TAPE SHUT. DO NOT STAPLE.

TAPE SHUT

TAPE SHUT

- - - FOLD HERE - - -

MAIL ≽ POSTE

Canada Post Corporation
Société canadienne des postes

Postage paid	Port payé
if mailed in Canada	si posté au Canada
Business Reply	Réponse d'affaires

0066102399   01

Nelson
Thomson Learning™

0066102399-M1K5G4-BR01

NELSON THOMSON LEARNING
HIGHER EDUCATION
PO BOX 60225 STN BRM B
TORONTO ON M7Y 2H1

TAPE SHUT

TAPE SHUT